4

Book 1 - Internal Auditing Basics

Chapter 1: Introduction to Internal Auditing

Purpose and Overview

Welcome to the world of internal auditing! This highly dynamic and ever-evolving field plays a crucial role in ensuring the smooth functioning and success of organizations. But what exactly is internal auditing and what do internal auditors do? In this chapter, we will provide a comprehensive overview of internal auditing, its purpose, and its key roles and responsibilities.

Internal auditing can be defined as an independent, objective assurance and consulting activity that is designed to add value and improve an organization's operations. It is a systematic approach to evaluating and improving the effectiveness of risk management, control, and governance processes. In simpler terms, internal auditors are responsible for assessing whether an organization is effectively managing risk, following proper procedures and controls, and complying with applicable laws and regulations.

Internal auditing is an integral part of an organization's risk management and governance framework, and its ultimate goal is to enhance the organization's operations, achieve its objectives, and create value for its stakeholders. It helps organizations identify potential risks and areas for improvement, provides assurance to management and stakeholders, and maintains the organization's ethical and legal responsibilities.

Key Terminology

Before delving further into the world of internal auditing, it's essential to understand some key terminology that is often used in this field.

Risk management:
The process of identifying, assessing, and controlling threats and opportunities that may affect an organization's ability to achieve its objectives.

Control:
Procedures designed to provide reasonable assurance that an organization's objectives will be achieved. They may include measures to prevent fraud, protect assets, ensure compliance with laws and regulations, and promote efficiency and effectiveness.

Governance:
The system by which an organization is directed and controlled. It includes processes, structures, and culture that are designed to achieve the organization's objectives, address risks, and comply with laws and regulations.

Role and Responsibilities

Internal auditors play a vital role in supporting an organization's governance and risk management processes. They work with management to evaluate and improve the effectiveness of the organization's risk management and control systems. They also provide assurances to stakeholders that the organization is operating in accordance with applicable laws and regulations.

Some of the key roles and responsibilities of internal auditors include:

1. Assessing risk management processes: Internal auditors are responsible for evaluating the effectiveness of an organization's risk management processes. They identify potential risks and recommend ways to mitigate or manage them.

2. Evaluating internal controls: Internal auditors review and assess the organization's internal controls to determine if they are adequate and functioning as intended. They make recommendations for improvements and help management implement them.

3. Conducting audits: Internal auditors plan and conduct audits of different areas within an organization, such as operations, finance, and compliance. They follow established audit methodologies to gather evidence and evaluate the effectiveness of processes and controls.

4. Reporting and communicating: Internal auditors communicate their findings and recommendations to management and stakeholders through audit reports. They also provide regular updates to management on the status of audit engagements.

5. Monitoring and follow-up: Internal auditors are responsible for tracking the implementation of their recommendations and ensuring that management takes appropriate action to address identified issues.

6. Providing consultation and advice: Internal auditors may also provide consulting services to management, such as guidance on risk management, control design, and compliance with laws and regulations.

In conclusion, internal auditing is a crucial function that helps organizations achieve their objectives, manage risks, and maintain good governance practices. In the following chapters, we will dive deeper into the various aspects of internal auditing and provide you with the knowledge and tools to excel in this exciting profession. So, buckle up, and get ready to explore the world of internal auditing!

Chapter 2: From Traditional Auditing to Modern Internal Auditing

Traditional auditing has been around for centuries, with records dating back to the ancient Egyptians and Romans. However, it wasn't until the 20th century that auditing began to evolve into its modern form. The rise of industrialization and the complexity of business operations led to the need for more systematic and formalized auditing processes. This chapter will explore the key milestones in the development of internal auditing and its transformation into a valuable tool for organizations.

Global Development

The growth of internal auditing has been a global phenomenon, with various countries contributing to its development. The United States played a significant role in promoting internal auditing, with the creation of The Institute of Internal Auditors (IIA) in

1941. The IIA is now an international organization with over 200,000 members worldwide, promoting and supporting the internal audit profession.

In Europe, the development of internal auditing was influenced by the establishment of the European Union and its accounting directives. As a result, internal auditing became an essential component of corporate governance and risk management practices in many European countries.

In Asia, the rise of Japanese manufacturing and the adoption of Total Quality Management (TQM) principles led to the development of internal auditing as a quality assurance tool. In recent years, internal auditing has also gained prominence in developing countries, as organizations recognize its value in improving governance and risk management.

Key Milestones

The 20th century was a critical period in the development of internal auditing, with various milestones that shaped its growth. Let's explore some of these milestones in more detail.

Creation of The Institute of Internal Auditors

The IIA was founded in 1941, with the mission of being a global leader in promoting and supporting the internal audit profession. It serves as the voice of the profession, setting the standards and providing guidance and resources for internal auditors worldwide.

Introduction of the CIA Certification

In 1974, the IIA launched the Certified Internal Auditor (CIA) certification program, a globally recognized designation for internal auditors. It is the only certification program specifically designed for internal auditors, covering the essential skills and knowledge required for the profession.

Sarbanes-Oxley Act of 2002

The Enron scandal in 2001 sparked the passing of the Sarbanes-Oxley Act (SOX) in the United States in 2002. This legislation requires companies to have effective internal controls and for their financial statements to be audited by external auditors. It resulted in increased demand for internal auditors in public companies, further elevating the importance of the internal audit function.

Publication of the International Professional Practices Framework

The IIA's International Professional Practices Framework (IPPF) was first published in 1999 and has undergone several updates. It provides a comprehensive guide for internal auditors, covering the Code of Ethics, International Standards for the Professional Practice of Internal Auditing (Standards), and Practice Advisories and Development and Practice Aids.

Focus on Risk Management

As the business landscape became increasingly complex, the focus of internal auditing shifted towards risk management. In 2005, the Committee of Sponsoring Organizations of the Treadway Commission (COSO) published its Enterprise Risk Management (ERM) framework, which emphasized the role of internal auditors in identifying and managing risks.

Advancements in Technology

With the rapid advancement of technology, internal auditors have had to adapt their approach to auditing. The use of data analytics, continuous auditing, and artificial intelligence has become essential tools for internal auditors to gather and analyze significant amounts of data efficiently.

Closing Thoughts

Internal auditing has come a long way from its traditional roots to become a vital component of organizational governance and risk management. Its evolution has been influenced by global developments and key milestones, resulting in a profession that continues to adapt and grow. As we move into a more interconnected and technologically advanced world, the role of internal auditors will only become more critical in providing assurance and promoting best practices for organizations.

Chapter 3: Auditing Standards and Frameworks

Auditing is a vital process for any organization, ensuring the accuracy and integrity of financial information, as well as the efficacy of internal controls and risk management. To conduct effective and efficient audits, internal auditors must adhere to rigorous standards and adhere to established frameworks. In this chapter, we will delve into the world of auditing standards and frameworks, exploring their evolution and their impact on the internal auditing profession.

Overview of International Standards

As businesses continue to expand globally and borders become increasingly blurred, it has become essential to have a set of universal standards for internal auditing. This led to the formation of the International Professional Practices Framework (IPPF) by the Institute of Internal Auditors (IIA). The IPPF consists of the International Standards for the Professional Practice of Internal Auditing (Standards), the Code of Ethics, the Practice Advisories, and the Implementation Guides. These standards provide a globally recognized framework for internal auditors to follow and ensure consistency in the profession.

The Standards are principles-focused, meaning they provide a framework for the practice of internal auditing and not specific mandates. They are divided into four sections: Attribute Standards, Performance Standards, Implementation Standards, and Supplemental Guidance. The Attribute Standards cover the characteristics that define excellent internal audit professionals, while the Performance Standards outline the expected outcomes of effective internal auditing. The Implementation Standards provide guidance on how internal audit work should be executed, and the Supplemental Guidance offers additional and more detailed information to enhance understanding and application.

One of the significant benefits of following the International Standards is that it allows for a consistent approach to internal auditing, regardless of geographic location or industry. It also promotes a level of professionalism and credibility for the internal audit profession.

COSO and COBIT Frameworks

Apart from the Standards set by the IIA, two other frameworks have become highly relevant for internal auditors: the Committee of Sponsoring Organizations of the Treadway Commission (COSO) framework and the Control Objectives for Information and Related Technology (COBIT) framework.

COSO was established in 1985 and released its Internal Control-Integrated Framework in 1992, which has since become the gold standard for internal control frameworks. It consists of five components: control environment, risk assessment, control activities, information and communication, and monitoring activities. The framework established a standard definition for internal control and provided guidelines for evaluating the effectiveness of internal controls.

On the other hand, COBIT was developed by ISACA (Information Systems Audit and Control Association) in the mid-1990s as a framework for IT governance and control. It has since evolved to become an all-encompassing framework that helps organizations achieve their IT objectives and manage associated risks. COBIT consists of five domains: governance and management, information architecture, technical architecture, IT services, and IT assets. Similar to the COSO framework, COBIT also provides guidance on the design and implementation of effective controls.

In recent years, the COSO and COBIT frameworks have become increasingly relevant for internal auditors, as organizations continue to rely on technology for their operations. These frameworks help internal auditors assess the effectiveness of internal controls related to IT systems and data.

Emerging Trends

As technology continues to advance and industries evolve, auditors must also adapt to emerging trends to ensure their audits remain relevant and effective. Some of the emerging trends in the auditing profession include data analytics, continuous auditing, and integrated reporting.

Data analytics allows internal auditors to mine large amounts of data to identify anomalies and patterns that may indicate potential fraud or other irregularities. This process is faster and more efficient than traditional methods, allowing auditors to uncover more significant insights and risks.

Continuous auditing involves conducting regular, real-time audits instead of the traditional annual audits. This approach allows auditors to identify and address issues promptly, reducing the risk of errors or fraud going undetected for extended periods. It also allows for a more proactive approach to risk management.

Integrated reporting is a framework that combines financial and non-financial information to provide a comprehensive view of an organization's performance. This approach allows internal auditors to assess an organization's overall health and identify potential issues that may not be apparent when looking at financial information alone.

In addition to these trends, the use of emerging technologies like artificial intelligence and blockchain in auditing is also gaining traction. These advancements have the potential to simplify and optimize the auditing process, making it more efficient and effective.

As the world continues to evolve, so will the auditing profession. It is crucial for internal auditors to stay updated on emerging trends and adapt their practices to ensure they continue to add value to their organizations.

In conclusion, auditing standards and frameworks play a critical role in the internal auditing profession, providing a framework for consistency and professionalism. While the International Standards set by the IIA act as a unifying platform for internal auditors globally, the COSO and COBIT frameworks offer guidance on specific areas of internal control and governance. As the world continues to change, internal auditors must also evolve to stay relevant and add value to their organizations.

Chapter 4: Essential Skills for Internal Auditors

Internal auditors are not just number crunchers; they are trusted advisors who help organizations achieve their objectives. To effectively perform their role, auditors need a wide range of skills beyond financial and accounting expertise. In this chapter, we will explore the essential skills for internal auditors, including communication, critical thinking, and analytical skills.

Communication

Effective communication is crucial for internal auditors as they need to interact with individuals at all levels of an organization, from front-line staff to C-suite executives. Auditors must be able to articulate complex ideas and findings in a clear and concise manner, both verbally and in writing.

In addition to communication skills, auditors must also be good listeners. By actively listening, they can better understand the organization's operations and identify any areas for improvement. Good communication also involves being able to build rapport and establish trust with stakeholders, which is essential for effective collaboration and communication.

To improve their communication skills, internal auditors should seek opportunities to present their findings and recommendations to different audiences and receive feedback to continuously improve their communication abilities. They should also stay up to date with the latest communication technologies and tools to effectively collaborate with team members and stakeholders.

Critical Thinking

Critical thinking is the ability to objectively analyze and evaluate information to form a well-reasoned judgment or decision. It is a fundamental skill for internal auditors as they need to make sense of complex and sometimes conflicting data to identify risks and opportunities.

Critical thinking requires auditors to challenge assumptions and biases, ask probing questions, and consider multiple perspectives to arrive at an objective and logical conclusion. It also involves being able to identify patterns, connections, and trends to gain a deeper understanding of an organization's operations and risks.

To hone their critical thinking skills, internal auditors should continuously seek out challenging assignments and opportunities to develop their analytical abilities. They should also regularly review and evaluate their thought processes to identify any potential biases or flaws.

Analytical Skills

Analytical skills go hand in hand with critical thinking. These skills involve breaking down complex information into manageable parts, identifying patterns and relationships, and using data to inform decision-making.

Internal auditors need strong analytical skills to gather and interpret data, evaluate controls and processes, and identify potential risks and opportunities. They must also be proficient in using data analytics tools and techniques to analyze large datasets and identify areas for improvement.

To develop their analytical skills, internal auditors should seek out opportunities to work with different data sets and learn new tools and techniques. They should also stay up to date with the latest data analytics trends and technologies to enhance their abilities and support their findings and recommendations.

Incorporating Creativity and Innovation

While the above skills are essential for internal auditors, it is also important to incorporate creativity and innovation into their work. Auditors should not be afraid to think outside the box and explore new and innovative ways to approach their audits. This can help identify potential risks and opportunities that may have otherwise been overlooked.

Additionally, auditors should continuously seek ways to improve and streamline their processes and procedures to enhance their efficiency and effectiveness. This requires a mindset of continuous improvement and a willingness to embrace change.

The Role of Emotional Intelligence

Emotional intelligence is often overlooked but is a crucial skill for internal auditors. This skill involves the ability to understand and manage one's emotions and the emotions of others. It also includes building and maintaining positive relationships with stakeholders, managing conflicts, and adapting to changing situations.

In the often high-stress and complex world of internal auditing, emotional intelligence helps auditors maintain composure and professionalism while adapting to different scenarios and effectively managing stakeholder relationships.

Diversify Your Skill Set

In addition to the above skills, internal auditors should continuously seek opportunities to expand their skill set. This can include attending trainings and workshops, obtaining new certifications, or even learning new languages. By diversifying their skill set, auditors can stay current and enhance their capabilities, making them even more valuable to organizations.

Final Thoughts

In today's fast-paced business world, internal auditors need more than just technical skills to be successful. Effective communication, critical thinking, and analytical skills are essential for auditors to identify risks, provide valuable insights, and help organizations achieve their objectives. By continuously honing these skills and remaining open to new and innovative approaches, internal auditors can add tremendous value to their organizations and advance in their career paths.

Chapter 5: Understanding and Managing Risks

Types of Risks

Risk assessment and management are crucial components of internal auditing. Risks can arise from every aspect of a business and can potentially hinder its success. As an internal auditor, it is essential to identify, assess and mitigate risks to ensure the organization's objectives are achieved. Here are the different types of risks that can be encountered during the auditing process.

1. Financial Risks

Financial risks refer to the potential losses or damages that an organization may face due to changes in economic conditions or financial markets. This type of risk can arise from investments, fluctuations in interest rates, currency exchange rates, or credit defaults. As an internal auditor, understanding the organization's financial risks is crucial in evaluating its financial health and identifying potential areas of concern. Common financial risks include liquidity risk, credit risk, and market risk.

2. Operational Risks

Operational risks refer to potential disruptions or failures in an organization's daily operations. These risks can arise from human error, systems breakdown, or external events. Identifying and mitigating operational risks is vital to ensure the organization's smooth functioning and maintain its reputation. As an internal auditor, it is essential to assess the organization's processes and procedures to identify potential deficiencies and recommend improvements to minimize operational risks.

3. Compliance Risks

Compliance risks refer to the risk of non-compliance with laws, regulations or internal policies and procedures. Failure to comply with legal and regulatory requirements can result in legal penalties, fines, and damage to the organization's reputation. As an internal auditor, it is essential to understand the relevant laws and regulations applicable to the organization's industry and assess the organization's compliance with them.

4. Strategic Risks

Strategic risks refer to potential threats to an organization's strategic objectives and goals. These risks can arise from changes in the market, competition, or evolving customer demands. As an internal auditor, understanding the organization's strategic goals and evaluating any potential risks that may hinder their achievement is crucial in providing valuable insights to management to ensure long-term success.

5. Reputational Risks

Reputational risks refer to potential damage to an organization's reputation due to any negative publicity or events. These risks can arise from customer dissatisfaction, unethical practices, or failures to meet stakeholders' expectations. As an internal auditor, it is essential to identify any potential areas of reputational risk and provide recommendations to mitigate them to protect the organization's reputation.

6. Compliance Risks

Compliance risks refer to the risk of non-compliance with laws, regulations or internal policies and procedures. Failure to comply with legal and regulatory requirements can result in legal penalties, fines, and damage to the organization's reputation. As an internal auditor, it is essential to understand the relevant laws and regulations applicable to the organization's industry and assess the organization's compliance with them.

Risk Assessment Process

Now that we have a better understanding of the types of risks that can impact an organization, let's discuss the risk assessment process. This process involves identifying, analyzing, and evaluating risks to determine their likelihood and potential impact on the organization. Here are the four main steps in the risk assessment process:

1. Identifying Risks

The first step in the risk assessment process is to identify potential risks to the organization. This can be achieved through various methods such as brainstorming, surveys, interviews, and reviewing historical data. As an internal auditor, it is essential to involve key stakeholders from different departments to ensure a comprehensive list of risks is identified.

2. Analyzing Risks

Once potential risks have been identified, the next step is to analyze them. This involves determining the likelihood and impact of each risk on the organization. Likelihood refers to the chances of the risk occurring, while impact refers to the consequences should the risk materialize. This step requires a thorough understanding of the organization's operations and industry to accurately assess the risks.

3. Evaluating Risks

After analyzing the risks, the next step is to evaluate them based on their likelihood and impact. This step involves assigning a risk score to each risk, which can be used to prioritize the risks and determine the appropriate mitigation strategies. Risks with a high likelihood and impact should be given more attention and addressed first.

4. Reporting

The final step in the risk assessment process is to report the identified risks and their associated risk scores to management. This step may also include providing recommendations for mitigation strategies and the potential impact on the organization if the risks are not addressed. As an internal auditor, clear and effective communication of the risks is crucial to ensure management can make informed decisions.

Mitigation Strategies

Once risks have been identified, analyzed, and evaluated, the next step is to develop and implement mitigation strategies. Here are some common mitigation strategies used by internal auditors:

1. Risk Avoidance

Risk avoidance involves completely eliminating the risk by not engaging in the activity that poses the risk. This is often the least desirable option as it may limit the organization's opportunities for growth and success. However, it may be necessary for risks with severe consequences.

2. Risk Transfer

Risk transfer involves shifting the risk to another party, typically through insurance or outsourcing. This can be beneficial for risks that the organization has no control over and cannot be avoided. However, the organization will still need to monitor the risk to ensure it is appropriately managed by the other party.

3. Risk Reduction

Risk reduction involves implementing controls and procedures to minimize the likelihood and impact of a risk. This is often the most common mitigation strategy used by internal auditors. It can include implementing additional internal controls, procedures, or training programs to reduce the likelihood of the risk occurring.

4. Risk Acceptance

Risk acceptance involves acknowledging the risk and accepting that there may be potential consequences. This is often used for risks with a low likelihood and impact or when the cost of mitigation strategies outweighs the potential consequences. However, it is essential to monitor the risk to ensure it does not escalate in the future.

Conclusion

In conclusion, understanding and managing risks is a crucial aspect of internal auditing. Internal auditors should have a thorough understanding of the different types of risks and their potential impact on the organization. By following a structured risk assessment process and implementing effective mitigation strategies, internal auditors can help mitigate potential risks and ensure the organization's success in achieving its objectives.

Chapter 6: Internal Control and Corporate Governance

Importance of Corporate Governance

In today's fast-paced business landscape, corporate governance has become a crucial aspect of organizational success. With constant changes in technology, markets, and regulations, organizations are faced with increasing levels of risks and uncertainties. In this context, the role of corporate governance cannot be overstated. At its core, corporate governance is the system of rules, practices, and processes that ensure the accountability, transparency, and ethical decision-making of an organization's management and board of directors.

An effective corporate governance framework creates a clear system of checks and balances, promoting accountability and transparency in the decision-making process. It also provides stakeholders with the confidence that their interests are safeguarded and that the organization is being managed ethically and responsibly. Strong corporate governance is a vital component of sustainable growth and value creation and is a deciding factor in attracting investors, customers, and employees.

Control Frameworks

In the world of internal auditing, standards and frameworks are essential tools that help guide and shape the practice of internal control. Control frameworks provide a comprehensive structure for internal control activities, enabling organizations to identify, assess, and manage risks effectively. They also provide a valuable reference point for internal auditors to determine the adequacy and effectiveness of controls.

One of the widely recognized control frameworks is the Committee of Sponsoring Organizations of the Treadway Commission (COSO) Internal Control Framework. This framework comprises five interrelated components: Control Environment, Risk Assessment, Control Activities, Information and Communication, and Monitoring Activities. The framework serves as a roadmap for organizations looking to develop an effective system for internal control.

Another widely used framework is the International Organization for Standardization (ISO) 31000, which provides guidelines for implementing risk management processes. The ISO 31000 framework is an invaluable resource for organizations as it helps them identify, assess, and manage risks in a systematic and controlled manner. It also promotes a culture of risk awareness and continuous improvement within an organization.

Internal Control Components

Internal control is a process designed to provide reasonable assurance regarding the achievement of an organization's objectives in the following categories: effectiveness and efficiency of operations, reliability of financial reporting, and compliance with laws and regulations. There are two primary types of internal control components: preventive and detective controls.

Preventive controls are designed to prevent errors, fraud, and other undesirable events from occurring in the first place. Examples of preventive controls include segregation of duties, physical controls, and authorization processes. These controls reduce the likelihood of errors and fraud, thereby protecting the organization's assets. On the other hand, detective controls are put in place to identify and correct errors or irregularities that have already occurred. These controls help identify vulnerabilities in the system and mitigate the risks associated with them. Examples of detective controls include reconciliations, exception reports, and periodic audits.

In addition to preventive and detective controls, internal control components also include monitoring activities and information and communication. Monitoring activities involve the regular review and evaluation of internal controls to ensure they are operating effectively. Information and communication, on the other hand, involves the timely flow and sharing of information within an organization, ensuring that all relevant parties have access to accurate and relevant information.

Uncommon Insights into Internal Control and Corporate Governance

In today's digital age, effective internal control and corporate governance are essential for organizations to thrive. With the increasing use of technology, internal controls must adapt and evolve to keep pace with the ever-changing risk landscape. This requires organizations to continuously review, assess, and modify their control processes to stay ahead of potential risks and ensure that their objectives are achieved.

Additionally, corporate governance is not just limited to the management and board of directors; it is a shared responsibility of all stakeholders. Employees at all levels play a crucial role in maintaining effective internal control and promoting an ethical corporate culture. It is essential to foster a culture where employees are encouraged to speak up and raise concerns about any potential control weaknesses or unethical behavior without fear of retaliation. Furthermore, internal control and corporate governance are not just about compliance; they are also about creating value. Effective internal controls not only mitigate risks but also help improve operational efficiency and effectiveness, leading to cost savings and ultimately resulting in value creation for the organization.

In conclusion, internal control and corporate governance are instrumental in ensuring an organization's long-term success. With the ever-changing business landscape, it is crucial for organizations to have robust control frameworks in place to adapt and thrive. By following recognized frameworks and continuously monitoring and adapting their control processes, organizations can effectively manage risks, safeguard their assets, and create sustainable value for all stakeholders.

Chapter 7: CIA Certification: Becoming a Certified Internal Auditor

Internal auditing is a vital function of any organization, ensuring the effectiveness and efficiency of operations, as well as the integrity of financial reporting. As the field of internal auditing continues to evolve, the demand for highly skilled and qualified professionals also increases. This is where the Certified Internal Auditor (CIA) certification comes in.

Eligibility Requirements

The CIA certification is globally recognized as the gold standard for internal audit professionals. It is awarded by the Institute of Internal Auditors (IIA), the leading professional organization for internal auditors worldwide. To be eligible for the CIA certification, individuals must meet specific criteria set by the IIA. These requirements include:

1. Education: Candidates must have a bachelor's degree or its equivalent from an accredited institution. This can be in any field of study, as the CIA certification is open to professionals from various backgrounds.

2. Work Experience: Candidates must have a minimum of two years' work experience in a related field, such as internal auditing, external auditing, or accounting. However, candidates with a master's degree or other relevant certifications may be eligible for certain exemptions.

3. Character Reference: Candidates must submit a character reference from a current or previous supervisor, educator, or industry leader, attesting to the candidate's ethical and professional conduct.

Exam Format

The CIA certification exam is a rigorous and comprehensive test of an individual's knowledge and skills in internal auditing. It is divided into three parts, each focusing on a different aspect of internal auditing. The exam can be taken at any of the IIA's testing centers worldwide and is available in multiple languages to accommodate candidates from diverse backgrounds.

Part 1: Internal Audit Basics - This part covers the fundamental principles and concepts of internal auditing, including governance and risk management, business processes, and communication and information technology.

Part 2: Internal Audit Practice - This part covers the practice of internal auditing, including conducting an audit engagement, fraud risks and controls, and managing the audit function.

Part 3: Internal Audit Knowledge Elements - This part focuses on specific knowledge areas, such as business acumen, financial management, and information technology, that are essential for successful internal auditors.

The CIA exam is a computer-based exam and consists of multiple-choice questions. Candidates have four hours to complete each part, and they must score a minimum of 600 out of 800 points to pass. It is recommended that candidates take the exam in sequential order, starting with Part 1.

Continuing Education

Earning the CIA certification is not a one-time achievement; it requires dedication to continued professional development. To maintain the certification, CIAs must complete a minimum of 40 hours of continuing professional education (CPE) each year, with a total of 120 hours over a rolling three-year period. This ensures that CIAs are continuously updating their knowledge and skills to meet the evolving demands of the profession.

The IIA offers a wide range of CPE opportunities, including conferences, webinars, and self-study courses. As internal auditors must stay current with industry developments and trends, the IIA also requires a certain number of CPE hours to be earned in specific subject areas, such as ethics, fraud, and governance. This ensures that CIAs have a well-rounded and up-to-date understanding of the field.

In conclusion, the CIA certification is highly sought after by organizations seeking top-notch internal audit professionals. It not only demonstrates an individual's expertise in the field but also highlights their commitment to continuous learning and professional growth. With its globally recognized reputation and rigorous requirements, the CIA certification is a valuable asset to any internal auditor looking to advance their career and make a significant impact in their organization.

Chapter 8: Audit Planning - Setting the Course for a Successful Audit

Internal auditing is a vital component of any organization's governance and control structure. It serves as an objective and independent assurance function, providing valuable insights to improve the organization's operations and mitigate risks. However, to be effective, internal auditors must have a roadmap for their audit engagements. This is where audit planning comes into play.

Audit Planning: The Foundation of a Well-Executed Audit

As the saying goes, "failing to plan is planning to fail." This couldn't be any truer when it comes to internal auditing. Audit planning is the process of developing a roadmap that outlines the scope, objectives, and approach of an audit engagement. It is a critical first step that sets the stage for a successful and efficient audit.

Understanding the Business: Know Thyself, Know Thy Audit Objectives

Before setting out to plan an audit, it is essential to have a thorough understanding of the organization's business operations. This includes the processes, systems, and people involved in delivering the organization's goods and services. This understanding should also extend to the organization's strategic objectives, its industry, and its regulatory environment.

Knowing the business is crucial because it lays the foundation for identifying areas of potential risk and establishing relevant audit objectives. By having an in-depth understanding of the business, internal auditors can tailor their audit approach to address the organization's most critical risks and provide valuable insights that align with its strategic goals.

Establishing Objectives: A Clear Path to Success

The next step in audit planning is establishing clear and concise objectives. Audit objectives are the goals that the internal audit function aims to achieve through an audit engagement. These objectives must be specific, measurable, attainable, relevant, and time-bound (SMART). In simpler terms, they must answer the questions of what is being audited, why it's being audited, and what the auditors hope to achieve.

Establishing objectives is a crucial part of audit planning because it helps auditors focus their efforts and ensures that the audit adds value to the organization. It also serves as a benchmark against which the audit's success can be measured. Without clear objectives, an audit can meander off course and fail to provide the desired results.

Uncovering Uncommon and Insightful Concepts: Materiality and Risk Assessment

In addition to the standard steps of audit planning discussed above, there are two commonly used concepts that play a significant role in internal audit planning - materiality and risk assessment.

Materiality refers to the significance of an item or issue in the context of an organization's financial or operational performance. In other words, it is the threshold at which an issue becomes significant enough to warrant attention and action. In audit planning, materiality is used to determine the level of detail and effort that should be put into assessing and reporting on specific risks or areas of the organization.

Risk assessment, on the other hand, is the process of identifying, analyzing, and prioritizing the organization's risks. It involves evaluating the likelihood of an event occurring and its potential impact on the organization. By conducting a comprehensive risk assessment, auditors can identify the areas of highest risk and tailor their audit approach to address those risks.

A Creative and Cherished Tone: The Art of Building Rapport with Auditees

Another crucial aspect of successful audit planning is building rapport with auditees. Auditees are the people responsible for the processes and activities being audited. Building rapport with them is essential because it can impact the quality of information they provide to auditors.

As auditors, it is important to remember that auditees are not the enemy. They are an integral part of the organization and should be treated with respect and professionalism. Taking the time to build a friendly rapport with them can make the audit process smoother and more effective.

Bringing It All Together: The Importance of an Integrated Approach

In conclusion, audit planning is a crucial first step in conducting an effective and efficient audit. By understanding the business, establishing clear objectives, and incorporating concepts like materiality and risk assessment, internal auditors can lay the foundation for a successful audit. Additionally, building rapport with auditees is essential for gaining their cooperation and ensuring a smooth audit process. An integrated approach to audit planning is key to setting the course for a successful audit engagement.

Chapter 9: Conducting an Effective Audit

In previous chapters, we have explored the fundamentals of internal auditing, as well as the essential skills and competencies that must be possessed by a successful auditor. Now, it is time to delve into the actual process of conducting an audit. In this chapter, we will discuss the key techniques and approaches that can be used to ensure that your audit is effective and thorough. We will cover the three main aspects of any audit: Sampling Techniques, Document Review, and Interviews.

Sampling Techniques

When conducting an audit, it is not always possible to review every single piece of data or information. This is where sampling techniques come into play. Sampling allows the auditor to select a smaller, representative sample of data for review, rather than trying to analyze the entire population. This not only saves time and resources, but also allows the auditor to focus on the most critical and relevant areas. One commonly used sampling technique is known as random sampling, where each item in the population has an equal chance of being selected for review. This ensures that the sample is unbiased and truly representative of the whole. Another method is stratified sampling, where the population is divided into smaller groups and a sample is selected from each group. This approach allows for more targeted sampling, as the auditor can focus on specific areas or segments of the population.

However, it is important for auditors to understand that sampling does not eliminate the need for proper risk assessment. Sampling is just a tool to help manage the workload and focus on high-risk areas, but it should not be used as a substitute for proper risk assessment procedures.

Document Review

Document review is a crucial part of any audit, as it allows the auditor to gain a deeper understanding of the organization's operations, processes, and controls. Documents such as financial statements, policies and procedures, contracts, and records provide valuable insights into the company's activities and can help identify potential risks and areas for improvement.

But document review is not just about reading through piles of papers. It requires a systematic and organized approach to ensure that all relevant documents are reviewed, and nothing is overlooked. It is important to establish a comprehensive document request list before the audit begins, and to continuously update it as new documents become available.

During the review, auditors should pay attention to key details, such as dates, signatures, approvals, and any discrepancies or inconsistencies. This can help identify potential red flags or areas that require further investigation. It is also important to document all findings and conclusions from the document review process.

Interviews

While documents can provide a wealth of information, they do not always tell the full story. This is why interviews are a critical aspect of any audit. Conducting interviews allows the auditor to gain a better understanding of the organization's operations, processes, and controls directly from key personnel.

Before conducting interviews, it is important to have a clear understanding of the purpose of each interview and to prepare relevant and targeted questions. It is also important to establish rapport with the interviewee and create a comfortable and open atmosphere for them to share their insights and perspectives.

During the interview, the auditor should actively listen to the interviewee's responses and ask follow-up questions to clarify any information that may be unclear. It is also important to document the responses accurately and objectively. Interviews can provide valuable insights and confirm or contradict information obtained through document review, making it an essential technique in conducting an effective audit.

Incorporating Technology

In today's digital age, auditors have access to a plethora of tools and technologies that can make the audit process more efficient and effective. The use of technology can help streamline data analysis, document review, and even communication with key personnel. One popular technology used in auditing is data analytics software, which can help auditors identify patterns and anomalies in large datasets. This can save a significant amount of time and resources, while also providing valuable insights into potential risks or areas that require further investigation.

Collaboration and project management tools can also help streamline the audit process and facilitate communication between team members. These tools can enhance organization and coordination within the audit team, ensuring that all tasks are completed on time and key findings are shared effectively.

Conclusion

In conclusion, conducting an effective audit requires careful planning, proper risk assessment, and the use of various techniques and approaches. Sampling, document review, and interviews are just some of the key techniques that auditors can use to ensure a comprehensive and thorough audit. With the use of technology and a systematic approach, auditors can improve the efficiency and effectiveness of their audits, ultimately providing valuable insights and recommendations to their organization.

Chapter 10: Conducting an Effective Audit

Internal auditing is a critical function within any organization, providing independent and objective assessments of the organization's operations, risk management, and internal controls. At the heart of internal auditing lies the audit itself - a systematic, disciplined approach to evaluating an organization's processes, systems, and activities. In this chapter, we will explore the different types of audits that internal auditors may conduct, and discuss best practices for conducting an effective audit.

Compliance Audits

Compliance audits are designed to assess an organization's adherence to laws, regulations, and internal policies. These audits help identify any gaps or weaknesses in the organization's compliance program, and provide recommendations for improvement. Compliance audits are essential for organizations operating in highly regulated industries such as finance, healthcare, and government.

During a compliance audit, internal auditors will assess the organization's compliance with relevant laws and regulations, as well as its internal policies and procedures. They will review documentation, interview employees, and may perform sample testing to determine the effectiveness of the organization's compliance controls.

To ensure a successful compliance audit, internal auditors must have a thorough understanding of the relevant laws and regulations, as well as the organization's internal policies and procedures. They must also maintain their independence and objectivity, to provide an unbiased assessment of the organization's compliance efforts.

Operational Audits

Operational audits, also known as performance audits, are focused on evaluating the efficiency and effectiveness of an organization's operations. These audits can cover a wide range of business functions, from customer service and production processes to marketing and supply chain management.

The aim of an operational audit is to identify opportunities for improvement and cost-saving measures, as well as potential risks that may impact the organization's operations. Internal auditors will use a combination of data analysis, interviews, and observations to assess the organization's processes and performance.

One key aspect of conducting an effective operational audit is to use benchmarking and industry best practices. By comparing the organization's processes and performance to those of its peers, internal auditors can identify areas where the organization can improve and catch up with the competition.

Financial Audits

Financial audits are perhaps the most well-known type of audit, and they are critical for providing assurance on the accuracy and reliability of an organization's financial statements. These audits are usually conducted by external auditors, but internal auditors may also participate to provide additional assurance to the organization's stakeholders.

During a financial audit, internal auditors will assess the organization's financial statements, looking for any errors, misstatements, or fraud. They will also assess the effectiveness of the organization's internal controls over financial reporting, to ensure the accuracy and reliability of the financial statements.

It is essential for internal auditors to have a deep understanding of accounting principles and financial reporting standards to conduct an effective financial audit. They must also be well-versed in audit techniques and procedures, including sample testing and analytical review.

Best Practices for Conducting an Effective Audit

While the specific steps and processes for conducting an audit may vary depending on its type, there are some best practices that can help internal auditors ensure the effectiveness and efficiency of their audits:

- Plan the audit carefully: A well-planned audit is more likely to be successful. Internal auditors should carefully consider the objectives, scope, and resources required for the audit.

- Use technology: Technology can help streamline and improve the audit process. For example, data analytics tools can help internal auditors identify patterns and trends in large datasets, making the audit more efficient and effective.

- Stay organized: Audits involve large amounts of information and documentation. It is essential for internal auditors to maintain organized and structured files to ensure they can easily retrieve and refer back to information throughout the audit.

- Communicate effectively: Internal auditors must communicate effectively with all stakeholders involved in the audit, including management, employees, and external auditors. Clear and concise communication can help ensure everyone is on the same page and avoid misunderstandings.

- Be open-minded: Auditors must maintain an open mind throughout the audit process and be willing to consider different perspectives and possibilities. This helps ensure the audit remains unbiased and objective.

- Document everything: All audit work should be well-documented, including the procedures followed, results obtained, and conclusions made. This provides evidence of the audit's thoroughness and supports any recommendations or findings presented.

Conclusion

Conducting an effective audit is critical for organizations looking to improve their operations, ensure compliance, and provide assurance to stakeholders. Internal auditors must remain knowledgeable, organized, and objective to conduct successful audits. By following best practices and using technology, internal auditors can provide valuable insights and recommendations that help organizations thrive.

Chapter 11: Risky Business - The Art of Internal Auditing

Identifying Risk Areas

Internal auditors play a vital role in helping organizations identify and manage risks. In today's rapidly changing business environment, the need for effective risk management is essential for organizations to remain competitive and sustain their operations. Therefore, it is crucial for internal auditors to have a thorough understanding of an organization's risk profile and key risk areas.

To identify risk areas, internal auditors must have a deep understanding of the organization's business operations, objectives, and strategies. They must also be aware of industry trends, regulations, and emerging risks. This knowledge will help auditors prioritize their work and focus on areas that pose the greatest risk to the organization.

In addition to these internal and external factors, internal auditors can use various tools and techniques to identify and assess risk areas. These can include risk assessments, data analytics, and benchmarking. By utilizing these tools, internal auditors can gather valuable insights into an organization's risk landscape and identify potential areas of concern.

Testing Methods

Once risk areas have been identified, the next step for internal auditors is to devise an appropriate testing methodology. This involves determining the most efficient and effective ways to examine the identified risk areas. The testing methods used can vary depending on the nature and complexity of the risk.

One common testing method used by internal auditors is the control testing approach. This involves evaluating the design and operating effectiveness of an organization's controls to mitigate identified risks. Control testing is an integral part of internal auditing and can provide valuable insights into the effectiveness of an organization's risk management processes. Another testing method is data analytics. With the increasing reliance on technology, organizations are generating vast amounts of data, making it an invaluable resource for internal auditors. By utilizing data analytics techniques, auditors can analyze large volumes of data to identify patterns, trends, and anomalies that may indicate potential risks. This approach can also help auditors identify and prioritize high-risk areas for further investigation.

In addition to these testing methods, internal auditors may also use expert judgment, interviews, and surveys to gather additional information and insights. These techniques can provide a deeper understanding of risks and their potential impact on the organization, making it an essential part of the testing process.

Reporting Findings

After the testing phase is complete, internal auditors must report their findings to key stakeholders. It is crucial for auditors to present their findings in a clear and concise manner, highlighting the potential impact of identified risks on the organization's objectives and operations. The report should also provide recommendations for mitigating the risks and improving risk management processes.

To ensure the effectiveness of the report, internal auditors must understand the needs and expectations of their stakeholders. These can include management, the board of directors, and external regulators. By understanding their audience, auditors can tailor their reports to communicate the most critical information in a way that is easily understood and actionable. In addition to written reports, internal auditors may also present their findings in person to key stakeholders. This can provide an opportunity for direct communication and discussion to clarify any points and ensure that the stakeholders fully understand the potential risk areas and recommended solutions.

Reporting findings also involves follow-up and monitoring. Internal auditors must track the implementation of their recommendations and assess if they have effectively addressed the identified risks. This helps to ensure that the organization's risk management processes are continually improved and kept up-to-date with any changes in the business environment.

In conclusion, identifying risk areas, testing methods, and reporting findings are crucial aspects of internal auditing. By utilizing a combination of tools and techniques, internal auditors can provide valuable insights into an organization's risk landscape and help mitigate potential risks. Effective risk management is an ongoing process, and internal auditors play a vital role in ensuring the organization's resilience and success in a constantly evolving business environment.

Chapter 12: Fraud and Ethics

Fraud is a deceptive action or misrepresentation of information done with the intention of gaining an unfair advantage. It is a common occurrence in the business world and can result in significant financial loss and damage to a company's reputation. As an internal auditor, it is your responsibility to detect and prevent fraud within your organization. In this chapter, we will discuss the various types of fraud, fraud detection techniques, and the ethical standards that every auditor should adhere to.

Types of Fraud

The first step in detecting fraud is understanding the different types that exist. There are three main categories of fraud: asset misappropriation, corruption, and financial statement fraud. Asset misappropriation refers to the theft of company resources, such as cash or inventory, by an employee. Corruption involves the misuse of power or influence for personal gain, such as accepting bribes. Financial statement fraud is the intentional misrepresentation of financial information in order to deceive stakeholders.

While these three categories encompass the majority of fraud cases, there are also various subcategories to be aware of. These include billing schemes, payroll schemes, inventory schemes, and many more. As an internal auditor, it is crucial to have a thorough understanding of all types of fraud and how they can be perpetrated.

Fraud Detection Techniques

Once you are aware of the types of fraud that exist, it is important to know how to detect them. One common technique that auditors use is data analytics. By analyzing large sets of data, anomalies and red flags can be identified that may indicate fraudulent activity. This can include unusual transactions, duplicate payments, or suspicious vendor relationships.

Another effective detection technique is conducting surprise audits or inventory counts. By randomly selecting a time to do an audit, employees will be less likely to have the opportunity to cover up fraudulent activity. Additionally, regularly reviewing and monitoring internal controls and conducting thorough background checks on new employees can also aid in detecting fraud.

Ethical Standards for Auditors

As an internal auditor, it is imperative that you adhere to strict ethical standards. The Institute of Internal Auditors (IIA) has established a code of ethics that all internal auditors should follow. This code includes principles such as integrity, objectivity, confidentiality, and competency. It is crucial for auditors to maintain independence and objectivity in their work in order to avoid any conflicts of interest that may lead to fraudulent behavior.

Beyond ethical standards set by professional organizations, auditors must also be aware of the legal and regulatory requirements in their industry. Adhering to laws and regulations not only ensures the validity of your audit findings but also protects the organization from legal consequences.

In addition to following ethical and legal guidelines, it is important for auditors to foster a culture of ethics within their organization. This can be achieved through promoting transparency, providing training on ethical standards, and encouraging employees to speak up if they suspect any fraudulent activity.

Conclusion

As an internal auditor, the task of detecting and preventing fraud can be daunting. However, by understanding the different types of fraud, utilizing effective detection techniques, and upholding ethical standards, you can effectively mitigate the risk of fraud within your organization. Remember that the responsibility lies on all employees, not just auditors, to maintain a culture of honesty and integrity in order to prevent and combat fraud. By doing so, we can promote a positive and ethical business landscape.

Chapter 13: The Power of Technology in Internal Auditing

In this digital age, technology has become an integral part of the business world and is continuously revolutionizing the way organizations operate. With the constant evolution of technology, it is not surprising that it has also greatly impacted the field of internal auditing. Gone are the days when auditors had to rely on manual and time-consuming processes to gather and analyze data. Today, with the use of data analytics and automation tools, internal auditors are able to streamline their processes and provide more valuable insights to organizations.

Use of Data Analytics

Data analytics is the process of using statistical analysis, predictive modeling, and machine learning techniques to uncover patterns, relationships, and anomalies in data. It enables internal auditors to analyze large volumes of data quickly and efficiently, allowing them to identify trends and anomalies that may be hidden in traditional audit methods. One of the primary benefits of data analytics is its ability to improve the efficiency and effectiveness of audits. With the traditional audit approach, auditors would typically sample a portion of the population and draw conclusions based on those samples. However, with data analytics, auditors can analyze entire data sets, providing a more comprehensive view of the organization's processes and controls.

Moreover, data analytics also enhances audit quality and helps auditors identify instances of fraud, waste, and abuse. By analyzing large volumes of data, auditors can identify patterns and anomalies that could indicate fraudulent activities. This enables organizations to take proactive measures to prevent and detect fraud, rather than waiting for it to be discovered in the future.

Automation Tools

Automation tools are another game-changer in the field of internal auditing. These tools are designed to automate manual and repetitive tasks, enabling auditors to focus on more critical and strategic activities. By automating tasks such as data entry, data analysis, report generation, and risk assessments, internal auditors can save time and resources, allowing them to perform audits more efficiently and effectively. One example of an automation tool used in internal auditing is robotic process automation (RPA). RPA uses software to automate tasks that would traditionally require human input, such as data entry and report generation. By implementing RPA, auditors can reduce errors and increase the speed of their audit processes.

Another useful automation tool for internal auditors is continuous auditing. Continuous auditing is the process of periodically analyzing data in real-time to identify potential risks and exceptions. This allows auditors to detect issues quickly, allowing organizations to take corrective action before they become significant problems.

Role of IT Auditing

The role of information technology (IT) in internal auditing has significantly increased with the rise of technology in the business world. IT auditors are responsible for evaluating the reliability, security, and integrity of an organization's information systems, which includes technologies such as databases, networks, and computer systems.

IT audits are critical for assessing risks associated with an organization's IT systems and ensuring that the necessary controls are in place to protect sensitive data. As technology continues to advance, IT auditors must stay up-to-date with emerging trends and threats to provide relevant and valuable insights to organizations.

Moreover, the integration of IT auditing with data analytics and automation tools has brought significant benefits to the field of internal auditing. By using these technologies, IT auditors can identify and assess risks more effectively and provide insights that go beyond traditional audit methods.

The Future of Technology in Internal Auditing

As technology continues to advance, the role of technology in internal auditing is only going to become more significant. With the increasing use of artificial intelligence (AI) and big data, internal auditors will be able to perform more complex analyses and provide more valuable insights to organizations.

AI-powered analytics tools can automatically identify patterns and abnormalities in data, helping auditors to detect potential risks and fraud more accurately and efficiently. Big data is also revolutionizing the way internal auditors perform risk assessments. By analyzing vast amounts of data, auditors can quickly identify potential risks and prioritize them based on their potential impact on the organization.

One concern with the increasing use of technology in internal auditing is the ethical implications it may bring. As auditors rely more on technology and automation, the reliance on human judgment and decision-making reduces. Therefore, it is crucial for auditors to maintain a balance between technology and human judgment to ensure that audit decisions are sound and ethical.

Conclusion

The use of technology in internal auditing has significantly improved the efficiency, effectiveness, and quality of audits. By leveraging data analytics, automation tools, and IT auditing, internal auditors can provide more valuable insights to organizations and help them mitigate risks and improve controls. As technology continues to evolve, it is essential for internal auditors to embrace these advancements and use them to their advantage. By doing so, internal auditors can significantly contribute to the success of organizations in the future.

Chapter 14: Auditing in the Digital Age

Components of an Audit Report

In today's constantly evolving business world, internal auditors are faced with the challenge of keeping up with new technologies and data sources while still maintaining a high level of efficiency and accuracy in their work. As a result, the role of internal auditors has shifted from traditional manual auditing methods to incorporating more advanced digital tools and techniques. The audit report, which is the final deliverable of an audit, must also evolve to reflect this digital shift.

An audit report is a formal communication document that summarizes the results and findings of an audit engagement. It serves as the primary way for internal auditors to communicate their observations, recommendations, and conclusions to management and stakeholders. The report must be well-organized and easy to understand to ensure that its recipients can make informed decisions based on the information provided. Therefore, it is essential to have certain components in an audit report to ensure its effectiveness.

Audit Scope and Objectives

The audit scope and objectives section define the boundaries and goals of the audit. It outlines what areas or processes were examined and the specific objectives that the audit aimed to achieve. This helps provide context for the findings and recommendations later in the report.

In the digital age, the scope and objectives may also include the use of technology and data analytics in the audit process. For example, if the audit is evaluating the effectiveness of an organization's data security measures, the scope may specify the assessment of security software and protocols.

Executive Summary

The executive summary is a concise overview of the audit report. It highlights the key findings and recommendations in an easily digestible format. This section is crucial for busy management and stakeholders who may not have time to read the entire report in detail. In the digital age, an executive summary may also include visual aids and data visualizations, making it more engaging and impactful.

Audit Findings and Recommendations

One of the most critical components of an audit report is the section that outlines the findings and recommendations. This section should be clear, detailed, and supported by evidence. In the digital age, audit findings may include weaknesses or gaps in technology systems or processes, and recommendations may revolve around implementing advanced digital tools or upgrading current systems.

It is essential to provide relevant and applicable recommendations that align with the organization's goals and objectives. Internal auditors must also consider the feasibility and cost-effectiveness of their recommendations to ensure they are realistic and achievable.

Communicating Results to Management and Stakeholders

Once the audit report is complete, the next step is to communicate the results to management and stakeholders. With the rise of technology, there are now more efficient and effective ways to share audit findings and recommendations.

Interactive Presentations

In today's digital age, simply presenting audit results in a traditional PowerPoint deck may not be enough to engage and educate stakeholders. With new presentation software and technology, auditors can create more interactive and visually appealing presentations. For example, they can use virtual reality to simulate potential risks or data analytics software to showcase trends and patterns in data.

Online Dashboards

Another way to share audit results is through online dashboards. These platforms allow stakeholders to view audit findings and recommendations in real-time, providing immediate access to important information. Dashboards can also include data visualization tools, making it easier for stakeholders to interpret complex data.

Social Media

Incorporating social media as a communication tool may also be effective in certain organizations. For example, a company may have a closed social media group for internal communications, where auditors can share audit results and engage in discussions with management and employees.

Digital Collaboration Tools

In the digital age, auditors can leverage various collaboration tools to facilitate discussions and engage in real-time communication with management and stakeholders. These tools allow for quick and efficient communication, making it easier for auditors to address any questions or concerns that may arise.

The Importance of Adaptability and Inclusivity

As the world becomes increasingly digital, it is crucial for internal auditors to embrace and adapt to these changes. However, it is also essential to ensure that all stakeholders are included and comfortable with the new methods of communication. Some individuals may not be as tech-savvy as others or may prefer more traditional forms of communication. Therefore, it is important to be adaptable and offer multiple channels for sharing audit results.

In conclusion, the digital age has brought about significant changes in the way internal auditors conduct audits and communicate their findings. With the use of advanced technology and digital tools, the components of an audit report have also evolved. It is crucial for internal auditors to embrace these changes and continue to find innovative ways to communicate results effectively to management and stakeholders. By staying up-to-date with the latest technology and being adaptable and inclusive in their approach, internal auditors can ensure their reports are impactful and provide value to their organizations.

Chapter 15: Performance-based Auditing

As internal auditors, our ultimate goal is to add value to the organization by providing insights and recommendations to improve operations and achieve strategic objectives. However, our work does not end when we submit the audit report. In fact, it is just the beginning. The success of our audits depends on how well management responds to our findings and recommendations, and how effectively the audit committee oversees the organization's response.

In this chapter, we will discuss the importance of tracking management's response to audit findings and the role of the audit committee in providing oversight and guidance in addressing these findings.

Tracking Management's Response to Audit Findings

One of the most crucial aspects of audit work is tracking management's response to audit findings and recommendations. This process ensures that the identified issues are addressed and the organization's operations are improved. It also serves as a reliable measure of the effectiveness of the internal audit function.

To effectively track management's response, the internal auditors should establish a system that allows for timely and accurate documentation of actions taken by management to address the identified issues. This system should also include procedures for follow-up reviews to ensure that the recommended actions are implemented and effective. The tracking process should start immediately after the completion of the audit, as it allows for timely resolution of issues and prevents them from recurring. Additionally, continuous tracking and follow-up reviews provide evidence to management and the audit committee that the internal audit function is an integral part of the organization's governance structure and adds significant value.

Apart from documenting the actions taken by management, the system should also facilitate the communication of audit findings and recommendations to relevant stakeholders. This communication can be through regular reports or presentations to the audit committee, management, and the board of directors. Open and transparent communication promotes accountability and helps build trust between the internal audit function and stakeholders.

It is essential to note that the tracking process is not only about ensuring that management takes action. It is also an opportunity for internal auditors to assess the effectiveness and efficiency of their recommendations. If the recommended actions are not producing the desired results, auditors should communicate with management and work together to find alternative solutions.

Audit Committee Oversight

The audit committee plays a critical role in overseeing the organization's response to audit findings and recommendations. As one of the principal governing bodies, the audit committee provides the necessary oversight to ensure that management is addressing issues promptly and effectively.

To fulfill its responsibilities, the audit committee should have a thorough understanding of the organization's operations, strategic objectives, and critical risks. It should also regularly review the internal audit function's performance, including the audits conducted, recommendations made, and management's response.

The audit committee should also monitor the implementation of the recommended actions by management and provide guidance and support where necessary. This support can involve requesting more information from the internal audit function, consulting with external experts, or involving other committees or the board of directors.

Furthermore, the audit committee should communicate with internal auditors on a regular basis to stay informed about the progress of audit recommendations and any identified issues that require their attention. This communication also allows for the audit committee to provide feedback and guidance on the internal audit function's performance and improvement opportunities.

Lastly, the audit committee should ensure that the internal audit function is adequately resourced and has the necessary skills and expertise to effectively carry out its responsibilities. This includes supporting professional development opportunities for internal auditors and evaluating the internal audit function's budget.

In conclusion, tracking management's response to audit findings and the audit committee's oversight play an integral role in the success of the internal audit function. An effective and transparent tracking process, coupled with regular communication and support from the audit committee, promotes accountability, trust, and continuous improvement within the organization. As certified internal auditors, it is our responsibility to ensure that these processes are in place and functioning effectively to enhance the organization's overall performance.

Chapter 16: Building Strong Relationships in Internal Auditing

Internal auditors play a critical role in organizations by providing independent and objective assessments of the company's operations, risks, and controls. To effectively carry out their duties, they must build strong relationships with different stakeholders, including management, employees, and external auditors. These relationships are essential for obtaining the necessary information, resources, and support to conduct efficient audits. In this chapter, we will explore the key elements of building strong relationships in internal auditing and how it contributes to the success of the internal audit function.

Building Relationships

Relationship building is the process of developing connections and establishing trust with others. In the world of internal auditing, this means establishing and maintaining professional relationships with various stakeholders who have a vested interest in the company's operations, such as the board of directors, senior management, and business unit heads. However, building relationships is not just a one-time effort; it requires continuous nurturing and genuine interest in understanding the needs and concerns of stakeholders.

Effective relationship building starts with having a positive attitude and approach towards others. This includes being respectful, open-minded, and empathetic. Internal auditors should strive to understand the perspectives of others and avoid making assumptions or judgments. By being approachable and actively listening to the concerns of stakeholders, auditors can build trust and rapport, making it easier to obtain information and support for audits.

Another critical aspect of relationship building is maintaining confidentiality. As internal auditors, we are privy to sensitive information that must be kept confidential to maintain the organization's integrity. Building strong relationships involves respecting the confidentiality of information shared by stakeholders and not disclosing it without proper authorization.

Communicating with Different Stakeholders

Effective communication is essential in any relationship, and the same applies to the internal audit function. Internal auditors must be skilled communicators, able to articulate complex issues and effectively convey the results of their audits to different stakeholders. In the world of internal auditing, there are various stakeholders with different levels of understanding of audit concepts and techniques. Therefore, internal auditors must communicate in a way that is easily understood and tailored to their audience.

When communicating with senior management and the board of directors, internal auditors should focus on providing high-level summaries, key findings, and recommendations. This allows them to understand the overall risks and control environment of the organization and make informed decisions. On the other hand, when communicating with business unit heads and department managers, internal auditors should be more detailed and provide specific, actionable recommendations to help drive change and improvement in processes and controls.

Communication with stakeholders should also be frequent and ongoing, as it helps to maintain trust and ensure that the audit process is transparent. This includes providing regular updates on the status of audits, addressing any concerns or questions, and seeking feedback on the audit process. By involving stakeholders in the audit process, internal auditors can gain valuable insights and build stronger relationships, leading to more effective audits.

Conflict Resolution

Despite our best efforts to build strong relationships, conflicts may arise between the internal audit function and stakeholders. These conflicts can stem from differing opinions, priorities, and goals. However, it is essential to address and resolve conflicts in a professional and respectful manner to maintain the integrity of the audit process.

Conflict resolution starts with active listening and seeking to understand the concerns and perspectives of all parties involved. Internal auditors should approach conflicts with an open mind and try to find common ground to address the issue. This may involve negotiating or compromising to find a mutually beneficial solution. It is also crucial to maintain professionalism and avoid taking conflicts personally, as this can damage relationships and hinder future collaborations.

In situations where conflicts cannot be resolved through dialogue, it is essential to escalate the issue to higher management or the board of directors for guidance and resolution. This demonstrates the internal audit function's commitment to maintaining independence and objectivity in the audit process.

In conclusion, building strong relationships is crucial for the success of the internal audit function. By having a positive attitude, effectively communicating with stakeholders, and addressing conflicts in a professional manner, internal auditors can build trust and rapport, leading to more effective audits and ultimately, the organization's success. Therefore, it is essential to continuously nurture and invest in building strong relationships in the world of internal auditing.

Chapter 17: International Internal Auditing

International business has become more interconnected and complex than ever before. Due to globalization, organizations are expanding their operations beyond borders, resulting in a need for international internal auditing practices. Internal auditors play a vital role in ensuring the smooth functioning of organizations by providing insights and recommendations on their governance, risk management, and control processes. In this chapter, we will explore the differences in international auditing practices, the challenges faced by internal auditors, and important considerations for conducting international audits.

Differences in International Auditing Practices

One of the main differences in international auditing practices is the varying regulatory environments and accounting standards in different countries. This poses a challenge for internal auditors as they not only have to comply with local laws and regulations, but also understand the international standards and cultural nuances of the countries they are operating in. Moreover, in some countries, there may be a lack of established standards and best practices for internal auditing, making it difficult to conduct audits that meet global standards. This can result in varying levels of effectiveness and consistency in audits across different countries.

Another major difference is the cultural and language barriers that can affect the communication and understanding between auditors and auditees. Internal auditors must be aware of these differences and adapt their communication and audit approaches accordingly, in order to effectively carry out their responsibilities.

Furthermore, the complexity and diversity of business operations in international organizations require internal auditors to have a deep understanding and expertise in a wide range of industries and business practices. This can be a challenge, especially for auditors who are not familiar with the industry or market they are auditing.

Challenges and Considerations

Conducting international audits also presents unique challenges for internal auditors. Some of these challenges include managing cultural differences in the workplace, dealing with language barriers, and navigating through unfamiliar legal and regulatory requirements. Additionally, due to the global nature of business, internal auditors may have to travel extensively, often to remote and unfamiliar locations, which can be physically and mentally taxing. Another major consideration for internal auditors is the diversity and complexity of technology systems used by multinational organizations. Auditors must have a strong understanding of these systems and their controls in order to effectively assess their effectiveness and identify potential risks.

Moreover, cross-border transactions, currency conversions, and valuation of assets and liabilities in different countries can also pose challenges for auditors. They must have a thorough understanding of these issues and consider them while conducting international audits to ensure accuracy and reliability of their findings.

In addition to these challenges, internal auditors must also be cognizant of the political, economic, and social environment of the countries they are operating in. Changes in any of these factors can impact the businesses and their operations, making it crucial for auditors to stay updated and consider them in their risk assessment and audit planning. Another important consideration for international internal auditors is the concept of cultural relativity. This refers to the cultural differences that can affect perceptions and behaviors, and ultimately impact how audits are conducted. Auditors must be culturally sensitive and aware of their own biases while conducting audits, in order to maintain objectivity and professionalism.

It is also important for internal auditors to have a strong understanding of the organization's global objectives, strategies, and risks. This will help them focus their audit objectives and scope, and provide valuable insights and recommendations that are aligned with the organization's goals.

In conclusion, conducting international audits presents a unique set of challenges for internal auditors. They must be prepared to adapt to different regulatory and cultural environments, be aware of the diversity and complexity of international business operations, and consider various factors that can impact the audit process. By being aware of these differences and challenges, internal auditors can effectively carry out their duties and help organizations in achieving their global objectives.

Chapter 18: Auditing for Enterprise Risk Management

Healthcare

In the healthcare industry, the importance of effective risk management cannot be overstated. From patient safety to financial stability, healthcare organizations face a myriad of risks on a daily basis. As such, it is crucial for internal auditors to have a thorough understanding of enterprise risk management (ERM) and its role in the healthcare setting. One of the key challenges in auditing for ERM in healthcare is the ever-changing landscape of regulations and compliance requirements. Healthcare organizations must comply with numerous laws and regulations, including HIPAA, Medicare and Medicaid rules, and state-specific regulations. Auditors must be knowledgeable in these regulations to ensure the organization is in compliance and managing risks appropriately.

Another important consideration in healthcare ERM auditing is the technological advancements and digital transformation in the industry. With electronic health records, telemedicine, and other technological innovations, healthcare organizations are faced with new risks and vulnerabilities. Internal auditors must stay up-to-date on these advancements and incorporate them into their risk assessments and audits.

Financial Services

In the fast-paced world of financial services, enterprise risk management is paramount. Financial institutions are subject to a wide range of risks, from market fluctuations to cybersecurity threats. It is the responsibility of internal auditors to help mitigate these risks and ensure the organization is operating in a sound and secure manner.

One of the most significant risks facing the financial services industry is cyber threats. With the increasing use of technology and the digitization of financial services, the risk of cyber attacks has grown exponentially. Internal auditors play a crucial role in assessing and testing the effectiveness of cybersecurity controls and processes.

In addition to cyber risks, financial services organizations also face compliance risks. With numerous regulatory requirements and strict laws, auditors must possess a deep understanding of the industry's regulations to effectively audit for ERM. This includes staying informed of updates and changes to regulations and incorporating them into risk assessments and audits.

Manufacturing

Manufacturing organizations face a unique set of risks that require careful and continuous monitoring. From supply chain disruptions to product quality control, there are various factors that can impact a manufacturer's operations and financial stability. Auditing for ERM in these organizations requires a thorough understanding of the manufacturing process and supply chain management.

One significant risk in the manufacturing industry is supply chain disruptions. With global supply chains and just-in-time production methods, any disruption can have a significant impact on an organization's operations and financials. Internal auditors must work closely with supply chain management to identify potential risks and implement appropriate controls.

Another essential aspect of ERM auditing in manufacturing is ensuring product quality control. Defective products can not only result in financial losses but can also pose a risk to consumer safety. Auditors must assess the organization's quality control processes and procedures to mitigate these risks and ensure products meet industry standards.

Government

Enterprise risk management in the public sector is a complex and multi-faceted task. Government organizations are responsible for providing various services to citizens, and any risk or disruption can have far-reaching consequences. Internal auditors in the government sector play a crucial role in identifying and managing these risks.

One of the significant risks facing government organizations is budgetary constraints. With limited resources and increasing demands for services, internal auditors must ensure that funds are allocated and spent efficiently and effectively. This includes assessing the organization's financial controls and identifying areas for improvement. Another vital aspect of ERM auditing in the government sector is ensuring compliance with laws and regulations. Government organizations must adhere to strict regulations and laws, including those related to data privacy and security. Auditors must have a thorough understanding of these regulations and incorporate them into their risk assessments and audits.

Conclusion

Auditing for ERM is an essential function in any organization, regardless of the industry. In healthcare, financial services, manufacturing, and government organizations, internal auditors play a crucial role in identifying and managing risks to ensure the organization's overall success. By staying informed of industry-specific risks and regulations, auditors can help organizations build a strong and resilient risk management framework.

Chapter 19: Enterprise Risk Management

Integrated Approach to Risk Management

Risk management has become an essential part of organizational operations, regardless of industry or size. It involves identifying, assessing, and mitigating potential risks that could impact the achievement of organizational objectives. Traditionally, risk management was seen as a separate function within an organization, but with the increasing complexity and interconnectedness of business processes, it has become imperative to integrate risk management into overall organizational strategy.

An integrated approach to risk management goes beyond the traditional approach of identifying and mitigating risks after they have occurred. It involves identifying potential risks at the onset of any business decision and incorporating risk mitigation strategies into the decision-making process. This pro-active approach ensures that risks are managed in a timely manner and potential losses can be avoided.

Furthermore, an integrated approach to risk management also involves involving all levels of the organization in the process. This means that risk management is not the sole responsibility of a risk management team or department, but rather a collaborative effort across all departments, functions, and levels. This not only helps in identifying a broader range of risks but also encourages a culture of risk awareness and accountability throughout the organization.

In addition, integrating risk management with other organizational processes such as strategic planning, performance management, and budgeting ensures that risks are considered and addressed in all aspects of the organization's operations. This also helps in aligning risk management with organizational objectives, which leads us to our next heading.

Aligning with Organizational Objectives

Risk management can no longer be seen as a separate function that only works to mitigate potential risks. It has to be aligned with organizational objectives to be truly effective in mitigating risks and helping the organization achieve its goals. This alignment ensures that risks are managed in a way that is in line with the organization's values, mission, and vision.

To align risk management with organizational objectives, it is crucial to have a clear understanding of the organization's objectives and the risks that could potentially impact them. This understanding can be achieved through regular communication and collaboration across departments and levels.

Furthermore, risk management should be viewed as a strategic function that helps the organization achieve its objectives rather than a hindrance to obtaining them. This mindset shift can be achieved by involving risk management in strategic planning processes and considering potential risks and their mitigation strategies in all decision-making processes.

In addition, an integrated and aligned approach to risk management also means that it is not solely focused on avoiding risks, but also on taking calculated risks that can help the organization achieve its objectives. This requires a risk-aware culture where employees feel empowered to take risks while also being knowledgeable about the potential risks and consequences.

Another important factor in aligning risk management with organizational objectives is to ensure that it is in line with the organization's values and culture. This means that risk management strategies should reflect the organization's values and consider the impact on stakeholders and society as a whole. Moreover, by aligning risk management with organizational objectives, the organization is better able to prioritize risks and allocate resources accordingly. This ensures that the most critical risks are identified and addressed in a timely and effective manner.

In conclusion, the modern business landscape requires an integrated and aligned approach to risk management for organizations to thrive. This involves involving all levels of the organization, integrating risk management with other organizational processes, and aligning it with organizational objectives, values, and culture. By doing so, organizations can effectively mitigate risks and achieve their objectives while also creating a risk-aware culture that contributes to their long-term success.

Chapter 20: Evaluating Business Processes for Auditing Excellence

Internal auditors play a crucial role in evaluating the various business processes within an organization. They are responsible for ensuring that these processes are effective and efficient in achieving the organization's objectives. As a CIA, it is essential to understand the methodology and best practices for evaluating business processes to ensure accuracy and reliability in our audits. In this chapter, we will dive deep into the process of evaluating business processes, including determining their effectiveness and efficiency and identifying opportunities for improvement.

Evaluating Business Processes

Before diving into the evaluation process, it is essential to understand what business processes are. Business processes are a series of activities that an organization performs to achieve its desired outcomes. These processes can range from simple to complex, involving multiple departments and stakeholders. By evaluating these processes, internal auditors can identify any flaws or inefficiencies that may hinder the organization's success.

The first step in evaluating business processes is to understand and document the current processes. This includes analyzing the process flow, identifying key stakeholders involved, and outlining the objectives of the process. As auditors, we must review this documentation to gain a thorough understanding before proceeding with the evaluation.

The next step is to evaluate the process based on the organization's objectives and industry best practices. This involves examining the process's effectiveness and efficiency, which we will discuss in detail in the next section. It is also crucial to assess the risks associated with the process and how they are managed. We must also identify any key performance indicators (KPIs) that are used to measure the process's success.

Once the process evaluation is complete, we must report our findings and recommendations to the relevant stakeholders. These recommendations may include changes to the process flow, control improvements, or implementing new technology to enhance efficiency. It is vital to communicate these recommendations effectively and ensure they align with the organization's objectives.

Determining Effectiveness and Efficiency

The effectiveness of a business process refers to how well it achieves its objectives. As internal auditors, it is our responsibility to ensure that the processes we evaluate are effective in achieving the organization's goals. To determine effectiveness, auditors must measure the process's output against its objectives and determine if it meets stakeholder expectations. It is also essential to assess if the process aligns with industry best practices and if any regulatory or compliance requirements are being met.

Efficiency, on the other hand, measures how well a process utilizes resources to achieve its objectives. As internal auditors, we should evaluate the efficiency of a business process by considering factors such as time, costs, and resources utilized. This assessment can help identify any wastage or inefficiencies within the process and suggest ways to improve them.

One critical aspect of evaluating effectiveness and efficiency is benchmarking. By benchmarking against industry peers or best practices, auditors can gain valuable insights into how well the organization's processes measure up. This comparison can help identify any gaps and areas for improvement, allowing the organization to stay competitive and efficient in its processes.

Identifying Opportunities for Improvement

During the process evaluation, internal auditors should also keep an eye out for opportunities to improve the process. This could include identifying areas where technology could be implemented to automate manual processes or streamlining the process flow to eliminate redundancies. Auditors must also consider any potential risks associated with these changes and make recommendations accordingly.

Another way to identify opportunities for improvement is to gather feedback from stakeholders involved in the process. This feedback can provide valuable insights into pain points or bottlenecks within the process that may not be apparent in the documentation. As auditors, we must be open to constructive criticism and use it to identify areas for improvement in the process.

In addition to gathering feedback, auditors can also conduct interviews and surveys to gather data on the process's effectiveness and efficiency. This data can provide a more in-depth understanding of the process and help identify any underlying issues that may need to be addressed.

Closing Thoughts

Effective evaluation of business processes is crucial to maintaining the organization's success. As internal auditors, it is our responsibility to ensure that these processes are effective and efficient in achieving the organization's objectives. By understanding the methodology and best practices for evaluating business processes, we can provide valuable insights and recommendations to improve the organization's overall performance.

Chapter 21: Quality Assurance and Improvement Program

Purpose and Importance

Internal Auditing is crucial for organizations as it provides independent and objective assurance on their operations. To ensure the effectiveness and credibility of internal audit activities, it is essential to have a comprehensive Quality Assurance and Improvement Program (QAIP) in place. A QAIP is a structured approach to systematically evaluate and improve the internal audit function's performance, adherence to professional standards, and alignment with the organization's objectives. It serves as a vital tool to maintain the integrity and value of the internal audit function, which is why having a robust and well-developed QAIP is crucial for every Certified Internal Auditor (CIA).

One of the primary purposes of a QAIP is to provide assurance to key stakeholders, including senior management and the board of directors, that the internal audit function is meeting established professional standards and contributing to the organization's strategic objectives. It also enables internal audit leaders to identify areas for improvement, demonstrate the value of the internal audit function, and build confidence in the organization's overall governance and risk management processes.

Elements of a QAIP

A QAIP comprises multiple elements that work together to evaluate and enhance the internal audit function's performance. These elements include:

Internal Assessments - This involves periodic self-evaluations of the internal audit function's effectiveness, efficiency, and compliance with professional standards. Internal assessments help identify strengths and weaknesses within the function and provide valuable insights for improvement.

External Assessments - As the name suggests, external assessments involve seeking a third party's professional opinion on the internal audit function. External assessments could be conducted by qualified individuals or organizations, such as the internal audit profession's external quality assessment (EQA) program. This element is crucial as it provides an objective and independent perspective on the internal audit function's performance.

Internal Audit Charter and Policies - The internal audit function's charter defines its purpose, authority, responsibilities, and relationship with other functions in the organization. It sets the tone for the internal audit function and provides guidance for conducting audits. Policies, on the other hand, are more detailed and establish the framework for how the internal audit function will operate. Both the charter and policies should be reviewed and updated periodically to ensure they remain relevant and aligned with the organization's objectives.

Professional Ethics - Internal Auditors are bound by a code of ethics that outlines their responsibilities and expectations. Therefore, a QAIP should include procedures to ensure ethical behavior and compliance with the code of ethics.

Staff Development - Having competent and knowledgeable internal auditors is crucial for the function's overall success. A QAIP should have procedures in place to support and promote staff development, such as providing training opportunities, mentoring programs, and career development plans.

Continual Improvement Cycle

To ensure the effectiveness and relevance of a QAIP, it is essential to establish a continual improvement cycle. This involves periodic evaluations of the QAIP elements and making necessary adjustments to enhance their effectiveness. The cycle typically includes the following steps:

Planning - This involves identifying the objectives, scope, resources, and timelines for the QAIP.

Execution - This step involves implementing the planned activities, such as conducting internal or external assessments, updating policies and procedures, or providing staff development opportunities.

Observation - Once the planned activities are executed, it is essential to observe their results and gather feedback from key stakeholders.

Evaluation - Based on the observations and feedback, the QAIP's effectiveness and impact on the internal audit function should be evaluated.

Improvement - The final step in the cycle is to make necessary improvements based on the evaluation results. This could include updating or revising procedures, implementing new processes, or providing additional resources.

Conclusion

A robust and well-developed QAIP is essential for the success of the internal audit function. It provides assurance to stakeholders, enhances the function's credibility, and contributes to the organization's overall objectives. As a CIA, it is crucial to understand the purpose and importance of a QAIP and be actively involved in its continual improvement to fulfill the internal audit profession's ethical and professional responsibilities.

Chapter 22: Managing Audit Engagements

Auditing is a vital component of any organization's operations, as it helps identify potential risks and control weaknesses. However, the success of an internal audit greatly depends on how it is managed. This is where the role of managing audit engagements comes into play. In this chapter, we will delve into the roles and responsibilities, coordination strategies, and common challenges that internal auditors face when it comes to managing audit engagements.

Roles and Responsibilities

Managing audit engagements involves a range of responsibilities that go beyond just reviewing financial statements and identifying control deficiencies. As a manager, you are responsible for overseeing the entire audit process, from planning to follow-up. This requires excellent organizational and leadership skills, as well as a deep understanding of auditing standards and techniques.

One of the key roles of managing audit engagements is setting clear objectives and expectations for the audit team. This involves defining the scope of the audit, establishing timelines, and assigning tasks to team members. As a manager, you must ensure that the team is well-equipped with the necessary resources and support to carry out their duties effectively.

In addition to project management, managing audit engagements also involves reviewing and evaluating audit work. This includes conducting quality assurance reviews and providing feedback to the audit team to enhance their performance. It is the manager's responsibility to ensure that the audit work is in compliance with the organization's policies and procedures, as well as external auditing standards.

Coordination Strategies

Effective coordination is essential for the success of any audit engagement. As a manager, it is your responsibility to promote collaboration and communication within the audit team. This can be achieved through regular team meetings, where progress is discussed and any issues or challenges are addressed.

Another important aspect of coordination is establishing a good working relationship with other departments and stakeholders within the organization. This includes building a rapport with management and gaining their cooperation and support throughout the audit process. It also involves coordinating with external auditors, if applicable, to ensure a smooth and efficient audit.

Utilizing technology and tools for coordination can also be beneficial. Internal audit software can help streamline the audit process and facilitate communication between team members. It can also provide real-time updates and progress tracking, making it easier to manage audit engagements remotely.

Common Challenges

Managing audit engagements comes with its fair share of challenges. One of the most common challenges is managing stakeholder expectations. The key to overcoming this challenge is by setting realistic objectives and timelines from the start and providing regular updates to stakeholders throughout the audit process.

Another challenge is managing conflicts within the audit team. In such situations, it is essential to have a clear communication channel and encourage open dialogue. Addressing conflicts promptly and effectively can help maintain team dynamics and ensure a successful audit.

Lastly, managing time and resources can be a challenge, especially when working with limited resources and tight deadlines. Careful planning and efficient resource allocation can help mitigate this challenge. It is also crucial to prioritize tasks and delegate responsibilities to team members as needed.

In conclusion, managing audit engagements is a crucial aspect of internal auditing that requires a combination of organizational skills, leadership abilities, and communication strategies. As a manager, it is your responsibility to effectively coordinate and lead the audit team, overcome challenges, and achieve successful outcomes for the organization. Utilizing the right tools and techniques can help streamline the process and ensure a smooth and efficient audit.

Chapter 23: Staffing, Budgeting, and Time Management for Internal Auditing Excellence

Internal audit functions play a critical role in ensuring the success and sustainability of organizations. As organizations face increasing complexity, volatility, and risks, the demand for skilled and effective internal auditors continues to grow. However, it is not just about having the right skills and competencies, but also about having the right staffing, budgeting, and time management strategies in place to achieve internal auditing excellence.

Staffing: Finding the Right Talent for Your Internal Audit Team

The first step in staffing for internal auditing excellence is finding the right talent for your team. This task can be quite daunting, as the role of an internal auditor requires a unique blend of technical skills, critical thinking abilities, and soft skills. Some organizations may opt to hire external candidates with extensive experience and qualifications, while others may choose to develop their team internally.

One key to successful staffing is creating a diverse and well-rounded team. Diversity in terms of skills, experiences, backgrounds, and perspectives can help improve the effectiveness and quality of internal audits. It also enables internal auditors to approach problems and challenges from different angles, leading to more insightful and value-adding recommendations. Another crucial element in staffing is ensuring the team has a mix of both technical and soft skills. While technical expertise is important, soft skills such as communication, relationship building, and adaptability are equally crucial, especially in a constantly evolving business landscape. Internal auditors must be able to effectively communicate their findings and recommendations to various stakeholders and build rapport with audit clients to gain their trust and cooperation.

Moreover, it is essential to have a continuous recruitment and development program for internal audit staff. This ensures a steady pipeline of talent and encourages team members to continuously enhance their skills and knowledge. Investing in the development of your internal audit team is investing in the future success of your organization.

Budgeting: Allocating Resources for Optimal Performance

One of the biggest challenges for internal audit functions is securing adequate resources to carry out their responsibilities effectively. Internal auditing excellence requires the appropriate allocation of resources, including staff, technology, and financial support. This means that budgeting for internal auditing must be strategically planned and managed.

The first step in budgeting for internal audit is establishing the necessary resources to carry out existing and upcoming audit engagements. This includes identifying the required number of personnel for each audit and ensuring they have access to the necessary technology and tools to perform their tasks effectively. One innovative approach to budgeting is activity-based budgeting, which allocates resources based on the level and complexity of activities and risks involved in each audit engagement. This method helps ensure that internal audit resources are used efficiently and effectively, reducing the likelihood of over or under-staffing.

Another key aspect of budgeting is incorporating risk-based budgeting, which allocates resources based on the level of risk associated with each audit engagement. High-risk areas may require more resources, while low-risk areas may need fewer resources. This approach also allows for flexibility in resource allocation, depending on the changing risk landscape.

Time Management: Maximizing Efficiency and Effectiveness

Time management is crucial in achieving internal auditing excellence. With tight deadlines and an ever-growing list of tasks and responsibilities, internal auditors must have strong time management skills to perform at their best.

Effective time management means having a clear understanding of priorities and making the most of available resources. This involves careful planning and scheduling of audit engagements, as well as efficient delegation of tasks within the team. Additionally, effective communication and coordination among team members can help prevent redundancy, ensuring that time is spent on high-value activities. Moreover, technology can be a game-changer in time management for internal auditors. Automation of routine tasks, such as data gathering and analysis, can save significant time and allow internal auditors to focus on more critical and value-adding activities. It is crucial to regularly assess and invest in new technologies that can improve the efficiency and effectiveness of the internal audit function.

In conclusion, staffing, budgeting, and time management are essential elements in achieving internal auditing excellence. By investing in the right talent, strategically allocating resources, and practicing effective time management, organizations can ensure the success of their internal audit function and ultimately contribute to the overall success of their organization.

Chapter 24: Remote Auditing in a Virtual World

As technology continues to advance, the way we work and conduct business is constantly evolving. This is especially true for the internal auditing profession, where the traditional method of on-site audits is being challenged by the need for virtual audits. This shift towards remote auditing presents both challenges and opportunities for internal auditors. In this chapter, we will explore the challenges of conducting remote audits and discuss strategies for overcoming them. We will also delve into the use of technology for virtual audits and how it can be leveraged to improve the efficiency and effectiveness of the audit process.

Challenges and Strategies for Remote Auditing

One of the biggest challenges of remote auditing is the loss of the personal touch that is often present in on-site audits. Building relationships and establishing rapport with audit clients is crucial for effective communication and collaboration. When conducting virtual audits, it can be more difficult to establish this personal connection. Additionally, the lack of physical presence may make it more challenging for auditors to observe and assess the organization's culture and tone at the top. To overcome these challenges, auditors must adapt and find ways to build relationships and maintain effective communication in a virtual setting. This could include scheduling regular video conferences to discuss audit progress and findings, setting clear expectations and objectives for the audit, and utilizing virtual collaboration tools to facilitate team work. It is also important to be proactive and communicate frequently with audit clients to address any concerns or issues that may arise.

Another challenge of remote auditing is the limited access to the organization's physical premises. This may hinder the ability of auditors to gather sufficient evidence and perform physical inspections, which are essential for certain types of audits. To overcome this challenge, auditors must find ways to obtain evidence through alternative means, such as reviewing electronic documents and utilizing data analytics tools. It may also be necessary to conduct on-site visits at a later stage, once conditions allow for it.

Use of Technology for Virtual Audits

With the advancement of technology, auditors now have access to a wide range of tools and resources that can enhance the audit process. Virtual audits rely heavily on technology, and auditors must be proficient in utilizing these tools to effectively perform their duties. One of the most valuable resources for virtual auditing is data analytics. By analyzing vast amounts of data, auditors can identify trends, patterns, and anomalies that may not be apparent through traditional auditing methods. This helps to improve the efficiency of audits and provides a deeper understanding of the organization's operations. Collaboration and communication tools are also essential for conducting virtual audits. Virtual meetings, video conferencing, and online document sharing platforms allow for effective communication and collaboration between auditors and audit clients. These tools also make it easier to organize and manage audit workpapers and findings.

Technology also plays a significant role in data security and confidentiality for remote audits. As auditors may be accessing sensitive information from a remote location, it is crucial to ensure that proper security measures are in place to protect the organization's data. Encryption, firewalls, and password protection are some of the ways to safeguard data during virtual audits.

In addition to these tools, artificial intelligence (AI) and robotic process automation (RPA) are also being increasingly utilized in the audit process. AI-powered audit tools can analyze and interpret large amounts of data, identify potential risks, and assist in planning the audit. RPA, on the other hand, can automate routine audit tasks, freeing up auditors to focus on more complex and value-added activities.

Incorporating Creativity and Innovation

With the shift towards virtual audits, there is also an opportunity for auditors to incorporate creativity and innovation into their approach. As remote audits may not have the same limitations as on-site audits, auditors can develop new and innovative ways to gather evidence and assess controls. This could include virtual walkthroughs, remote interviews, and using drones for physical inspections. Another emerging trend in remote auditing is gamification. By using game-like elements, auditors can engage audit clients and make the audit process more interactive and enjoyable. This not only improves collaboration but also allows for a more thorough understanding of the organization's operations.

Embracing a Virtual Future

The COVID-19 pandemic has accelerated the adoption of virtual audits and has shown that it is possible to effectively conduct audits remotely. While there are challenges to overcome, the use of technology and innovative approaches can facilitate the transition to a virtual audit environment. Internal auditors must continue to adapt and embrace new ways of working to ensure that audits can be conducted efficiently and effectively in a virtual world. By utilizing the right tools and strategies, auditors can continue to add value to their organizations and uphold the integrity of the internal auditing profession.

Chapter 25: Training and Development for Internal Auditors

Internal auditors play a crucial role in ensuring the effectiveness of an organization's internal controls and overall risk management. To be successful in their roles, it is essential for auditors to continuously develop their skills and knowledge. However, with the rapidly changing business landscape and emerging technologies, it can be challenging to keep up with the constantly evolving expectations and demands of the field. This is why investing in training and professional development opportunities for internal auditors is crucial for maintaining and enhancing the quality of internal audit functions.

Skills Gap Analysis

Before determining the appropriate training plans and opportunities for internal auditors, it is essential to conduct a skills gap analysis. This involves identifying the current skills and competencies of the audit team and comparing them to the skills and competencies required to perform their roles effectively. This analysis will help identify any areas where the team may need additional training or development. One way to conduct a skills gap analysis is through a performance evaluation process. This can involve a self-assessment from the auditor, as well as feedback from their supervisor and colleagues. Identifying areas where auditors feel they need more training or where their performance may have been lacking can help determine the necessary training plans.

Additionally, organizations can also conduct a more formal skills assessment, such as a competency assessment, to identify individual and team strengths and weaknesses. This process can involve testing or observation of auditors' performance to assess their skills and knowledge in key areas such as risk assessment, data analysis, and communication.

Training Plans

Once the skills gap analysis has been completed, it is crucial to develop a training plan that addresses the identified gaps. This can include internal training programs, external courses, conferences, and other forms of professional development opportunities.

Internal training programs can be tailored to meet the specific needs of the team and organization. These can include workshops, seminars, or webinars on topics such as audit methodologies, risk management, or data analytics. Internal training can also involve shadowing experienced auditors or cross-training within different areas of the organization to broaden auditors' skill sets.

External courses and conferences can provide auditors with the opportunity to learn from industry experts and stay updated with the latest trends and developments in the field. It is essential to choose training opportunities that align with the specific needs of the team and organization. These opportunities can also allow auditors to network with other professionals in the field and exchange best practices.

Professional Development Opportunities

In addition to formal training programs, there are many other professional development opportunities that internal auditors can take advantage of. These can include certifications, memberships in professional organizations, and mentorship programs.

Certifications, such as the Certified Internal Auditor (CIA) designation, are highly valued in the industry and can provide auditors with a competitive edge. These certifications demonstrate a high level of skill and knowledge in the field of internal auditing and can open up opportunities for career advancement. Joining professional organizations, such as the Institute of Internal Auditors (IIA), can offer auditors access to a wealth of resources, networking opportunities, and educational events. These organizations also offer continuing education opportunities, which are essential for maintaining certifications and staying current in the field.

Mentorship programs can also be highly beneficial for internal auditors, especially those early in their careers. Mentors can provide valuable guidance, support, and knowledge sharing, helping to bridge the skills gap and accelerate the growth and development of junior auditors.

In Conclusion

As the internal audit field continues to evolve, it is essential to invest in the training and development of auditors to ensure the success of internal audit functions. Conducting a skills gap analysis, developing appropriate training plans, and providing professional development opportunities are crucial for maintaining audit quality and staying ahead of the curve in today's fast-paced business world. By continuously investing in the development of internal auditors, organizations can ensure the effectiveness of their internal audit function and support the growth and success of the organization as a whole.

Chapter 26: Internal Audit Quality and Improvement

Evaluating Audit Quality

As internal auditors, our primary responsibility is to provide assurance to our organization's management and stakeholders that risks are being effectively managed. In order to fulfill this role, it is crucial that the quality of our audits is continuously evaluated and improved upon. This not only allows us to uphold the highest standards of our profession, but also helps build trust in our organization's processes and controls.

One way to evaluate the quality of our audits is through the use of quality assurance and improvement programs (QAIPs). An effective QAIP should include both internal and external assessments, as well as ongoing monitoring of audit activities. These assessments should be conducted using a comprehensive set of criteria, such as the International Standards for the Professional Practice of Internal Auditing (Standards), to ensure a thorough evaluation of all aspects of our audit process. Another key aspect of evaluating audit quality is taking into consideration the expectations and needs of our stakeholders. This includes understanding their level of satisfaction with our work, as well as their perception of the value added to the organization through our audits. Regular communication with stakeholders is crucial in gauging their satisfaction and identifying areas for improvement.

Monitoring for Improvement

Once we have evaluated the quality of our audits, the next step is to implement improvements to enhance our performance. This can be achieved through the use of monitoring activities, which involve tracking and analyzing our audit processes and outcomes on a continuous basis. One important aspect of monitoring is performing root cause analysis. This involves investigating the underlying reasons for any identified deficiencies or deviations from our audit objectives. By understanding these root causes, we can take corrective action to prevent such issues from recurring in the future. Additionally, internal auditors can use data analytics and technology to monitor and analyze large sets of audit data. This allows us to identify trends and patterns, helping us to proactively identify potential risks and areas for improvement.

Furthermore, it is important to regularly review and update our audit methodologies and tools to keep up with changing business environments and emerging technologies. This ensures that our audit processes are efficient, effective, and aligned with relevant regulations and best practices.

Managing Risks

As internal auditors, we not only evaluate and monitor risks within our organization, but we also have a responsibility to manage the risks within our own audit function. This includes identifying and managing potential threats to our independence, objectivity, and integrity.

One of the ways to manage these risks is through regular training and development for internal auditors. By continuously acquiring new skills and knowledge, we can stay relevant and adapt to the evolving needs and expectations of our stakeholders. Another important aspect of managing risks is fostering a culture of ethics and compliance within the internal audit function. This involves promoting ethical behavior and creating a safe environment for whistleblowers to report any concerns or violations. It is also crucial to regularly communicate with management and the audit committee, providing them with updates on our risk management processes and any potential risks or threats to the internal audit function.

In conclusion, evaluating and continuously monitoring the quality of our audits is essential to ensure the effectiveness of our role as internal auditors. By implementing improvements and effectively managing risks, we can uphold the highest standards of our profession and provide valuable assurance to our organization and stakeholders.

Chapter 27: Governmental and Regulatory Requirements

As internal auditors, it is important for us to not only have a deep understanding of auditing standards and frameworks, but also of the various regulations and guidelines that govern our profession. Compliance with these requirements is crucial for maintaining the integrity and credibility of the internal audit function. In this chapter, we will explore the different facets of governmental and regulatory requirements and their impact on internal auditing.

Compliance Audits

One of the key roles of internal auditors is to assess the organization's level of compliance with laws, regulations, and internal policies. Compliance audits help to identify any potential risks and non-compliant practices within an organization and provide recommendations for improvement. These audits also provide assurance to stakeholders, including management, board of directors, and regulatory bodies.

In order to conduct effective compliance audits, internal auditors must possess a deep understanding of the relevant laws and regulations, as well as the organization's internal policies and procedures. They must also have a keen eye for detecting potential areas of non-compliance and be able to effectively communicate their findings to stakeholders. It is important for auditors to remain independent and objective in their assessment, while also being sensitive to the organization's culture and values.

Sarbanes-Oxley Act

In the wake of major corporate scandals, such as Enron and WorldCom, the Sarbanes-Oxley Act (SOX) was enacted in 2002 to restore trust in the financial markets. This legislation applies to all public companies in the United States and requires them to maintain strict internal controls over financial reporting and to disclose any material weaknesses in those controls. The internal audit function plays a critical role in SOX compliance by providing an independent assessment of the company's internal controls and identifying any potential weaknesses or deficiencies. This not only helps to ensure accurate financial reporting, but also strengthens the overall control environment of the organization.

However, it is important for internal auditors to keep in mind that SOX compliance is not just a box-ticking exercise. It is about continuously improving and strengthening the internal control framework to prevent future scandals and protect the interests of stakeholders.

Other Regulations and Guidelines

Apart from SOX, there are various other regulations and guidelines that internal auditors need to be familiar with. These include industry-specific regulations, such as the Health Insurance Portability and Accountability Act (HIPAA) for healthcare organizations, as well as global regulations like the General Data Protection Regulation (GDPR) in Europe. Additionally, audit standards and frameworks, such as the International Standards for the Professional Practice of Internal Auditing (Standards), also contain guidelines and requirements related to regulatory compliance. For example, Standard 2100: Nature of Work requires internal auditors to have sufficient knowledge of laws, regulations, and industry-specific practices relevant to the organization being audited.

It is important for internal auditors to continuously stay updated on any changes in regulations and guidelines to ensure their audits are conducted in accordance with the latest requirements.

In the world of internal auditing, staying on top of regulatory requirements is vital for maintaining integrity, credibility, and effectiveness. Compliance audits, the Sarbanes-Oxley Act, and other regulations and guidelines serve as guidelines for internal auditors to ensure that organizations are operating in an ethical and compliant manner. By continuously strengthening these controls, internal auditors contribute to the overall success and sustainability of the organization.

Chapter 28: Corporate Social Responsibility Auditing

In today's business world, there is growing pressure from stakeholders for companies to not only focus on profitability, but also on their impact on society and the environment. Corporate Social Responsibility (CSR) has become a crucial aspect of business operations, and companies are expected to be transparent and accountable for their actions. This has led to the rise of CSR reporting and audits, with the role of internal auditors becoming increasingly important in ensuring companies adhere to CSR standards. In this chapter, we will explore the definition and benefits of CSR audits, the role of internal auditors, and the reporting on CSR.

Definition and Benefits

Corporate Social Responsibility (CSR) can be defined as the responsibility of a company for its impact on society and the environment, beyond its legal and economic obligations. This includes a company's ethical, social and environmental practices. CSR audits are independent assessments of a company's impact and compliance with CSR standards. They provide assurance to stakeholders that the company is taking responsibility for its actions, and can help identify areas for improvement.

One of the main benefits of CSR audits is improved transparency and accountability. By undergoing a CSR audit, a company is making a public commitment to being responsible and sustainable. This can improve its reputation and trust with consumers, investors, and other stakeholders. CSR audits can also help companies identify areas of risk and improve their operations, leading to cost savings and increased efficiency. Additionally, CSR audits can help companies attract and retain top talent, as employees are increasingly looking for companies that align with their personal values.

Role of Internal Auditors

Internal auditors play a crucial role in ensuring a company's compliance with CSR standards. They are responsible for evaluating the effectiveness of a company's systems and processes to manage risks related to CSR. This includes assessing the company's policies, procedures, and controls to ensure they align with CSR principles and standards. Internal auditors also play a key role in assessing the accuracy and completeness of CSR reporting, providing assurance to stakeholders that the information presented is reliable.

It is important for internal auditors to have a strong understanding of CSR principles and standards, as well as the company's industry and operations. This will enable them to effectively evaluate the company's CSR practices and identify areas for improvement. Internal auditors also need to have strong communication skills and be able to work collaboratively with stakeholders from different levels of the organization. By partnering with the company's CSR team, internal auditors can help drive positive change and ensure the company's reputation and sustainability goals are met.

Reporting on CSR

CSR reporting is an important aspect of CSR audits, as it provides stakeholders with information on the company's CSR practices and performance. Internal auditors play a key role in evaluating the accuracy and completeness of CSR reporting, and providing assurance to stakeholders that the information presented is reliable.

CSR reporting can take various forms, including standalone CSR reports, integrated reports, and sustainability reports. Companies may choose to report on their CSR performance using internationally recognized frameworks such as the Global Reporting Initiative (GRI) or the UN Sustainable Development Goals (SDGs). These frameworks provide guidelines for reporting on a company's economic, environmental, and social impacts.

There are also external assurance services available to provide independent verification of a company's CSR reporting. Internal auditors may work with external auditors to assess the company's CSR reporting and provide additional assurance to stakeholders.

In conclusion, CSR audits play an important role in ensuring companies uphold their responsibilities to society and the environment. Internal auditors have a crucial role in evaluating a company's CSR practices, ensuring compliance with standards, and providing assurance on CSR reporting. By doing so, they help companies build trust and maintain their reputation, while also driving positive change towards a more sustainable future.

Chapter 29: Auditing for Environmental, Social, and Governance (ESG)

Environmental, Social, and Governance (ESG) Auditing

In recent years, there has been a growing importance placed on Environmental, Social, and Governance (ESG) factors within organizations. This has led to the rise of ESG auditing, which is the process of evaluating an organization's ESG performance and practices. As internal auditors, it is important to understand the role of ESG auditing and its impact on organizations and stakeholders.

ESG encompasses a wide range of issues including environmental sustainability, social responsibility, and corporate governance. ESG audits involve assessing how the organization addresses these issues and whether their actions align with their stated ESG goals and values. This includes reviewing policies, procedures, and practices related to environmental impact, diversity and inclusion, employee relations, human rights, supply chain management, and ethical business conduct. One of the main challenges in ESG auditing is the lack of standardized frameworks and reporting requirements. This makes it difficult to compare ESG performance across companies and industries. However, there are various guidelines and standards that organizations can follow, such as the Global Reporting Initiative (GRI) and the Sustainability Accounting Standards Board (SASB), in order to provide more transparency and consistency in their ESG reporting.

Impact on Organizations

The motivation for organizations to undergo ESG audits is not just driven by ethical or moral reasons, but also by the potential impact on their bottom line. Companies that demonstrate strong ESG performance have been found to have better financial returns and higher valuations than their peers. This is because ESG factors can have a significant influence on an organization's operational efficiency, risk management, and reputation.

For example, an organization with a strong commitment to reducing their carbon footprint may reduce their energy consumption and waste production, resulting in cost savings. A company with a diverse and inclusive workforce may have higher employee satisfaction and therefore, higher productivity. And a business that follows ethical business practices may have a better reputation and attract more customers. On the other hand, poor ESG performance can have negative consequences for an organization. This can include regulatory fines, legal action, negative publicity, and damage to their brand and reputation. Therefore, ESG audits can help identify areas of improvement for an organization and mitigate potential risks.

Impact on Stakeholders

ESG issues not only affect organizations, but also their stakeholders such as employees, customers, suppliers, and investors. Stakeholders are increasingly demanding more transparency and accountability from organizations when it comes to ESG performance. This is why ESG audits have become an important tool for organizations to demonstrate their commitment to sustainability and responsible business practices. For employees, a strong ESG performance from their organization can positively impact their job satisfaction and sense of purpose. Customers may also be more inclined to support a company that aligns with their own values and beliefs. Suppliers can also benefit from working with a socially and environmentally responsible organization. And investors may see better financial returns and reduced risks from investing in companies with good ESG practices.

However, lack of transparency or poor ESG performance can lead to loss of trust and support from stakeholders. This can ultimately affect the organization's bottom line and long-term sustainability.

In conclusion

ESG auditing has become an important aspect of internal auditing as organizations strive to improve their ESG performance and meet the growing demands of stakeholders. By evaluating an organization's environmental, social, and governance practices, ESG audits can identify potential risks and opportunities for improvement. It is up to internal auditors to stay informed on the latest ESG guidelines and standards in order to effectively assess and report on an organization's ESG performance.

Chapter 30: Managing Audit Findings and Recommendations

Key Considerations

When it comes to managing audit findings and recommendations, there are a few key considerations that internal auditors must keep in mind. The first and most important consideration is objectivity. As internal auditors, it is crucial to remain unbiased and objective when presenting findings and recommendations to management. This means avoiding personal biases or conflicts of interest and strictly adhering to professional standards and ethical principles. Another consideration is the clarity of communication. Auditors must ensure that their findings and recommendations are communicated clearly and concisely to management. This includes using non-technical language and providing supporting evidence to help management understand the issues and their potential impact on the organization.

In addition, timing is also an important consideration. Auditors must present findings and recommendations in a timely manner so that management can take immediate action to address any issues identified. This also means avoiding any unnecessary delays in the reporting process.

Due Diligence

To effectively manage audit findings and recommendations, auditors must conduct thorough due diligence. This includes verifying the accuracy and validity of the findings and recommendations before presenting them to management. This may involve reviewing documentation, interviewing relevant individuals, and conducting additional testing to ensure the reliability of the audit results. Another aspect of due diligence is understanding the context of the findings and recommendations. Auditors must consider the organization's objectives, risks, and controls to provide meaningful and relevant recommendations. This also involves understanding the culture and operations of the organization to provide practical and feasible solutions.

Managing Vendor Relationships

In today's business landscape, organizations often rely on third-party vendors for various services and products. This means that internal auditors must also consider the vendor relationships in managing audit findings and recommendations. Auditors must ensure that the vendor relationships are properly managed and that any potential risks or issues are identified and addressed.

Key considerations in managing vendor relationships include conducting thorough due diligence before engaging with a vendor, developing a strong vendor risk management program, and regularly monitoring the vendor's performance and compliance with contractual obligations.

Internal auditors also have a role in managing potential conflicts of interest with vendors. This means ensuring that vendors are selected based on objective criteria and that any potential conflicts are disclosed and addressed appropriately. Moreover, auditors must also consider the impact of any findings or recommendations on the vendor relationships. This includes communicating with vendors and collaborating with them to address any issues and improve processes, ultimately benefiting both the organization and the vendor.

Overall, managing vendor relationships is a crucial aspect of managing audit findings and recommendations. By understanding and addressing potential risks and issues with vendors, internal auditors can help mitigate operational and financial risks for the organization.

Uncommon and Insightful Concepts

One uncommon and insightful concept that internal auditors should keep in mind is the importance of empathy in managing audit findings and recommendations. While it is essential to maintain objectivity, auditors must also consider the perspectives and feelings of the individuals and teams that will be affected by the findings and recommendations. By empathizing with their concerns and needs, auditors can work together with management to develop practical and effective solutions that are well-received by all parties involved. Another concept to consider is proactive communication. Internal auditors should not wait until the end of an audit to communicate with management about potential issues. Instead, regular communication throughout the audit process can help build trust and collaboration, and ultimately lead to more effective management of findings and recommendations.

Lastly, auditors must also consider the power of data analytics in managing audit findings and recommendations. With advancements in technology, auditors have access to vast amounts of data that can provide valuable insights and support their findings and recommendations. By leveraging data analytics tools, auditors can analyze trends, identify potential risks, and provide data-driven recommendations to management.

Conclusion

In conclusion, managing audit findings and recommendations requires careful consideration of key factors such as objectivity, clarity of communication, and timing. It also involves due diligence, effective management of vendor relationships, and incorporating uncommon and insightful concepts such as empathy, proactive communication, and data analytics. By incorporating these aspects into their approach, internal auditors can effectively manage audit findings and recommendations and help organizations achieve their objectives while mitigating risks.

Chapter 31: The Evolution of Internal Auditing

Internal auditing has come a long way since its inception in the early 20th century. What started as a means to detect and prevent fraud within companies has evolved into a vital function that helps organizations achieve their objectives and improve overall governance, risk management, and control processes. As the business landscape becomes increasingly complex and globalized, the role of internal auditors continues to expand and evolve.

Root Cause Analysis

One of the primary responsibilities of internal audit is identifying the root causes of issues and problems within an organization. This is crucial for ensuring that effective solutions are implemented to address the underlying problems, rather than just treating the symptoms. Conducting a root cause analysis requires a thorough understanding of the organization's processes and systems, as well as the ability to ask the right questions and gather relevant data.

Internal auditors must possess strong analytical skills to identify the underlying causes of issues. This involves looking beyond the obvious and understanding the broader context in which problems arise. It also requires the ability to assess the potential risks and impacts of the root causes and make recommendations for effective solutions.

Tracking and Monitoring Implementations

Identifying and recommending solutions is only one part of the internal auditor's job. To truly add value, auditors must also ensure that their recommendations are implemented and are effective. This involves tracking and monitoring the progress of implementation and identifying any barriers or challenges that may arise. Tracking and monitoring implementations also require effective communication and collaboration with management and other stakeholders. Internal auditors must maintain open and transparent communication to ensure that the recommended solutions are effectively implemented and that any issues are addressed promptly.

In addition to tracking and monitoring the implementation of recommendations, internal auditors can also play a crucial role in identifying opportunities for process improvements and value creation. By keeping a pulse on the organization's operations, auditors can proactively identify areas for improvement and make recommendations to optimize processes and resources.

Closing the Audit Loop

The final step in an internal audit is closing the loop. This involves communicating the audit findings and recommendations to management, addressing any concerns or questions, and ensuring that the audit's objectives were met. Closing the loop also includes following up on the implementation of recommendations and assessing their effectiveness.

Effective communication is key in closing the audit loop. Internal auditors must have the ability to present complex information in a clear and concise manner, tailored to their audience. This not only involves technical skills but also the ability to understand and relate to the concerns and priorities of management. Furthermore, internal auditors must have a culture of continuous learning and improvement to ensure that the audit function adds value and remains relevant. This involves staying up to date with industry trends and best practices, as well as professional development and training opportunities.

Closing the loop also involves providing feedback on and improving internal audit processes. By analyzing the results of audits and obtaining feedback from management and stakeholders, internal auditors can continually enhance their procedures and methods to better address the organization's needs.

The Role of Technology

Technology has significantly transformed the field of internal auditing. From data analytics to robotic process automation, auditors now have access to powerful tools that can analyze large volumes of data and identify patterns and anomalies that may not be apparent to the human eye. This has not only improved the efficiency and effectiveness of the audit process but also enabled auditors to provide deeper insights and add more value to the organization. However, with the increased use of technology in internal auditing comes the need for auditors to continuously develop their skills in data analytics and technology. It is no longer enough to have a traditional audit background; auditors must also possess technical skills to leverage the latest technology and tools effectively.

The Future of Internal Auditing

While the core principles of internal auditing remain the same, the profession is constantly evolving and adapting to the changing business landscape. As organizations face new challenges and risks, the role of internal auditors will continue to expand and evolve. This requires auditors to be adaptable, continuously learning, and staying informed of the latest trends and best practices.

Moreover, the internal audit function must remain independent and objective to be truly effective. This involves maintaining a healthy balance between providing assurance and consulting services and ensuring that the organization's objectives and interests are also considered.

In Summary

In conclusion, the role of internal auditing has evolved from its origins in fraud detection to a critical function that helps organizations achieve their objectives and improve overall governance, risk management, and control processes. To be effective and add value, internal auditors must possess a diverse set of skills, from analytical and technical competencies to effective communication and collaboration skills. With the constant evolution of technology and the business landscape, internal auditors must also continuously adapt, learn, and enhance their processes to meet the organization's changing needs.

Chapter 32: The Advancements of Technology in Internal Auditing

Internal auditing has come a long way in recent years, and a significant part of that progress can be credited to the advancements of technology. With the increasing complexity and volume of data, traditional auditing methods are no longer sufficient. Internal auditors must now incorporate technology into their practices to effectively assess and manage risk.

Advantages

The use of technology in internal auditing has numerous advantages that contribute to the overall efficiency and effectiveness of the internal audit function. One of the primary advantages is the ability to analyze large amounts of data quickly and accurately. With the help of technology, internal auditors can perform a variety of analytical procedures, such as trend analysis and outlier detection, which were previously time-consuming and prone to errors.

Moreover, technology has also enabled real-time auditing, which is essential for staying on top of rapidly changing risks. With the availability of data in real-time, internal auditors can now provide timely assurance and insights to management and stakeholders. This enables them to identify and address potential issues before they become significant problems. Another notable advantage of technology in internal auditing is the ease of communication and collaboration. With the help of various communication tools and platforms, internal auditors can share information and collaborate with stakeholders across different locations, improving efficiency and reducing the cost of conducting audits.

Use of Technology

The use of technology in internal auditing is not limited to just one aspect of the audit process. It can be applied in various stages, from planning and risk assessment to reporting and follow-up. Some of the commonly used technologies in internal auditing include data analytics software, artificial intelligence, and robotic process automation. Data analytics software has revolutionized the way internal auditors handle data. It allows auditors to efficiently and accurately analyze large datasets, providing insights into potential areas of risk and fraud. This technology also offers the flexibility to customize and programmatically test controls, reducing the risk of human error.

Artificial intelligence (AI) and robotic process automation (RPA) have also gained popularity in internal auditing. AI can be used to perform predictive analysis and risk assessment, while RPA can automate repetitive tasks, freeing up time for auditors to focus on more complex and critical tasks.

Moreover, technology solutions such as electronic workpapers and data visualization tools have also significantly improved internal auditing processes. Electronic workpapers enable auditors to access and organize documents and evidence easily, while data visualization tools help auditors communicate complex data in a more straightforward and understandable manner.

Challenges and Mitigation Strategies

Despite the numerous benefits of using technology in internal auditing, there are also some challenges that need to be addressed. One of the most significant challenges is keeping up with the fast pace of technological advancements. With new technologies emerging constantly, it can be challenging for internal auditors to stay updated and adapt their skills and processes accordingly.

Another challenge is the security and privacy risks associated with using technology in internal auditing. With the sensitive and confidential nature of audit data, it is crucial to ensure that proper security measures are in place to protect against cyber threats and unauthorized access. To address these challenges, internal auditors must prioritize continuous learning and staying up-to-date with the latest technology. This may include attending training programs, conferences, and obtaining relevant certifications. It is also essential to have a thorough understanding of the organization's IT environment and implement robust security controls to safeguard data. Collaboration and communication among all stakeholders are also vital to ensuring the successful integration of technology in internal auditing. By involving different departments, such as IT and data analytics, internal auditors can obtain valuable insights and support for incorporating technology into their processes.

In conclusion, the advancements of technology have brought significant benefits to the practice of internal auditing. By utilizing technology, internal auditors can enhance their capabilities, provide timely and valuable insights to management and stakeholders, and ultimately improve the overall effectiveness of the internal audit function. However, it is essential to address the challenges and ensure that appropriate mitigation strategies are in place to leverage technology successfully.

Chapter 33: Building High-Performing Internal Audit Teams

Introduction

In the fast-paced and complex world of internal auditing, having a high-performing team is crucial for success. A high-performing team is one that consistently achieves outstanding results, works together harmoniously, and continuously improves their performance. In this chapter, we will explore the key elements of building and managing a high-performing team in the realm of internal auditing.

Building High-Performing Teams

The foundation of a high-performing team is built upon understanding the team's goals and objectives and working towards them collaboratively. As an internal auditor, it is essential to establish a shared vision and set clear and achievable goals for the team. This creates a sense of purpose and direction, motivating team members to work towards a common goal. Regular team meetings are another essential aspect of building a high-performing team. These meetings provide an opportunity for team members to discuss progress, share ideas and concerns, and brainstorm solutions. It also allows for open and effective communication, which is crucial in promoting a positive team dynamic.

Creating a culture of trust within the team is also crucial for its success. This means fostering an environment where team members feel comfortable sharing their thoughts and opinions without fear of judgment. Trust is the foundation of effective teamwork and is built through open communication, respect, and transparency among team members. Another critical aspect of building a high-performing team is balancing individual skills and collective abilities. A diverse team with varying backgrounds, expertise, and skill sets can bring a unique perspective and contribute to the team's success. As a leader, it is important to recognize and utilize each team member's strengths and assign tasks accordingly.

Managing Conflict

Conflict within a team is inevitable, but it is how it is managed that determines whether it can have a positive or negative impact. Effective conflict management involves acknowledging and addressing the conflict rather than ignoring or avoiding it. It is important to encourage open and honest communication to understand the root cause of the conflict and work towards a resolution together.

As a leader, it is also essential to lead by example and model positive conflict resolution behavior.

This includes actively listening to all parties involved, remaining calm and composed, and finding a mutually beneficial solution. By managing conflict effectively, teams can build stronger relationships and work together more efficiently.

Recognizing and Utilizing Individual Strengths

Every team member brings a unique set of strengths and weaknesses to the table. As a leader, it is important to not only recognize these strengths but also to actively utilize them for the team's benefit. This involves delegating tasks to individuals with expertise in that area and encouraging team members to share their knowledge and skills with one another.

It is also crucial to create opportunities for team members to build and develop new skills. This not only helps them grow as professionals but also adds to the team's collective knowledge and capabilities. Encouraging continuous learning and development can foster a culture of innovation and improvement within the team.

Conclusion

Building a high-performing team in the field of internal auditing involves setting clear goals, effective communication, trust, diversity, conflict management, and recognizing individual strengths. As a leader, it is important to continuously assess and adjust team dynamics to ensure optimal performance and achievement of goals. By implementing these strategies, internal auditors can create a high-performing team that consistently delivers exceptional results.

Chapter 34: Professionalism and Career Development for CIA

Internal auditing is a profession that demands the highest level of professionalism and integrity. As a Certified Internal Auditor (CIA), it is imperative to adhere to a strict code of ethics, avoid conflicts of interest, and implement quality control measures. In this chapter, we will delve deeper into these important aspects of the internal auditing profession, and also discuss how to advance your career as a CIA.

Code of Ethics

The Institute of Internal Auditors (IIA) has established a Code of Ethics for internal auditors, which serves as a guide for conducting ethical and professional behavior. The Code of Ethics is based on five fundamental principles: integrity, objectivity, confidentiality, competency, and due care.

Integrity is the cornerstone of the internal auditing profession. It involves being honest and transparent in all professional and personal dealings. Objectivity means having an unbiased attitude and avoiding any conflicts of interest. Confidentiality is crucial in maintaining the trust of stakeholders and ensuring the security of sensitive information. Competency and due care relate to the qualifications and professional responsibilities of a CIA.

As a CIA, it is essential to continuously remind yourself of these principles and use them as a framework for making ethical decisions. Remember, integrity is not something that can be compromised, and it is your responsibility to uphold the reputation of the internal auditing profession.

Conflicts of Interest

One of the biggest challenges for internal auditors is managing potential conflicts of interest. These conflicts can arise in various forms, such as personal relationships, financial interests, or employment outside of the organization. As a CIA, it is crucial to identify and disclose any conflicts of interest to your employer and the IIA.

To avoid conflicts of interest, it is best to establish clear boundaries and maintain a professional relationship with stakeholders. It is also essential to recuse yourself from any potential conflicts of interest and not participate in the audit or decision-making process.

Additionally, internal auditors must avoid any real or perceived conflicts of interest to maintain their independence and objectivity. As a CIA, it is crucial to remember that your ultimate responsibility is to the organization and its stakeholders, not any individual or group within the organization.

Quality Control Measures

In the world of internal auditing, quality is paramount. To ensure quality, the IIA has established Standards for the Professional Practice of Internal Auditing, which includes guidelines for quality control.

As a CIA, it is crucial to implement quality control measures throughout the audit process. This includes identifying and addressing potential risks, ensuring all relevant laws and regulations are followed, and maintaining a high level of professionalism and competency. It is also essential to have a quality assurance and improvement program in place to continuously monitor and improve the quality of internal auditing services.

In addition to following the IIA Standards, it is also essential to stay updated on the latest industry trends and best practices. Invest in professional development opportunities, such as attending conferences and obtaining relevant certifications, to enhance your skills and knowledge as a CIA.

Advancing Your Career as a CIA

Being a CIA is not just about having the necessary skills and knowledge; it is also about continuous development and career advancement. Here are some tips to help you advance your career as a CIA:

- Network: Building relationships with other professionals in the internal auditing field can open up new opportunities and provide valuable insights. Attend industry events, join professional organizations, and don't be afraid to reach out to other CIAs for advice and guidance.

- Specialize: As the internal auditing profession evolves, there is a growing demand for specialists in specific areas such as IT, fraud, and risk management. Consider obtaining specialized certifications to set yourself apart from other CIAs and increase your marketability.

- Gain Experience: Experience is essential in any profession. Seek out opportunities to work on diverse audit engagements, take on leadership roles, and continuously challenge yourself. The more experience you gain, the more valuable you become as a CIA.

- Embrace Technology: Technology is changing the way internal audits are conducted. As a CIA, it is crucial to stay updated on emerging technologies and how they can be utilized to improve audit processes and provide valuable insights to organizations.

- Become a Trusted Advisor: The role of internal auditors is shifting from being just a compliance function to a trusted advisor. To advance your career as a CIA, develop strong communication skills, and establish yourself as a valuable business partner who provides strategic advice and adds value to the organization.

In conclusion, as a CIA, it is crucial to uphold the highest level of professionalism and ethical standards, avoid conflicts of interest, and continuously strive for quality in your work. By doing so, you will not only advance in your career but also contribute to the advancement of the internal auditing profession.

Chapter 35: Internal Auditing in Crisis Management

Internal auditors play a crucial role in disaster recovery and continuity planning for organizations. As trained professionals in risk management and governance, internal auditors are well-equipped to identify potential threats and develop strategies to mitigate them. In this chapter, we will explore the role of internal auditors in disaster recovery and continuity planning, as well as the importance of lessons learned in improving crisis management protocols.

Role in Disaster Recovery

When a disaster strikes, it can have a devastating impact on an organization's operations and reputation. This is where internal auditors step in. They are responsible for evaluating the effectiveness of disaster recovery plans and procedures in place to mitigate the impact of unforeseen events. Internal auditors work closely with management to identify critical processes and systems that need to be restored in the event of a disaster. This includes identifying backup plans and contingency measures to keep the organization functioning during and after a crisis.

One of the key roles of internal auditors in disaster recovery is to ensure that the organization's disaster recovery plans are regularly tested and updated. This helps to identify any weaknesses in the plans and make necessary adjustments. It is essential for internal auditors to have a thorough understanding of the organization's operations and processes to assess the adequacy and effectiveness of disaster recovery plans.

Continuity Planning

In addition to disaster recovery, internal auditors also play a crucial role in continuity planning. Continuity planning involves identifying critical functions and processes that must be maintained in the event of a disruption. This is especially important for organizations that provide essential services or products that can have a significant impact on the public or economy. Internal auditors are responsible for assessing the adequacy of the organization's continuity plans and identifying any potential gaps. They work closely with management to ensure that continuity plans are regularly updated and tested to ensure they can effectively support the organization's critical functions in case of a crisis. This proactive approach allows businesses to resume operations as quickly as possible and minimize any negative impact on stakeholders.

Lessons Learned

When a disaster occurs, it is inevitable that there will be some lessons to be learned. Internal auditors play a vital role in identifying these lessons and incorporating them into the organization's crisis management protocols. They analyze the organization's response and recovery efforts, identifying any weaknesses or gaps that were not addressed in the disaster recovery and continuity plans. This helps to improve the organization's readiness for future crises.

Lessons learned from previous disasters can also help internal auditors identify potential risks and develop strategies to mitigate them in the future. This proactive approach is essential in ensuring that the organization is prepared to handle any future crises effectively. Internal auditors also play a critical role in communicating these lessons to senior management and educating employees on their roles and responsibilities in crisis management.

In conclusion, internal auditors play a crucial role in ensuring an organization's readiness for disasters and crises through disaster recovery and continuity planning. Their expertise in risk management and governance allows them to assess and improve the effectiveness of the organization's plans. They also help the organization learn from past experiences and anticipate future risks. With their proactive approach, internal auditors play a vital role in protecting the organization from the impact of disasters and ensuring its resilience in the face of adversity.

Chapter 36: Managing Whistleblower Allegations

From time to time, organizations may encounter situations where employees or third parties raise concerns about potential wrongdoing within the company. These concerns can range from minor issues to serious allegations of fraud, corruption, or other misconduct. As internal auditors, it is our responsibility to investigate and address these allegations in a timely and effective manner. In this chapter, we will discuss the role of internal audit in managing whistleblower allegations, investigative techniques, confidentiality considerations, and reporting considerations.

Role of Internal Audit

The role of internal audit in managing whistleblower allegations is crucial. As the independent and objective assurance function within an organization, internal audit is responsible for evaluating and improving the effectiveness of risk management, control, and governance processes. This includes investigating allegations of unethical or illegal behavior within the company.

Internal auditors must approach each allegation with professionalism and impartiality. They should maintain a skeptical mindset and conduct detailed investigations to gather sufficient evidence and determine the veracity of the allegations. Internal auditors must also ensure that the investigation process is fair and unbiased, devoid of any personal biases or conflicts of interest.

Another important aspect of the internal audit role is to collaborate with other departments, such as compliance and legal, to ensure that all investigative steps align with relevant policies, procedures, and legal requirements. Internal auditors must also keep senior management and the audit committee informed of the progress and findings of the investigation.

Investigative Techniques

Investigating whistleblower allegations requires specific skills and techniques to ensure a thorough and unbiased process. Internal auditors must use a combination of analytical, interviewing, and forensic accounting techniques to uncover the truth and gather evidence. Analytical techniques involve analyzing data and information to identify relationships, trends, anomalies, or patterns that may suggest fraudulent or unethical behavior. This may include examining financial transactions, conducting a risk assessment, or using data analytics tools to identify irregularities.

Interviewing is another critical investigative technique that internal auditors must possess. Effective interviewing requires following a structured approach, building rapport with the interviewee, and asking open-ended questions to gather relevant information. It is essential to remain objective and maintain a professional demeanor throughout the interview process.

In cases where financial fraud or misappropriation of assets may be involved, internal auditors must possess a strong understanding of forensic accounting techniques. This involves examining financial documents, tracing transactions, and analyzing financial records to identify discrepancies or fraudulent activities.

Internal auditors must also document and preserve all evidence gathered during the investigation process while maintaining the confidentiality of sensitive information. This brings us to the next topic – confidentiality considerations.

Confidentiality Considerations

Maintaining the confidentiality of whistleblower allegations is of utmost importance to protect the rights of the individuals involved and avoid any potential retaliation. As such, internal auditors must follow strict confidentiality protocols when dealing with such cases. All information gathered during the investigation must be kept in a secure and locked location. Access to this information should be restricted to authorized personnel only, and any copies must be made with necessary permissions and proper labeling.

Internal auditors must also ensure that information is disclosed only to relevant parties who are involved in managing the allegation or have a legitimate need to know. Disclosure of confidential information without proper authorization can lead to legal consequences and adversely affect the organization's reputation. Data security is also an essential aspect to consider when investigating whistleblower allegations. As internal auditors, we must protect electronic data, such as emails, chat conversations, and other electronic records, from potential leaks or breaches.

Reporting Considerations

Reporting considerations are critical when managing whistleblower allegations. As part of their role, internal auditors must provide a detailed and unbiased report of their findings and recommendations to senior management and the audit committee.

The report should include the scope and objectives of the investigation, the key information gathered, and the evidence supporting the findings. It should also highlight any control weakness or gaps identified during the investigation and provide recommendations for improvement to prevent similar situations from occurring in the future. Internal auditors must communicate the report in a timely manner to ensure that corrective actions are taken promptly. It is also crucial to maintain accurate and comprehensive records of the investigation process and outcomes for future reference.

In conclusion, managing whistleblower allegations is a critical responsibility that falls on the shoulders of internal auditors. It requires a combination of technical skills, objectivity, and professionalism to conduct thorough and unbiased investigations. By understanding the role of internal audit, various investigative techniques, and maintaining confidentiality and reporting considerations, internal auditors can effectively manage these situations and protect the organization's best interests.

Chapter 37: Internal Auditing in Mergers and Acquisitions

As businesses grow and evolve, mergers and acquisitions are becoming increasingly common as a method to expand and diversify. While these transactions bring exciting possibilities for growth and expansion, they also pose significant challenges for internal auditors. The integration of two different companies, cultures, and systems can create complexities and vulnerabilities that require proper attention and diligence. In this chapter, we will explore the role of internal auditors in the merger and acquisition process, from due diligence to post-merger auditing.

Due Diligence

As with any major decision, proper due diligence is crucial before proceeding with a merger or acquisition. The goal of due diligence is to thoroughly evaluate the potential risks and opportunities of the transaction and identify any potential issues that may need to be addressed. This process involves an in-depth examination of the financial, operational, and cultural aspects of the companies involved. Internal auditors play a critical role in conducting due diligence, as they possess the expertise and knowledge to thoroughly assess the risks and controls of the targeted company. They can also evaluate the effectiveness and efficiency of the company's internal controls and identify any red flags that may require further investigation. Additionally, internal auditors can evaluate the cultural compatibility of the two companies and advise on any necessary measures to ensure a smooth integration process.

Integration Planning

Once the due diligence process is complete, the next step is integration planning. This stage involves developing a comprehensive plan to merge the two companies successfully. Integration planning requires thorough coordination between various departments, including finance, IT, human resources, and legal. It also requires careful consideration of the cultural aspects of the companies to ensure a smooth transition. Internal auditors can provide valuable input in the integration planning process, as they can identify potential risks and provide recommendations for mitigating them. They can also help develop a timeline and coordinate with different teams for a seamless integration process. Furthermore, internal auditors can assess the compatibility of IT systems and processes and identify any areas that may require additional security measures.

Post-merger Auditing

After the merger is complete, internal auditors play a crucial role in conducting post-merger audits to ensure the effectiveness of the integration process. These audits help identify any gaps or weaknesses in the newly merged company's internal controls and recommend necessary adjustments. Post-merger auditing also ensures that the integration process has not compromised the company's overall control environment and financial reporting.

Internal auditors can also provide valuable insights into the company's performance and help identify areas for improvement. By comparing the financial and operational data from pre and post-merger, internal auditors can identify potential issues and provide recommendations for addressing them. They can also support the newly merged company by providing guidance on risk management and internal control processes to maintain a strong control environment.

The Human Element

While mergers and acquisitions are primarily financial transactions, they also involve significant cultural aspects. A company's culture can have a significant impact on the success or failure of a merger. Internal auditors play a critical role in assessing the cultural compatibility of the two companies during the due diligence process. They can also provide insights and recommendations for addressing any cultural differences and ensuring a smooth integration process.

Embracing Change and Innovation

Mergers and acquisitions bring significant changes to the company's systems, processes, and culture. Internal auditors must embrace these changes and adapt to the new environment to continue to add value to the organization. It is also essential for auditors to stay updated on emerging technologies and incorporate them into their audit processes. This will allow them to provide valuable insights on the impact of technology and innovation on the newly merged company's control environment.

Ethics and Integrity

The merger and acquisition process can also give rise to ethical and integrity issues, particularly when there is pressure to achieve the deal. It is the responsibility of internal auditors to remain vigilant and identify any potential fraud or unethical behavior. They must ensure that the due diligence process includes a thorough evaluation of the target company's ethical and compliance practices. Post-merger, internal auditors must continue to monitor for any potential ethical issues and provide guidance on maintaining a culture of integrity within the merged company.

In conclusion, mergers and acquisitions pose unique challenges for internal auditors, requiring a thorough understanding of the target company, effective coordination with different departments, and adaptability to change. By actively participating in due diligence, integration planning, and post-merger auditing, internal auditors can add value to the merger process and support the newly merged company's success. It is essential to keep in mind that a successful merger not only requires financial and operational success but also cultural compatibility and ethical integrity. With the right approach, internal auditors can play a crucial role in the success of a merger.

Chapter 38: Emerging Technologies in Internal Auditing

The world of internal auditing is constantly evolving, and staying on top of the latest technological developments is crucial for auditors to effectively fulfill their roles. In recent years, two technologies have gained significant traction and have the potential to greatly impact the field of internal auditing

- Artificial Intelligence (AI) and Blockchain. In this chapter, we will examine the potential impact of these emerging technologies on auditing practices and how internal auditors can embrace them to enhance their effectiveness.

Artificial Intelligence

AI, also known as machine intelligence, is the simulation of human intelligence processes by computer systems. It involves the creation of algorithms that can learn from data and make decisions without explicit programming. With the increasing availability and accessibility of data, AI has the potential to revolutionize the field of internal auditing.

One of the key areas where AI can have a significant impact is in data analysis. Auditors are often faced with massive amounts of data, and manually analyzing and identifying patterns can be time-consuming and prone to errors. With AI, auditors can leverage machine learning algorithms to quickly analyze data and identify potential risks, anomalies, or fraud patterns. This can greatly enhance the efficiency of audits, allowing auditors to focus on analyzing more complex and high-risk areas.

Another way AI can enhance internal auditing is through automation. AI-powered tools can automate routine tasks such as data extraction, cleansing, and analysis, freeing up auditors' time to focus on more critical tasks. This can also help auditors to identify and address potential control gaps or deficiencies more efficiently.

Blockchain

Blockchain, a decentralized digital ledger technology, has gained significant popularity due to its potential to disrupt traditional financial systems. However, its applications go beyond finance and have the potential to greatly impact the field of internal auditing.

One of the key areas where blockchain can enhance internal auditing is in data integrity. As auditors rely on data to perform their audits, ensuring the accuracy and integrity of that data is crucial. Blockchain technology uses cryptography to create a secure and immutable record of transactions, ensuring that data cannot be altered or deleted. This can greatly enhance the reliability and trustworthiness of data auditors use in their audits.

Another area where blockchain can be beneficial is in improving the accuracy and efficiency of audit trails. With blockchain, every transaction is recorded in a transparent and tamper-proof manner, creating a reliable audit trail for auditors to follow. This can also help auditors to identify potential control deficiencies or control gaps more quickly.

Impact on Auditing Practices

The emergence of AI and blockchain has the potential to greatly impact auditing practices as we know them. With these technologies, auditors can perform faster, more efficient, and more accurate audits, ultimately enhancing the value they bring to their organizations. However, these technologies also present some challenges for internal auditors. As AI and blockchain are relatively new technologies, there is a learning curve for auditors to fully understand and leverage their capabilities. Internal auditors must continuously update their skills and knowledge to effectively embrace these technologies and stay ahead of the game.

Moreover, as these technologies rely heavily on data, auditors must also be mindful of potential privacy and security risks. With AI, there is a risk of bias in algorithms, which can lead to incorrect conclusions and decisions. It is the responsibility of auditors to ensure that proper controls and measures are in place to mitigate these risks and maintain the integrity of their audits.

Embracing Emerging Technologies

To effectively embrace AI and blockchain, internal auditors must keep an open mind and be willing to adapt to new ways of working. This includes enhancing their skills and knowledge in data analytics, coding, and machine learning. Additionally, auditors must work closely with IT teams to understand the organization's technology landscape and identify opportunities for using AI and blockchain in their audits. Internal audit departments must also invest in the right tools and technologies to effectively utilize AI and blockchain. This may include acquiring AI-powered audit software or partnering with external experts to implement blockchain solutions. Ultimately, it is the responsibility of internal auditors to stay at the forefront of these emerging technologies and continuously find ways to leverage them to enhance their auditing practices.

Conclusion

The emergence of AI and blockchain has the potential to greatly impact internal auditing practices. These technologies offer auditors the opportunity to perform faster, more efficient, and more accurate audits, ultimately bringing more value to their organizations. However, to fully embrace these technologies, internal auditors must continuously update their skills, be aware of potential risks, and invest in the right tools and technologies. By doing so, internal auditors can stay ahead of the curve and continue to add value to their organizations.

Chapter 39: Advancing the Internal Audit Profession

Networking

As a Certified Internal Auditor (CIA), networking is an essential factor in advancing your career. It not only helps you stay updated with the latest industry trends and best practices, but it also provides opportunities for collaboration and knowledge sharing with other professionals. Building a strong network of peers, mentors, and industry leaders will not only enhance your professional development but also open up avenues for career growth.

One of the best ways to network within the internal audit profession is by joining professional associations such as the Institute of Internal Auditors (IIA). The IIA has a global network of over 200,000 members, providing access to a diverse group of professionals with varying levels of experience and expertise. The IIA offers networking events, conferences, and online communities to connect with other internal auditors and share insights and ideas.

Another effective networking strategy is to attend local and regional IIA chapter meetings. These meetings provide opportunities to interact with other professionals in your area, exchange ideas, and gain insights into the local internal audit landscape. It also allows you to showcase your skills and knowledge, making you stand out as a valuable and knowledgeable member of the internal audit community.

As the internal audit profession continues to grow and expand, it is crucial to build and maintain relationships with professionals in related fields such as accounting, finance, risk management, and compliance. These connections can provide valuable insights and perspectives on the broader business landscape, strengthening your overall understanding of the business and enhancing your audit approach.

Career Opportunities

One of the significant benefits of being a CIA is the numerous career opportunities available. Internal auditors not only play a critical role in evaluating and improving organizational processes and systems, but they also contribute to strategic decision-making and risk management. This strong and diverse skill set opens up a wide range of career paths within and outside the internal audit profession.

Within the internal audit field, there are opportunities for career advancement through different levels of auditing, including senior, manager, and executive positions. The CIA designation is highly regarded by employers and can increase your chances of promotion and higher-paying positions. Moreover, there are specialized areas within internal audit, such as compliance auditing, IT auditing, and financial auditing, that provide opportunities for specialization and growth.

Outside of the internal audit profession, there are several executive-level positions that require or prefer candidates with internal audit experience. These positions include Chief Financial Officer (CFO), Chief Risk Officer (CRO), and Chief Compliance Officer (CCO). The comprehensive skill set of internal auditors makes them well-suited for these roles as they have a deep understanding of the business's operations and risks.

Future of Internal Auditing

The role of internal auditors is continuously evolving, and it is essential to stay updated with the changing landscape to advance in this profession. As organizations become more complex and interconnected, the risk landscape becomes increasingly dynamic, making internal audit a critical function to ensure the organization's success.

One of the significant changes in the future of internal auditing is increased automation and the use of technology. As auditors move away from manual processes and reliance on paper-based documentation, they can leverage technology to analyze data and identify trends and anomalies more efficiently. This shift will enable internal auditors to focus on more strategic initiatives, providing value beyond traditional audit processes. Moreover, the rapidly changing business environment requires internal auditors to continuously upskill and stay updated on the latest industry developments and trends. The IIA offers a variety of professional development opportunities, such as webinars, e-learning courses, and conferences, to help internal auditors stay relevant and competitive in the industry.

The future of internal auditing is bright, with increasing demand for skilled and knowledgeable professionals in this field. The evolving role of internal auditors and their critical contribution to organizational success make this a promising career choice for individuals looking for growth and opportunities.

Conclusion

In conclusion, networking, career opportunities, and the future of internal auditing are crucial aspects of advancing in this profession. As a CIA, building a strong network, exploring diverse career paths, and staying updated on industry developments will not only enhance your skills and knowledge but also open up numerous opportunities for career growth. The internal audit profession is continuously evolving, and it is essential to stay updated and embrace change to thrive in this dynamic and critical role within organizations.

Book 2 - Internal Audit Practices

Chapter 1: Introduction to CIA and Internal Audit

Definition of CIA

Certified Internal Auditor (CIA) is a globally recognized professional certification for individuals working in the field of internal audit. It is offered by the Institute of Internal Auditors (IIA) and is considered the gold standard in the industry. A CIA is a competent and ethical professional who possesses the necessary skills and knowledge to effectively manage and conduct audits within an organization.

The certification is awarded after successfully completing a rigorous exam that covers three main areas: essentials of internal auditing, practice of internal auditing, and business knowledge for internal auditing. Candidates must also meet strict education and experience requirements to be eligible for the CIA certification.

History of Internal Audit

The concept of internal audit dates back to ancient times, where it was primarily used to ensure accountability and prevent fraud and corruption in government agencies. However, it was not until the early 20th century that internal audit evolved into a formal profession.

In 1941, the IIA was established to promote the profession and provide international standards for internal audit practices. The first formal training and certification program for internal auditors was introduced in 1974, and in 1978, the IIA launched the Certified Internal Auditor (CIA) certification. Since then, the certification has been recognized and valued by organizations worldwide.

Role and Responsibilities of a CIA

The role of a CIA is multifaceted and critical in today's business landscape. A CIA's primary responsibility is to assess and evaluate an organization's internal controls and risk management processes to ensure the effectiveness and efficiency of operations, reliability of financial reporting, and compliance with laws and regulations. CIAs are also responsible for detecting and preventing fraud, conducting investigations, and providing recommendations to improve processes and mitigate risks. They serve as trusted advisors to management and help organizations achieve their objectives through systematic and disciplined approach to internal audit.

As the business world becomes increasingly complex and global, CIAs must possess a diverse range of skills and knowledge to effectively fulfill their responsibilities. This includes expertise in areas such as risk management, IT auditing, data analytics, and international practices.

In addition to technical abilities, CIAs must also possess strong communication and interpersonal skills to effectively collaborate with all levels of management and handle sensitive situations with diplomacy and tact. They must also uphold the highest ethical standards and continuously strive for professional growth and development.

In conclusion, the role of a CIA is crucial in ensuring accountability, transparency, and long-term success of organizations. The CIA certification provides individuals with the necessary skills and knowledge to fulfill this role and contribute to the overall success of businesses and society. In the following chapters, we will delve deeper into the various aspects of internal audit practices and how CIAs can effectively fulfill their responsibilities.

Chapter 2: Assessing and Enhancing Internal Control

Internal control is a vital component of any organization's operations, ensuring that resources are used efficiently and effectively, and that accountability and compliance are maintained. Certified Internal Auditor (CIA) professionals play a critical role in assessing and enhancing internal control to protect organizations against potential risks and vulnerabilities.

In this chapter, we will dive into the principles of internal control, the process of assessing and enhancing internal control, and various strategies for implementing effective control measures.

Principles of Internal Control

As defined by the Committee of Sponsoring Organizations (COSO) of the Treadway Commission, internal control is a set of processes and procedures that provide assurance that an organization's objectives are achieved in an efficient and effective manner, and that its resources are safeguarded against potential risks. These processes and procedures cover the entire organization, including financial transactions, operations, and compliance. The COSO framework outlines five interrelated components that make up effective internal control: Control Environment, Risk Assessment, Control Activities, Information and Communication, and Monitoring Activities. While these components are not exhaustive, they provide a comprehensive structure for organizations to evaluate and enhance their internal control systems.

Control Environment

The control environment sets the tone for internal control by establishing the foundation for all other components. It is influenced by the organization's leadership and is manifested by the policies, procedures, and values that guide its operations. A strong control environment promotes an ethical and supportive culture, fosters accountability, and empowers employees to take responsibility for their actions.

Risk Assessment

Risk assessment involves identifying potential risks and evaluating their likelihood and impact on the organization's objectives. This process helps organizations prioritize their control activities and allocate resources appropriately. A thorough risk assessment considers both internal and external factors, such as changes in the business environment and emerging technologies.

Control Activities

Control activities are the policies and procedures that are established to mitigate identified risks. These activities can take many forms, such as approvals and authorizations, segregation of duties, and physical safeguards. Effective control activities are tailored to an organization's specific risks and are continuously monitored and improved upon.

Information and Communication

Information and communication play a critical role in internal control by ensuring that relevant and timely information is communicated to the right people. This includes recording and processing transactions accurately, maintaining necessary records, and providing clear and concise communication to key stakeholders. An effective information and communication system also ensures that relevant information is shared with those responsible for risk management and compliance.

Monitoring Activities

Monitoring activities involve ongoing evaluations of internal control effectiveness. This can be done through self-assessments, internal audits, or other evaluations. By regularly monitoring and evaluating internal control, organizations can identify weaknesses or gaps and make necessary improvements to enhance their control systems.

Assessing and Enhancing Internal Control

Assessing and enhancing internal control is an ongoing process that requires a systematic and disciplined approach. Continuous risk assessment, control evaluation, and monitoring activities are crucial for ensuring the effectiveness of internal control. Here are some key steps to follow when assessing and enhancing internal control:

Conduct a Risk Assessment

The first step in assessing and enhancing internal control is to conduct a thorough risk assessment. This involves identifying potential risks and evaluating their likelihood and impact. The information gathered during this process will help determine the appropriate control activities to mitigate these risks.

Evaluate Existing Control Activities

Organizations must regularly evaluate their current control activities to determine their effectiveness. This can be done through self-assessments or internal audits. By examining control activities, organizations can identify weaknesses or gaps and make necessary improvements.

Implement Additional Control Measures

Based on the risk assessment and evaluation of existing control activities, organizations may need to implement additional control measures to address any identified gaps or risks. These measures can vary depending on the organization's size, industry, and operations and may include new policies, procedures, or technology.

Communicate Changes to Relevant Stakeholders

Any changes made to internal control must be effectively communicated to relevant stakeholders. This includes employees, management, and external stakeholders such as auditors and regulators. Transparent and ongoing communication is crucial for ensuring that everyone understands their roles and responsibilities in maintaining effective internal control.

Control Implementation Strategies

Implementing control measures requires careful planning and execution to ensure their effectiveness. Here are some strategies for successful control implementation:

Start with the Highest Risk Areas

When implementing control activities, it's essential to prioritize the highest risk areas first. This ensures that the most significant risks are addressed and mitigated promptly.

Involve Key Stakeholders

Effective internal control requires collaboration and buy-in from all key stakeholders. This includes management, employees, auditors, regulators, and other relevant parties. By involving stakeholders in the control implementation process, organizations can gather valuable insights and support.

Utilize Technology

In today's digital world, technology plays a vital role in internal control. Automation and data analytics tools can help organizations streamline processes, identify potential risks, and monitor control effectiveness. By utilizing technology, organizations can enhance their control systems, reduce human error, and improve efficiency.

Provide Training and Education

To ensure that control measures are successfully implemented, it's crucial to provide training and education to all employees. This includes training on new policies and procedures, as well as ongoing education about the importance of internal control and compliance.

Chapter 3: Fraud Detection and Prevention

Fraud. It's a word that no one wants to hear, but unfortunately, it is a reality that exists in our society. From large corporations to small family-owned businesses, no one is immune from the threat of fraud. However, it is important for organizations to be proactive in detecting and preventing fraud, as it can have detrimental effects on their financial stability, reputation, and ultimately, their survival.

Types of Fraud

Fraud comes in many forms and can be committed by both internal and external parties. Understanding the different types of fraud can help organizations in identifying and preventing them.

1. Employee Fraud
Employee fraud occurs when an employee deceives their employer for personal gain. This can include a variety of fraudulent activities such as falsifying expense reports, stealing office supplies, or even embezzlement. It is estimated that employee fraud accounts for approximately 5% of a company's revenue each year.

2. Vendor Fraud
Vendor fraud is when a vendor or supplier deceives a company by providing false or inflated invoices for products or services. This can also occur in the form of kickbacks or bribes to employees in exchange for a contract or business.

3. Financial Statement Fraud
Financial statement fraud involves intentionally misstating or omitting information in company financial statements in order to deceive stakeholders. This type of fraud is often committed by top executives and can have severe consequences for the organization.

4. Cyber Fraud
With the rise of technology, cyber fraud has become a prevalent threat to organizations. This can include hacking, identity theft, and phishing scams. It is estimated that cybercrime costs businesses over $400 billion globally each year.

Red Flags of Fraud

While fraud can be difficult to detect, there are certain red flags that organizations should be aware of. These warning signs can alert organizations to a potential fraud and allow them to take preventative measures.

1. Unusual Behavior
An employee who suddenly starts displaying unusual behavior, such as being secretive about their work or becoming defensive when asked about their actions, could be a red flag for fraud.

2. Unexplained Transactions
Unexplained or undocumented transactions in company records, such as missing receipts or invoices, can be a sign of fraudulent activity. These discrepancies should be investigated and resolved immediately.

3. Lifestyle Changes
An employee who suddenly starts living beyond their means without a justifiable increase in salary or assets could be an indication of fraud. This could include lavish vacations, expensive purchases, or a sudden increase in their personal wealth.

4. Lack of Internal Controls
Organizations without proper internal controls in place are at a higher risk for fraud. Lack of segregation of duties, no oversight or audits, and poor record-keeping can all contribute to making it easier for fraud to occur.

Techniques for Detecting and Preventing Fraud

While fraud can be difficult to detect, there are techniques that organizations can implement to prevent and identify fraudulent activities.

1. Implement Strong Internal Controls
Having strong internal controls in place can help prevent fraud by limiting the opportunity for it to occur. This includes proper segregation of duties, regular audits, and oversight.

2. Conduct Background Checks
It is important for organizations to conduct thorough background checks on potential employees, especially for positions that involve handling sensitive financial information.

3. Foster an Ethical Culture
Organizations should promote an ethical culture and encourage employees to speak up if they notice any suspicious behavior. This can help prevent fraud and create a culture of trust and integrity.

4. Regularly Review Financial Statements
Regularly reviewing financial statements can help identify any potential red flags or inconsistencies that may indicate fraudulent activity. It is important for organizations to have a

system in place to regularly monitor and reconcile financial records.

5. Educate Employees
Educating employees on the risks of fraud and how to prevent it can go a long way in deterring fraudulent activities. This can include training on internal controls, identifying red flags, and promoting an ethical workplace.

In conclusion, fraud is a reality that organizations cannot afford to ignore. By understanding the different types of fraud, recognizing red flags, and implementing preventative techniques, organizations can protect themselves from the devastating effects of fraud. It is important for companies to be proactive in creating a culture of integrity and ethical behavior to help prevent and detect fraudulent activities.

Chapter 4: Internal Audit Practices – Creating Effective Audit Plans

Creating an Internal Audit Plan

Creating an internal audit plan is the foundation of a successful and efficient internal audit process. It involves determining the scope and objectives of the audit, identifying the key risks and controls, and developing a strategy to address them. A well-designed audit plan not only ensures that all significant risks are addressed, but also helps to allocate resources effectively and provide timely and useful information to stakeholders. To create an effective internal audit plan, the first step is to understand the organization's overall objectives and goals. This will help to identify the key business processes, departments, and systems that need to be audited. It is also important to consider any potential changes in the organization's operations, such as new systems or processes, mergers or acquisitions, or regulatory changes, which may impact the risk profile of the organization. The next step is to conduct a risk assessment, which involves identifying and evaluating the risks associated with each business process and system. This can be done through interviews with key stakeholders, review of previous audit reports, and use of risk assessment tools and techniques. The key risks identified should be prioritized based on their potential impact on the organization's objectives and likelihood of occurrence.

Once the key risks have been identified, the audit team can then develop a detailed audit plan that outlines the scope, objectives, and procedures for each audit. This should include a timeline for the completion of the audit, as well as the resources and expertise required. It is important to involve all relevant stakeholders, such as management and other department heads, in the planning process to ensure that their concerns and priorities are taken into account.

Conducting Risk Assessments

Risk assessments are an integral part of the internal audit process. They provide an understanding of the risks facing the organization and help to prioritize audit activities. However, conducting risk assessments requires skill and expertise to ensure that all significant risks are identified and properly evaluated. To conduct an effective risk assessment, the audit team should use a combination of qualitative and quantitative methods. Qualitative methods involve the use of interviews, surveys, and workshops to gather information about risks and their potential impact. Quantitative methods, on the other hand, involve the use of data and statistical analysis to determine the likelihood and potential consequences of risks.

One commonly used tool for risk assessment is the risk heat map, which helps to visualize the likelihood and impact of risks. By plotting risks on a color-coded grid, this tool helps to identify high-risk areas that require more attention. It is important to note that risk assessments should be conducted periodically, as risks and their impact may change over time.

Developing Audit Procedures

The final step in creating an internal audit plan is developing the audit procedures. These are the steps and tests that the audit team will perform to gather evidence and determine the effectiveness of controls in mitigating risks. The procedures should be tailored to the specific audit objectives and risks identified, and should take into consideration any regulatory requirements or industry best practices. Audit procedures may include a combination of document reviews, interviews, observations, and analytical tests. It is important to select the most appropriate procedures for each audit, based on the objectives and risks identified. The audit team should also consider the cost and time required for each procedure, and balance these with the benefits to be gained. It is also crucial to ensure that audit procedures are clearly documented and communicated to all relevant stakeholders. This will help to avoid any misunderstandings and ensure that the audit is conducted in a consistent and efficient manner. Additionally, the audit team should be prepared to adapt the procedures as needed, based on any unexpected findings or changes in the organization.

In conclusion, creating an effective internal audit plan is essential for conducting a successful audit. It involves understanding the organization's objectives, conducting a thorough risk assessment, and developing appropriate audit procedures. By following these steps, the audit team can ensure that all significant risks are addressed, and provide valuable insights to stakeholders. Remember, a well-designed audit plan not only helps to mitigate risks, but also adds value to the organization by identifying opportunities for improvement.

Chapter 5: Conducting an Internal Audit

Internal audit plays a crucial role in ensuring that an organization's operations are in compliance with internal policies and external regulations. As a Certified Internal Auditor (CIA), it is your responsibility to gather evidence, utilize sampling techniques, and analyze and document findings to provide valuable insights to your organization. In this chapter, we will explore the essential steps in conducting an internal audit.

Gathering Evidence

The first step in conducting an internal audit is to gather evidence. This evidence will serve as the foundation for your audit and support the conclusions and recommendations you make. The sources of evidence can vary, depending on the nature and scope of the audit. However, here are some common methods of gathering evidence: - Reviewing documents and records: Documents such as financial statements, contracts, and policy manuals can provide valuable information about an organization's operations.

- Observing processes: Sometimes, it is essential to observe processes in action to understand how they work and identify potential areas of improvement.

- Conducting interviews: Talking to employees, management, and other stakeholders can provide valuable insights into their roles and responsibilities and the organization's operations.

- Performing physical inspections: In some cases, it may be necessary to physically inspect assets or facilities to validate their existence and condition.

- Analyzing data: With the increasing use of technology, data analysis plays a crucial role in audits. By analyzing data, you can identify trends, patterns, and anomalies that may require further investigation.

When gathering evidence, it is essential to keep in mind the audit's objectives and maintain a professional and ethical approach. All evidence should be documented and appropriately supported to ensure its accuracy and integrity.

Sampling Techniques

Given the vast amount of data and information available, it is impossible to review every single transaction or document during an audit. Therefore, sampling techniques are a crucial tool in internal auditing. Sampling helps auditors gather enough evidence to make accurate conclusions while ensuring the efficient use of resources. Here are some common sampling techniques used in internal auditing: - Random Sampling: In this method, items or transactions are selected randomly from the total population. This technique ensures that every item has an equal chance of being selected, thereby reducing the risk of bias.

- Stratified Sampling: This technique involves dividing the population into strata and selecting a proportionate number of items from each stratum. This method is used when the population has different characteristics that need to be considered.

- Systematic Sampling: In this method, items are selected at a regular interval, such as every 5th item. It is a quick and straightforward technique but may not be suitable for populations with underlying patterns.

- Block Sampling: This technique involves selecting a sample from a particular block or group of items based on a characteristic or criteria. It is commonly used when looking for specific types of transactions within a population.

- Haphazard Sampling: In this method, items are selected based on the auditor's judgment or without a specific pattern. While convenient, this method may introduce bias into the sample.

- Judgmental Sampling: This technique relies on the auditor's judgment to select items that they believe are most relevant and representative of the population. It is commonly used in situations where there is limited data or when the audit objectives require a targeted approach.

When selecting a sampling technique, it is crucial to consider the audit's objectives, the population's characteristics, and the level of risk associated with the specific area being audited.

Analyzing and Documenting Findings

Once the evidence has been gathered and a sample has been selected, the next step is to analyze the findings. The analysis should be thorough and based on the audit objectives and criteria. The extent of the analysis will also depend on the nature and complexity of the audit. After analyzing the findings, it is essential to document them accurately. Documentation serves as evidence of the work performed and allows for transparency and credibility. The documentation should include the scope and objectives of the audit, the methods used, the evidence gathered, and the conclusions and recommendations made. It is crucial to ensure that the documentation is clear, concise, and easily understood by the intended audience. As a CIA, it is necessary to maintain a professional and ethical approach when documenting findings. All information should be kept confidential, and any issues or concerns should be reported to the appropriate stakeholders.

In conclusion, conducting an internal audit involves gathering evidence, utilizing sampling techniques, and analyzing and documenting findings. It is a complex and crucial process that requires a combination of technical skills, professional judgment, and ethical behavior. By following these steps, a CIA can provide valuable insights to their organization and contribute to its success. Remember, the quality of an audit depends on the quality of the evidence gathered and the analysis and documentation of findings.

Chapter 6: IT Auditing

Understanding IT Risks

The Growing Importance of IT Auditing

The world of business is constantly evolving and with this evolution comes increased reliance on technology and the digital world. As a result, companies are now more vulnerable to IT risks which can have a significant impact on their operations and ultimately their bottom line. This is where IT auditing comes in. It is the process of evaluating and assessing the organization's IT infrastructure, systems and processes to identify any potential risks and weaknesses. IT auditors are responsible for verifying that these systems and processes are functioning as intended and identifying any areas for improvement.

The Role of IT Auditing in Mitigating Risks

IT auditing is not only about identifying risks, it is also about mitigating them. By performing regular and thorough IT audits, organizations can identify and address potential risks before they become major issues. This helps to strengthen the organization's overall risk management strategy and ensures that they remain compliant with industry and government regulations. In today's technology-driven world, maintaining a strong IT auditing program is crucial for any organization's survival.

The Evolution of IT Risks

The landscape of IT risks is constantly changing. With new technologies emerging and increasing interconnectivity, the potential for cyber attacks, data breaches and other IT risks is higher than ever before. IT auditors must stay on top of these developments in order to effectively assess and mitigate risks. This means staying informed about the latest cyber security threats, understanding new technologies and their potential risks, and being well-versed in regulatory requirements and compliance standards.

The Importance of a Risk-based Approach to IT Auditing

One of the key principles of IT auditing is taking a risk-based approach. This means focusing on the areas of highest risk and prioritizing efforts accordingly. This allows for a more efficient and effective audit process, as auditors can spend more time on the most critical areas. It also ensures that organizations are proactively addressing the most significant risks to their IT systems and processes.

The Role of the IT Auditor in Risk Management

IT auditors play a critical role in risk management within an organization. They are responsible for assessing and evaluating the organization's technology infrastructure and identifying any vulnerabilities or weaknesses that could pose a risk to the organization. They also provide valuable insight and recommendations for mitigating these risks and ensuring the organization's IT systems are secure and resilient.

IT Audit Techniques

Thorough Documentation

Documentation is a crucial aspect of IT auditing. It provides a clear understanding of the current state of IT systems and processes and serves as a reference for future audits. This includes documenting policies, procedures, and controls, as well as identifying any potential risks or vulnerabilities. By having thorough documentation, auditors can easily track changes and trends over time and identify any areas that may need improvement.

Network and System Scanning

Network and system scanning is an essential technique used by IT auditors to assess the security of an organization's network and IT infrastructure. This involves using a variety of tools and techniques to identify any potential vulnerabilities or weaknesses. By performing these scans, auditors can identify potential risks, such as open ports or outdated software, and make recommendations for improvement.

Vulnerability Assessments

Similar to network and system scanning, vulnerability assessments involve a comprehensive review of an organization's IT systems and processes. This includes identifying any potential vulnerabilities and assessing the impact they could have on the organization. By performing vulnerability assessments, IT auditors can provide valuable recommendations for mitigating these risks and strengthening the organization's overall security posture.

Penetration Testing

Penetration testing, also known as "pen testing," is a simulated attack on an organization's IT systems to identify potential weak points and vulnerabilities. This is a crucial technique for IT auditors, as it allows them to see where an attacker could potentially gain access and what data could be compromised. By performing penetration testing, IT auditors can identify any critical risks and make recommendations for strengthening the organization's overall security.

Data Analytics

The amount of data being generated by organizations is increasing at an exponential rate. This makes data analytics an important tool for IT auditors to use in their assessments. By analyzing large amounts of data, auditors can identify any unusual patterns or anomalies that may indicate potential risks or security breaches. This can also help auditors to identify areas for process improvement and efficiency.

Evaluating IT Controls

The Purpose of IT Controls

IT controls are policies, procedures, and processes put in place to safeguard an organization's IT systems and data. These controls are designed to prevent, detect, and correct any potential risks or vulnerabilities. They are a critical component of IT auditing, as they provide a foundation for assessing the effectiveness of an organization's IT systems and processes.

Understanding Different Types of IT Controls

There are several types of IT controls that auditors must be familiar with in order to effectively evaluate them. These include preventive, detective, and corrective controls. Preventive controls are designed to prevent potential risks or vulnerabilities from occurring. Detective controls are used to identify and alert when a potential risk does occur. Corrective controls are processes put in place to address and mitigate any risks that have been identified.

The Effectiveness of IT Controls

The effectiveness of IT controls is a critical aspect of IT auditing. Auditors must assess whether controls are properly designed and implemented and whether they are effectively mitigating risks. This involves testing controls to ensure they are working as intended and that any issues are appropriately addressed. By evaluating the effectiveness of IT controls, auditors can provide valuable recommendations for improvement and better risk management.

Continuous Monitoring of IT Controls

IT controls are not a one-time set-it-and-forget-it process. They must be continuously monitored and reviewed to ensure they remain effective. With technology constantly evolving, IT controls must also adapt to keep up with any new risks or vulnerabilities. IT auditors play a crucial role in regularly monitoring the organization's IT controls and identifying any areas that may need improvement.

The Human Element of IT Controls

While technology plays a major role in IT controls, it is also important to note the human element. People are often the biggest risk to an organization's IT systems and processes. This could be through unintentional actions, such as clicking on a malicious link, or intentional actions, such as insider threats. IT auditors must also assess the effectiveness of human controls, such as training and awareness programs, to mitigate these risks and ensure the organization is adequately protected.

Overall, IT auditing is a crucial aspect of risk management for every organization. With technology playing an increasingly important role in business operations, the potential risks and vulnerabilities are also on the rise. IT auditors play a critical role in identifying these risks and mitigating them through a risk-based approach and evaluating the effectiveness of IT controls. By continuously monitoring and assessing IT systems and processes, they help organizations stay secure and compliant in an ever-changing digital landscape.

Chapter 7: Effective Report Writing, Communicating with Management, Follow-up and Monitoring

Effective Report Writing

When it comes to internal audit, one of the most crucial aspects is effective report writing. This process involves communicating the findings and recommendations of an audit to management in a clear and concise manner. The purpose of a report is to inform and guide management towards improving the overall internal control and risk management processes of the organization. Report writing requires a balance between providing enough detail to support the findings and recommendations, while also being concise and using accessible language. It is important to avoid using technical jargon and terminology that may be unfamiliar to the readers. The goal is to communicate complex concepts in a way that is easily understandable to non-auditors. To ensure effective report writing, internal auditors should follow a structured approach. This includes clearly identifying the objective of the audit, providing background information and context, outlining the methodology and procedures used, and presenting the key findings with supporting evidence. The report should also include recommendations for improvement and a conclusion summarizing the overall results of the audit.

In addition to the content, the format and layout of the report are also important. A well-organized and visually appealing report will make it easier for management to digest the information and take action on the recommendations. The use of bullet points, charts and tables can help to present information in a clear and concise manner.

Communicating with Management

Effective communication is essential for internal auditors to successfully carry out their responsibilities. It is important for auditors to establish a good working relationship with management, as they will be relying on their cooperation and understanding to address any issues identified during the audit process. Communication should be ongoing throughout the audit process, from planning to reporting. It is important for auditors to clearly communicate the purpose and scope of the audit, as well as any significant findings and recommendations. This will provide management with an opportunity to provide additional information and address any concerns they may have. When communicating with management, it is important for auditors to remain objective and unbiased. Auditors should also be mindful of the language and tone used, as it can greatly impact the effectiveness of their message. Communication should be clear, respectful and professional at all times.

In addition to written reports, auditors should also engage in verbal communication with management. This can include meetings, presentations, and follow-up discussions. Verbal communication allows for a more interactive and dynamic exchange of information, and can help to clarify any misunderstandings that may arise from written reports.

Follow-up and Monitoring

The final stage of an internal audit is follow-up and monitoring. This involves tracking the progress of management's response to the audit findings and recommendations. Follow-up is crucial to ensure that the necessary action has been taken to address any deficiencies and improve the overall internal control and risk management processes. The follow-up process should include a monitoring schedule, outlining when and how progress will be assessed. This can include regular meetings with management, periodic progress reports, and verification through testing and sampling. In addition, it is important for auditors to have open communication with management during the follow-up process. This will allow for any delays or challenges to be addressed in a timely manner, and ensure that the action plan is still relevant and effective.

The results of follow-up and monitoring should also be documented in a report and provided to management and relevant stakeholders. This will provide transparency and accountability, and also serve as a record of the progress made and any outstanding issues.

Conclusion

Effective report writing, communication with management, and follow-up and monitoring are essential components of a successful internal audit. These processes require strong communication skills, a structured approach and ongoing engagement with management. By following these best practices, internal auditors can ensure that their findings and recommendations are clearly and effectively communicated to management, and that the necessary actions are taken to improve the overall internal control and risk management processes of the organization.

Chapter 8: Corporate Governance and Internal Audit

Importance of Corporate Governance

Corporate governance can be defined as the system of rules, practices, and processes by which a company is directed and controlled. It encompasses the relationships between a company's stakeholders, such as shareholders, management, and the board of directors. The main purpose of corporate governance is to ensure that the company is managed and operated in an ethical and responsible manner, with a focus on maximizing long-term value for all stakeholders. In today's complex business landscape, corporate governance has become increasingly important. The actions and decisions of companies have a significant impact on the wider society and the environment. Therefore, it is essential for companies to have strong governance structures in place to ensure transparency, accountability, and ethical behavior.

One of the major reasons why corporate governance is crucial is that it can help a company achieve and maintain its competitive advantage. By promoting good governance practices, companies can attract and retain top talent, gain the trust of investors, and enhance their reputation in the market. It also facilitates effective decision-making and risk management, ensuring the long-term sustainability of the company.

Responsibilities of Internal Audit in Corporate Governance

Internal audit plays a critical role in corporate governance. As the third line of defense, internal auditors are responsible for evaluating and monitoring the effectiveness of a company's governance processes and controls. In addition to assessing the adequacy of internal controls, internal auditors also provide valuable insights and recommendations on how to improve governance practices. The responsibilities of internal audit in corporate governance vary, depending on the size and complexity of the organization. However, some of the key areas that internal auditors should focus on include:

- Evaluating the effectiveness of the company's risk management processes and controls

- Reviewing compliance with laws, regulations, and company policies

- Assessing the integrity of financial and non-financial reporting

- Monitoring the company's ethical culture and adherence to ethical standards

- Examining the effectiveness of the company's control environment and corporate governance structure

Moreover, internal auditors should also be proactive in identifying potential risks and areas for improvement in the company's governance processes. By providing objective and independent assurance, internal audit can help strengthen the company's corporate governance practices.

Legal and Ethical Considerations

When it comes to corporate governance, there are several legal and ethical considerations that companies and internal auditors need to be aware of. These considerations not only help ensure compliance with laws and regulations but also promote ethical behavior and foster trust and credibility in the company. One of the key legal considerations in corporate governance is compliance with laws and regulations, particularly those related to financial reporting and corporate disclosures. Internal auditors should have a thorough understanding of these laws and regulations and ensure that all relevant requirements are followed.

Ethics also play a significant role in corporate governance. Companies are expected to operate in an ethical manner, with a focus on fairness, transparency, and social responsibility. Internal auditors should be well-versed in the company's code of ethics and conduct and assess whether employees are adhering to ethical standards. Moreover, internal auditors themselves are held to a high standard of ethical behavior. They must maintain objectivity and independence in their work and avoid conflicts of interest. This ensures that their findings and recommendations are unbiased and serve the best interests of the company.

In conclusion, corporate governance is an essential component of effective and responsible management. It involves not only complying with laws and regulations but also promoting ethical behavior and transparency. Internal audit, as the independent assurance function, plays a crucial role in evaluating and improving corporate governance practices. By fulfilling their responsibilities with a focus on legal and ethical considerations, internal auditors can help companies achieve and maintain strong governance structures for long-term success.

Chapter 9: International Standards and Best Practices for CIAs

As internal auditors, we strive to provide credible, independent, and objective assurance to our organizations. In order to achieve this, it is essential for us to adhere to internationally recognized standards and best practices. In this chapter, we will delve into the various standards and practices that govern the professional practice of internal auditing, including the International Standards for the Professional Practice of Internal Auditing (Standards), the Code of Ethics, and the Quality Assurance and Improvement Program.

International Standards for the Professional Practice of Internal Auditing (Standards)

The International Standards for the Professional Practice of Internal Auditing (Standards) were developed by the Institute of Internal Auditors (IIA), the leading global professional association for internal auditors. These standards serve as a framework for the internal audit profession, providing guidance on the fundamental principles of internal auditing, as well as the implementation of these principles. One of the key components of the Standards is the definition of Internal Auditing, which is "an independent, objective assurance and consulting activity designed to add value and improve an organization's operations. It helps an organization accomplish its objectives by bringing a systematic, disciplined approach to evaluate and improve the effectiveness of risk management, control, and governance processes."

The Standards also provide guidance on governance, risk management, and control, as well as the core principles of internal auditing. These principles include integrity, objectivity, confidentiality, competency, and due care, among others. As CIAs, it is crucial for us to uphold these principles in order to maintain the trust and credibility of our profession. Furthermore, the Standards emphasize the importance of independence and objectivity in internal auditing. This means that internal auditors should remain free from any conflicts of interest and should not be influenced by personal feelings or biases when conducting their work. This ensures that the conclusions and recommendations made by internal auditors are impartial and unbiased.

It is important for CIAs to stay up-to-date with the Standards and incorporate them into their work practices. This not only ensures consistency and quality in internal auditing processes but also demonstrates our commitment to professionalism and ethical conduct.

Code of Ethics

Along with the Standards, the IIA has also developed a Code of Ethics that outlines the ethical principles and guidelines that CIAs should adhere to. This includes integrity, objectivity, confidentiality, and competency, which are aligned with the principles outlined in the Standards. Integrity is a fundamental principle in the Code of Ethics, emphasizing the importance of honesty and fairness in all aspects of internal auditing. This includes being truthful in all communications, maintaining confidentiality of information, and disclosing any potential conflicts of interest.

Objectivity is also crucial in maintaining the credibility and trust of the internal audit profession. This principle highlights the importance of remaining impartial and unbiased in our work, avoiding any personal or professional biases that may influence our judgment.

Confidentiality is another key aspect of the Code of Ethics, requiring CIAs to safeguard any confidential or sensitive information obtained during the course of their work. This ensures the protection of organizational and personal data, preventing any misuse or unauthorized access.

Competency is also emphasized in the Code of Ethics, requiring CIAs to possess the necessary skills, knowledge, and experience to perform their duties effectively. This includes staying updated with industry developments and continuously expanding our skills and expertise.

As CIAs, it is our responsibility to uphold the Code of Ethics and demonstrate ethical behavior in all aspects of our work. Failure to comply with these ethical standards may result in disciplinary action by the IIA.

Quality Assurance and Improvement Program

To ensure the adherence to these standards and ethics, it is essential for CIAs to have a Quality Assurance and Improvement Program (QAIP) in place. This program is designed to evaluate the quality and effectiveness of internal audit processes and provide opportunities for improvement. The IIA recommends conducting external quality assessments every five years and internal quality assessments annually. These assessments provide an independent evaluation of the internal audit function and help identify areas for improvement. It also ensures that internal audit processes are in line with the Standards and Code of Ethics.

Through quality assurance and improvement programs, internal auditors can continuously enhance their skills and knowledge, and fine-tune their processes to deliver high-quality work. This leads to improved credibility and trust in the internal audit function and adds value to the organization.

In addition to these external assessments, it is important for CIAs to conduct self-assessments regularly. This involves evaluating our own work and adhering to the Standards and Code of Ethics in every aspect of our job. It also provides an opportunity to reflect on our performance and identify areas for growth and development.

In conclusion, International Standards, Code of Ethics, and Quality Assurance and Improvement Programs are essential components of the professional practice of internal auditing. As CIAs, it is our responsibility to adhere to these standards and continuously strive for excellence in our work, ultimately contributing to the success and sustainability of our organizations.

Chapter 10: Skills and Competencies of a CIA

The role of a Certified Internal Auditor (CIA) requires a diverse range of skills and competencies to effectively execute the responsibilities of an internal audit professional. In this chapter, we will explore the technical, analytical, communication, and leadership skills necessary for a successful CIA.

Technical Skills

Technical skills are the foundation of a CIA's knowledge and expertise in the field of internal auditing. These skills are acquired through education, training, and on-the-job experience. A CIA must possess a deep understanding of accounting principles, financial reporting, and auditing standards. They must also have a strong grasp of internal control systems and risk management frameworks.

While technical skills can be learned through formal education and practical experience, it is important for CIAs to continuously update and expand their knowledge to keep up with the ever-evolving business environment. This can be achieved through attending training and development programs, reading industry publications, and participating in professional organizations and networks.

Analytical Skills

The ability to analyze and interpret data is crucial for a CIA. An important aspect of internal auditing is identifying patterns and trends in data to uncover risks and potential areas of fraud. CIAs must possess strong critical thinking and problem-solving skills to effectively evaluate and analyze information. They must also be able to think strategically and have an eye for detail to identify potential deficiencies and discrepancies.

In addition to their analytical skills, CIAs must also possess strong research and investigative skills. They must be able to gather and analyze information from various sources and use critical judgment to draw conclusions. These skills are essential in conducting thorough and effective audits.

Communication Skills

Effective communication is a vital skill for CIAs to possess. They must be able to comfortably interact and build relationships with individuals at all levels of an organization, from front-line staff to top executives. CIAs must also be able to clearly articulate complex information in a way that is easily understood by others.

In addition to verbal communication, written communication is also important for CIAs. They must be able to write accurate and concise audit reports, which may often be read by non-technical stakeholders. These reports must effectively convey findings, observations, and recommendations to drive positive change within an organization.

Leadership Skills

As a CIA, one must have strong leadership skills to successfully manage and lead audit teams. CIAs must be able to motivate and support team members, delegate tasks, and provide guidance and feedback to ensure the successful completion of audit projects. In addition to leading audit teams, CIAs must also be able to demonstrate leadership within the organization they work for. They must have the ability to influence and collaborate with colleagues and management to promote a culture of internal control and ethical behavior.

Moreover, CIAs must possess the skills to adapt to change and be resilient in challenging situations. They must also be able to manage stakeholder expectations, handle conflicts, and make decisions in the best interest of the organization.

The Importance of Soft Skills

Apart from the technical and specialized skills required for an internal auditor, certain soft skills are also essential for a CIA's success. These skills include time management, organization, adaptability, and the ability to handle pressure and stress. As audit projects often have tight deadlines and require working with multiple stakeholders, CIAs must possess the ability to manage their time effectively and prioritize tasks.

In addition, CIAs must also be able to work well under pressure and manage stress to maintain the quality and accuracy of their work. They must be able to adapt to a dynamic and ever-changing environment and remain focused on achieving audit objectives.

Diversity and Inclusivity in CIA Program

In recent years, there has been a growing emphasis on diversity and inclusivity in the CIA program. This includes the importance of diversity in terms of race, gender, age, and culture, among others. A diverse and inclusive workforce brings different perspectives and experiences to the table, leading to better decision-making and more effective internal audits.

Recognizing this, the Institute of Internal Auditors (IIA) has made efforts to promote diversity and inclusivity within the CIA program. This includes increasing resources for minority and underrepresented groups, as well as providing guidance and support for organizations looking to promote diversity within their internal audit departments.

The Future of CIAs

The role of a CIA is continually evolving, and the skills and competencies required for success will also change over time. As the business landscape becomes more complex and technology continues to advance, CIAs must adapt and develop new skills to remain relevant and effective in their roles. To prepare for the future, CIAs must embrace a culture of continuous learning and development. They must also be open to new ideas and embrace technological advancements to enhance their audit processes and produce more efficient and effective results.

In conclusion, a successful CIA not only possesses technical and analytical skills, but also strong communications, leadership, and soft skills. These skills are essential to effectively fulfill the responsibilities of an internal audit professional and contribute to the success of an organization. As the role of a CIA continues to evolve, continuously honing and developing these skills will be crucial for achieving success in the field of internal auditing.

Chapter 11: Job Opportunities and Advancement in the CIA Field

Job Opportunities

A career as a Certified Internal Auditor (CIA) can open up a world of opportunities for professionals in the audit and accounting field. With the growing importance of internal controls and the need for companies to prevent fraud, the demand for qualified CIAs is on the rise. One of the major benefits of becoming a CIA is the flexibility in job opportunities. CIAs are needed in various industries, including finance, healthcare, government, and manufacturing. This diverse range of industries allows CIAs to gain experience in different settings and industries, expanding their knowledge and skills.

Apart from the variety of industries, CIAs also have a range of job titles to choose from. Some examples include internal auditor, risk analyst, senior auditor, audit manager, and compliance manager. This diversity in job titles gives CIAs the opportunity to find a role that aligns with their interests and strengths.

In addition, being a CIA also opens the door for global job opportunities. As companies expand their operations globally, the need for internal auditors with a broad understanding of different cultures, laws, and regulations increases. This creates opportunities for CIAs to work for multinational companies or to even travel for assignments in different countries.

Advancement Opportunities

Becoming a CIA not only offers diverse job opportunities, but also provides opportunities for career advancement. CIAs have the potential for a successful and fulfilling career path, with the ability to move up the ladder within their organization or in the industry. With their specialized skills and knowledge in areas such as internal control, fraud detection, and IT auditing, CIAs are highly valued and sought after by organizations. This demand for qualified CIAs often leads to higher salaries, bonuses, and other benefits.

Furthermore, having a CIA certification opens up opportunities for career advancement within the internal audit field. CIAs can become audit managers, internal audit directors, or even Chief Audit Executives (CAEs). These roles come with increased responsibilities and higher pay, making CIAs a highly desired asset for any organization.

Apart from moving up in their career, CIAs also have the option to branch out into other areas such as risk management, compliance, or even executive positions. The versatile skillset and knowledge gained as a CIA allows professionals to take on different roles within their organization or even switch to a different industry.

Continuing Professional Education

Continuing professional education (CPE) is essential for maintaining the CIA certification. It is a requirement for CIAs to complete 40 hours of CPE every year, with at least 20 of those hours directly related to internal auditing. However, CPE not only helps CIAs maintain their certification, but it also plays a crucial role in their career development. As the business landscape constantly evolves, CIAs need to stay updated with the latest trends, best practices, and regulations to remain relevant and valuable to their organizations.

CPE also provides CIAs with the opportunity to expand their knowledge, skills, and network. Attending training programs, conferences, and seminars not only increases their understanding of internal auditing, but also offers opportunities to connect with other professionals in the industry. Moreover, CPE gives CIAs the chance to explore other areas of interest and pursue new challenges within their organization. It allows them to gain new perspectives and insights, leading to personal and professional growth.

In conclusion, a career as a Certified Internal Auditor offers a wealth of job opportunities and opportunities for advancement. With the ever-increasing demand for qualified CIAs, professionals in this field have the potential for a lucrative and fulfilling career. By continuously engaging in CPE, CIAs can stay updated with the latest developments in their field and open doors to even more opportunities for growth.

Chapter 12: CIA Exam

Exam Structure

The CIA Exam is one of the most rigorous and prestigious certifications in the financial and auditing industry. It consists of three parts, each focusing on different aspects of internal auditing. Part 1 covers the essentials of internal auditing, Part 2 focuses on the practice of internal auditing, and Part 3 tests your knowledge of business knowledge for internal auditing. The exam is computer-based and consists of multiple-choice questions, with each part containing approximately 125 questions. The time limit for each part is 2.5 hours, with a total of 7.5 hours for the entire exam.

Study Tips

Preparing for the CIA Exam requires discipline, dedication, and a solid study plan. Here are some tips to help you succeed in your exam preparations:

- Start Early: Begin preparing for the exam at least three to four months in advance. This will give you enough time to cover all the material and revise before the exam.
- Choose Study Materials Wisely: There are various resources available to help you prepare for the CIA Exam, including textbooks, practice exams, and review courses. It's crucial to choose materials that are updated and align with the exam's content outline.
- Create a Study Plan: Make a study schedule and stick to it. Allocate enough time for each part of the exam, and make sure to include review sessions and practice exams in your plan.
- Use Practice Exams: Practice exams are a great way to assess your knowledge and identify weak areas that need more attention. Make sure to take at least one practice exam for each part of the exam.
- Stay Focused: Avoid distractions while studying and stay focused on the task at hand. Turn off your phone and find a quiet study space to avoid interruptions.
- Study Smart, Not Hard: Understanding the concepts rather than just memorizing them is crucial for success in the CIA Exam. Take breaks and use different study techniques, such as creating flashcards or using mnemonic devices, to help you retain the material.

Resources

Having the right resources can make a huge difference in your exam preparations. Here are some recommended resources to help you prepare for the CIA Exam:

- The IIA's CIA Learning System: This is the official study guide for the CIA Exam, created by The Institute of Internal Auditors (IIA). It includes textbooks, online practice tests, and flashcards.

- Practice Exams: There are various practice exams available online, such as Gleim, Wiley, and Surgent CIA Review, that can help you assess your knowledge and prepare for the real exam.
- Review Courses: Many review courses offer comprehensive study materials, practice exams, and video lectures to help you prepare for the exam. Some popular review courses include Becker, HOCK, and CIA Exam Academy.
- IIA's Global Knowledge Center: The IIA's Global Knowledge Center offers various resources, such as e-books, articles, and case studies, to help you prepare for the CIA Exam.

Passing the Exam

Passing the CIA Exam requires hard work, dedication, and effective preparation. Here are some tips to help you increase your chances of passing the exam on your first attempt:

- Understand the Content Outline: The IIA's content outline is the blueprint for the CIA Exam. Make sure to understand the topics and subtopics covered in each part of the exam.
- Focus on Weak Areas: Use the results from your practice exams to identify weak areas that need improvement. Focus on these areas in your review sessions to increase your chances of passing.
- Pay Attention to Time Management: Each part of the exam has a time limit of 2.5 hours. Practice managing your time wisely during your study sessions and on practice exams to ensure you can complete each part within the allotted time.
- Read the Questions Carefully: Make sure to read each question carefully and understand what it is asking before selecting your answer.
- Don't Change Answers Unless Necessary: Studies have shown that your first instinct is usually correct. Only change an answer if you are confident that your first choice was incorrect.
- Don't Get Discouraged: If you do not pass the exam on your first attempt, don't get discouraged. Use your results to identify areas that need improvement and keep studying. Many candidates pass the exam after multiple attempts.

Remember, success in the CIA Exam is not just about passing the exam but also gaining a thorough understanding of internal auditing principles. The knowledge and skills you acquire while preparing for the CIA Exam will not only help you pass the exam but also be a valuable asset in your career as a Certified Internal Auditor. Good luck on your journey to becoming a CIA!

Chapter 13: CIA Exam Preparation

Certified Internal Auditor (CIA) is one of the most renowned certifications in the field of Internal Audit. It not only enhances your knowledge and understanding of internal audit practices, but also showcases your expertise and credibility in the industry. Being a CIA can open doors to new opportunities and career growth. However, obtaining this prestigious certification requires hard work, dedication, and a well-planned study approach. In this chapter, we will discuss the various aspects of CIA Exam preparation in detail.

Study Plan

Having a structured study plan is crucial for the success of any exam, and CIA is no exception. As you begin your CIA Exam preparation, it is essential to create a study plan that suits your needs and schedule. Allocate sufficient time for each topic and make sure you cover all the exam syllabus. Make use of study materials provided by the Institute of Internal Auditors (IIA) or other reputable sources to supplement your understanding. Moreover, it is also beneficial to join a study group or get a study partner to keep yourself motivated and accountable.

While creating your study plan, keep in mind that the CIA exam is divided into three parts, namely Part 1: Essentials of Internal Auditing, Part 2: Practice of Internal Auditing, and Part 3: Business Knowledge for Internal Auditing. Each part has a different weightage and covers specific topics. It is crucial to understand the weightage and focus on the topics accordingly. For example, Part 2 has the highest weightage, so you may need to allocate more time for it compared to the other two parts.

Time Management

Time management plays a vital role in your CIA Exam preparation. With a vast syllabus to cover, it is essential to manage your time efficiently. Besides allocating time for studying, make sure you also take regular breaks to avoid burnout. Use techniques such as the Pomodoro method, where you study for 25 minutes and take a 5-minute break, to maintain your focus and productivity. Also, try to study during your most productive hours, whether it is early in the morning or late at night. As you get closer to the exam date, make sure you revise and practice more, rather than just studying new topics.

Practice Questions

Practice questions are a great way to assess your knowledge and identify your weak areas. The IIA provides a sample practice exam for each part of the CIA exam, which can give you an idea of the type and difficulty level of questions that may appear in the actual exam. You can also find practice questions from other sources such as study materials, online forums, or previous exam papers. Make sure you not only solve the practice questions but also understand the concept behind each question. This will help you in answering similar questions in the real exam.

Mock Exams

Taking mock exams is an excellent way to simulate the actual exam environment and assess your readiness for the CIA exam. The IIA also offers mock exams for each part of the CIA exam, which can help you understand the format and structure of the exam and identify your strengths and weaknesses. You can also find mock exams from other sources, such as review courses or study materials. Taking these mock exams will help you evaluate your progress and make necessary adjustments to your study plan, if required. In addition to the above, it is crucial to also focus on your mental and physical well-being during your CIA Exam preparation. Make sure you get enough rest, exercise, and maintain a healthy diet to keep your mind and body in top shape. Remember to stay positive and believe in yourself, as you have already taken the first step towards becoming a Certified Internal Auditor.

In conclusion, becoming a CIA requires hard work, dedication, and a well-planned study approach. With a structured study plan, efficient time management, regular practice, and mock exams, you can increase your chances of success in the CIA exam. Keep in mind that there is no shortcut to success, and it is essential to put in the effort and stay disciplined throughout your preparation. Good luck on your journey to becoming a CIA!

Chapter 14: Fundamentals of Internal Auditing

Internal auditing is a crucial component of any organization's success, providing essential insights and recommendations for improvement. It is the process of evaluating and assessing an organization's operations, finances, and processes to ensure they are efficient, effective, and compliant with laws and regulations. In this chapter, we will delve deeper into the fundamentals of internal auditing, including governance, risk management, and control.

Fundamentals of Internal Auditing

To understand the fundamentals of internal auditing, we must first understand the role of internal auditors. Internal auditors are independent and objective professionals who provide assurance on an organization's operations, risk management, and internal controls. They act as the eyes and ears of the organization, providing valuable insights and recommendations to improve their overall functioning.

Internal Audit's Role in Governance

Governance is the system of rules and processes that govern an organization's decision-making and operations. A strong governance framework is essential for organizations to achieve their objectives and meet regulatory requirements. Internal audit plays a crucial role in governance by providing assurance on the effectiveness of the organization's governance processes and controls.

Internal auditors assess the effectiveness of the board of directors and executive management in setting and implementing the organization's strategic objectives. They review the organization's policies, procedures, and processes to ensure they align with the internal and external environment's requirements. Internal audit also evaluates the organization's code of conduct and the ethical culture's strength, ensuring it is in line with the organization's values and objectives.

Risk Management in Internal Audit

Risk management is the process of identifying, assessing, and managing potential risks that could impact an organization's ability to achieve its objectives. A robust risk management framework is crucial for organizations to proactively identify and mitigate potential risks before they turn into crises. In the context of internal auditing, risk management involves assessing the organization's risk management processes and controls, providing assurance on their effectiveness, and making recommendations for improvement.

Internal auditors use a risk-based approach to identify areas of high risk and prioritize their audit activities accordingly. They review the organization's risk management processes and controls, ensuring they are adequate, effective, and comply with laws and regulations. Internal audit also evaluates the organization's risk culture, ensuring it is embedded in the organization's values and mission.

Control in Internal Audit

Internal control is the process of designing, implementing, and monitoring controls to help an organization achieve its objectives, mitigate risk, and ensure compliance with laws and regulations. Internal auditors play a critical role in evaluating and providing assurance on the effectiveness of internal controls.

Internal auditors assess the adequacy and effectiveness of the organization's internal control framework, covering areas such as financial controls, operational controls, and IT controls. They identify weaknesses and gaps in the controls and make recommendations for improvement to ensure the organization's resources are used efficiently and effectively.

Unpacking the Concept of Assurance

One of the key responsibilities of internal audit is to provide assurance to stakeholders on the organization's operations, risk management, and internal controls. But what exactly does assurance mean in the context of internal auditing?

In simple terms, assurance is the level of confidence or certainty that stakeholders have in the organization's processes and controls. It is the idea that the organization's operations are being carried out in an effective and efficient manner and that risks are being appropriately managed. Internal auditors play a crucial role in providing assurance by objectively evaluating and reporting on the organization's operations to provide stakeholders with a level of comfort regarding the organization's functioning.

The Importance of Independence and Objectivity

When it comes to internal auditing, independence and objectivity are critical. Internal auditors must be independent, both in fact and in appearance, to provide unbiased assessments of the organization's operations. This includes reporting directly to the board of directors or an audit committee and having unrestricted access to all levels of the organization.

Objectivity, on the other hand, ensures that internal auditors do not have any conflicts of interest that could compromise their professional judgment. They must approach each audit with an open mind and evaluate the organization's operations based on facts and evidence.

Technology's Impact on Internal Auditing

In today's digital age, technology plays a crucial role in almost every aspect of an organization's operations. This includes internal audit, where technology has significantly impacted the way auditors conduct their work. With the increasing use of data analytics, internal auditors can analyze large volumes of data to identify patterns, trends, and anomalies, providing a more comprehensive and accurate assessment of the organization's operations.

But along with its advantages, technology has also presented new challenges for internal auditors, such as cybersecurity risks and the impact of automation on traditional audit processes. As technology continues to evolve, it is essential for internal auditors to stay updated on the latest developments and adapt their audit approach accordingly.

The Importance of Communication

Effective communication is vital in all aspects of business, and this holds true for internal audit as well. Internal auditors must be able to convey their findings and recommendations in a clear, concise, and understandable manner to a wide range of stakeholders. Through effective communication, internal auditors can build trust and credibility with stakeholders, ensuring their recommendations are understood and implemented.

The Future of Internal Auditing

As the business world continues to evolve and organizations face new challenges, the role of internal audit will also evolve. Internal auditors must adapt to changes in technology, regulations, and organizational processes to continue providing valuable insights and recommendations to their organizations. The future of internal audit holds many opportunities, and it is up to internal auditors to embrace them and continue fulfilling their critical role in the organization's success.

Closing Thoughts

In this chapter, we have explored the fundamentals of internal auditing, including its role in governance, risk management, and control. Internal audit plays a crucial role in providing assurance to stakeholders and helping organizations achieve their objectives through efficient and effective processes. As technology and business landscapes continue to evolve, the role of internal audit will also evolve, presenting new challenges and opportunities. With its objective and independent approach, internal audit will continue to play a vital role in organizations' success.

Chapter 15: CIA Exam Part 2 - Practice of Internal Auditing

Audit Planning

Audit planning is a crucial step in the internal audit process. It involves the identification and assessment of risks, determination of audit objectives and scope, and development of a detailed audit plan. This plan serves as a roadmap for the audit and provides a framework for its successful execution. As a CIA, it is essential to understand the business operations and the risks associated with them. This knowledge will help in identifying areas that need to be audited and determining the level of risk for each area. It is also important to consider the organization's goals and objectives while planning the audit, as it should align with the overall strategy.

In addition to these factors, the audit plan should also include details on the resources required, timelines, and the audit approach to be followed. This approach can vary depending on the nature of the audit, such as financial, operational, or compliance. A well-thought-out audit plan increases the chances of a successful audit and ensures that no crucial areas are overlooked.

Conducting the Audit Engagement

Once the audit plan is in place, the next step is to conduct the audit engagement. This involves gathering evidence, testing controls, and evaluating the results. As auditors, it is our responsibility to ensure that the audit is conducted in a professional and unbiased manner. Effective communication is a critical element during the audit engagement. This involves keeping the stakeholders informed about the audit's progress, discussing any findings or issues that arise, and seeking their input when necessary. This approach promotes transparency and builds trust with clients, enhancing the effectiveness of the audit process.

During the audit, it is also essential to remain independent and objective. As CIAs, we must maintain an unbiased perspective and avoid any conflicts of interest that could compromise the audit's integrity.

Quality Assurance and Improvement Program

A quality assurance and improvement program (QAIP) is a systematic approach to evaluate the internal audit function's effectiveness and identify areas for improvement. It is a critical component of the internal audit process and is required by the International Standards for the Professional Practice of Internal Auditing (Standards). A QAIP typically includes a self-assessment, external assessment, and ongoing monitoring activities. The self-assessment involves regular evaluations of internal audit activities against the Standards and other best practices. This helps identify any gaps in the audit process and implement corrective actions.

External assessments, on the other hand, are conducted by an independent assessor who evaluates the internal audit function's effectiveness and provides suggestions for improvement. These assessments are usually conducted every five years and provide valuable insights into the organization's overall risk management and governance processes.

Ongoing monitoring is a continuous process that evaluates the internal audit function's performance against predetermined key performance indicators (KPIs). These KPIs could include the number of audits conducted, audit completion times, and client satisfaction ratings, among others. Regular monitoring ensures that the internal audit function remains efficient, effective, and relevant.

Uncommon Insights and Concepts

One key concept to understand when it comes to the practice of internal auditing is the concept of materiality. Materiality refers to the magnitude at which a misstatement or omission could influence the decision of a reasonable individual relying on the audit report. As auditors, we must assess the materiality of audit findings and report them accordingly, taking into consideration the impact they could have on the organization. Another important aspect is the concept of value-added auditing. As CIAs, we are not just there to identify and report on problems or inefficiencies. We should also strive to provide insights and recommendations that add value to the organization. This could include opportunities for cost savings, process improvements, or other suggestions that align with the organization's goals.

Lastly, effective communication is vital in the practice of internal auditing. This includes not only communicating with clients but also collaborating and sharing knowledge with other audit professionals. The internal audit function plays a crucial role in ensuring strong governance and risk management within an organization, and effective communication can help achieve this goal.

In conclusion, the practice of internal auditing is a crucial aspect of the CIA profession. It requires a thorough understanding of the business operations, a well-planned and executed audit process, and continuous improvement through quality assurance. By incorporating these uncommon insights and concepts, CIAs can enhance their skills and capabilities, ensuring the success of their internal audit engagements.

Chapter 16: CIA Exam Part 3 - Business Knowledge for Internal Auditing

Internal auditing is a constantly evolving field, and as a Certified Internal Auditor (CIA), it is crucial to have a comprehensive understanding of business processes, financial accounting, and finance. Part 3 of the CIA exam, titled "Business Knowledge for Internal Auditing," is designed to assess your knowledge and understanding of these important areas. In this chapter, we will explore the topics covered in this section and provide insights into how to prepare for this part of the exam.

Business Processes

Business processes are the core elements that drive an organization's operations and are essential for its success. As a CIA, it is vital to have a deep understanding of these processes to identify any weaknesses or inefficiencies that could potentially lead to fraud or errors. This section of the CIA exam covers topics such as organizational structure, business process flows, and risk management. To effectively assess business processes, it is essential to have a thorough understanding of an organization's operations. This includes understanding its objectives, strategies, and core processes. A CIA must also have a clear understanding of the organizational structure, including its different departments, roles, and responsibilities. This knowledge will help in identifying potential control gaps or areas of concern.

Business process flows are another critical aspect of this section of the exam. Understanding the flow of information and materials through an organization is crucial in identifying potential risks and control weaknesses. A CIA must have the ability to map out these flows and identify any vulnerabilities or opportunities for improvement.

Risk management is also a vital aspect of business processes. As a CIA, it is essential to have a thorough understanding of the risk management framework and how it is implemented within an organization. This includes identifying and assessing risks, implementing controls, and monitoring their effectiveness. Having a robust knowledge of risk management will help ensure that internal audit practices are aligned with an organization's overall risk management strategies.

Financial Accounting and Finance

Financial accounting and finance are crucial areas for a CIA to have a thorough understanding of. This section of the exam covers topics such as financial statement analysis, budgeting and forecasting, and investment analysis. Financial statement analysis is the process of evaluating an organization's financial performance by analyzing its financial statements. This includes understanding the different financial statements, such as the balance sheet, income statement, and cash flow statement, and interpreting the information they provide. A CIA must also have a good grasp of financial ratios and their significance in assessing an organization's financial health.

Budgeting and forecasting are also critical areas of knowledge for a CIA. This involves understanding the budgeting process, including its importance in planning and controlling an organization's operations. A CIA must also have a good understanding of forecasting techniques and their applications in assessing the future financial performance of an organization.

Investment analysis is another essential topic covered in this section of the exam. As a CIA, one must have a solid understanding of the different investment vehicles and their risks and returns. This includes knowledge of financial markets, securities, and the role of a financial analyst.

Managerial Accounting

Managerial accounting is a crucial aspect of internal audit, as it involves the analysis of an organization's internal financial information to assist in decision-making. This section of the CIA exam covers topics such as cost accounting, performance measurement, and variance analysis. Cost accounting is the process of identifying, measuring, and analyzing the costs associated with producing goods or services. A CIA must have a good understanding of different costing methods and their applications, as well as the principles of cost behavior and cost allocation.

Performance measurement and variance analysis are also key topics in this section of the exam. This involves understanding the different performance metrics used to evaluate an organization's financial and operational performance and analyzing variances between actual and expected results. A CIA must also have the ability to identify potential fraudulent activities or errors through variance analysis.

Preparing for the Exam

Preparing for Part 3 of the CIA exam requires a thorough understanding of all the topics mentioned above. It is essential to review and understand the exam syllabus and allocate sufficient time for studying each area covered. Taking practice exams and seeking feedback from experienced CIAs can also help in identifying areas that require further study. Additionally, staying up to date with current business trends and developments can also help in preparing for this section of the exam. This includes staying informed about changes in regulations, industry standards, and new technologies that may impact an organization's business processes, financial accounting, and finance.

In conclusion, Part 3 of the CIA exam, "Business Knowledge for Internal Auditing," covers a diverse range of topics that are essential for a CIA to have a comprehensive understanding of. These include business processes, financial accounting and finance, and managerial accounting. By dedicating sufficient time and effort to prepare for this part of the exam, a CIA can demonstrate their knowledge and skills in these areas and become a valuable asset to any organization.

Chapter 17: CIA Exam Preparation Tips

Preparing for the Exam Day

As the day of your CIA exam approaches, it is natural to feel some nerves and anxiety. However, through proper preparation and strategies, you can overcome these feelings and perform at your best on the exam day. Here are some tips to help you prepare for the exam day:

1. Know the Exam Format and Content

Before the exam day, make sure you are familiar with the exam format and content. This will help you plan your study schedule accordingly and focus on the key areas that will be tested. The CIA exam consists of three parts, with each part consisting of multiple-choice questions and a few essay questions. It is important to understand the structure of the exam and the weightage given to each section.

2. Get Adequate Rest

It is crucial to get a good night's sleep before the exam day. Your brain needs rest to function at its best, and lack of sleep can affect your performance on the exam. Make sure you get at least 7-8 hours of sleep to feel well-rested and alert on the day of the exam.

3. Plan Your Exam Day Schedule

It is important to plan your exam day schedule in advance to avoid any last-minute stress or confusion. Take into account the time it will take you to reach the exam center and factor in some extra time in case of any unexpected delays. Also, plan your meals and breaks in between the exam sections to keep your energy levels up.

Strategies for Answering Questions

The CIA exam is designed to test your knowledge, critical thinking, and decision-making skills. Here are some strategies to help you answer the questions effectively:

1. Read the Instructions Carefully

Before you start answering a question, make sure you read and understand the instructions carefully. Some questions may require you to choose the best answer, while others may ask you to eliminate incorrect options or provide a detailed explanation.

2. Manage Your Time Wisely

Time management is crucial on the exam day. You do not want to spend too much time on one question and then run out of time for other questions. It is recommended to spend an average of 1.2 minutes per multiple-choice question and 15-20 minutes for each essay question.

3. Practice Elimination Technique

If you are struggling with a multiple-choice question, you can use the elimination technique. Start by eliminating the obviously wrong answers, which will increase your chances of choosing the correct answer. This is an effective strategy, especially when you are unsure about the correct answer.

Managing Test Anxiety

It is normal to feel anxious before and during the exam. However, if the anxiety becomes overwhelming, it can affect your performance. Here are some tips to help you manage test anxiety:

1. Breathe and Stay Calm

Deep breathing exercises can help relax your mind and body. Take a few deep breaths before starting the exam and during breaks to stay calm and focused.

2. Avoid Cramming

Studying at the last minute can increase anxiety and make it difficult for you to retain information. Avoid cramming and focus on your study plan to feel confident and prepared on the exam day.

3. Stay Positive

Positive self-talk can go a long way in managing anxiety. Instead of being self-critical, tell yourself that you have prepared well and are capable of passing the exam. This will help boost your confidence and reduce anxiety.

4. Take Breaks

It is important to take breaks during the exam to give your mind and body a chance to relax and recharge. Use these breaks to stretch, take a quick walk, or have a light snack to refresh yourself.

5. Visualize Success

Visualization is a powerful tool for overcoming anxiety. Before the exam, take a few moments to visualize yourself successfully completing the exam. This will help boost your confidence and reduce anxiety.

In conclusion, proper preparation, effective strategies, and managing test anxiety can greatly improve your chances of success on the CIA exam. Keep a positive attitude, stay focused, and trust in your abilities. Good luck on your exam day!

Chapter 18: Continuing Education for Certified Internal Auditors

In order to maintain their certification and stay up-to-date on industry standards and best practices, Certified Internal Auditors (CIAs) are required to participate in continuing professional education (CPE). This chapter will explore the importance of CPE for CIAs and provide insights into the requirements, ethics, and reporting of CPE credits.

Continuing Professional Education Requirements

The Institute of Internal Auditors (IIA) sets the requirements for CPE for CIAs. As stated in the CIA Handbook, CIAs are required to complete a minimum of 40 hours of CPE every year, with at least 20 hours being related to internal audit. The remaining 20 hours can be in any relevant field such as accounting, finance, or business. CIAs must also ensure that their CPE activities are relevant to their current job responsibilities and contribute to their professional development.

Ethics and Professional Development

The IIA's Code of Ethics serves as a guide for CIAs in performing their duties ethically and with integrity. Part of these ethics includes the responsibility to stay up-to-date on the latest industry requirements and practices. Engaging in regular CPE activities not only fulfills this ethical obligation, but also allows CIAs to continuously develop their skills, knowledge, and competencies.

CPE also plays an important role in career development for CIAs. It allows them to stay current with changes in the industry and demonstrate their commitment to professional development to employers and clients. By completing relevant and high-quality CPE, CIAs can not only enhance their job performance, but also increase their marketability for future opportunities.

Reporting CPE Credits

As part of maintaining their certification, CIAs are required to report their CPE credits to the IIA on an annual basis. This is done through the IIA's Certification Management System, where CIAs can input their completed CPE activities and upload supporting documentation. The IIA conducts random audits to ensure that CIAs are accurately reporting their CPE credits.

It is important for CIAs to keep thorough records of their CPE activities, including certificates of completion or other proof of attendance, to ensure a smooth reporting process. The IIA also offers resources for CIAs to track their CPE credits, such as the CPE Tracker Tool available on its website.

The Importance of Quality CPE Activities

Not all CPE activities are created equal. It is important for CIAs to carefully evaluate the quality of their CPE activities to ensure that they are relevant, current, and meet the requirements set by the IIA. Some activities may offer CPE credit, but may not be directly related to internal audit or may not effectively contribute to the CIA's professional development. CIAs should also be cautious of activities that are solely marketing or sales pitches, rather than educational opportunities.

One way to ensure quality in CPE activities is to seek out those offered or recognized by the IIA or other reputable organizations. These activities often have a thorough review process to ensure their relevancy and value to CIAs. Additionally, CIAs can look for activities that offer practical application and opportunities for networking and sharing best practices with other internal auditors.

Innovative CPE Options

In today's fast-paced world, where professionals are often busy with work and personal commitments, it can be challenging to find time for traditional CPE activities. However, there are many innovative options available for CIAs to fulfill their CPE requirements, such as online courses, webinars, and podcasts. These can offer flexibility and convenience, while still providing valuable learning opportunities. Another emerging trend in CPE is gamification, or the use of gaming elements in learning. This approach can make the learning experience more engaging and interactive, while still providing valuable knowledge and skills. CIAs should consider incorporating these innovative options into their CPE plans to keep their learning experience fresh and engaging.

In conclusion, continuing education is an essential part of being a Certified Internal Auditor. It not only fulfills ethical and professional obligations, but also allows CIAs to continuously develop their skills and stay up-to-date on industry standards and best practices. By carefully selecting high-quality and innovative CPE activities, CIAs can ensure that they are meeting their requirements and furthering their professional development.

Chapter 19: Dealing with Challenges and Changes in Internal Audit

Internal auditors are faced with various challenges and changes in their role to ensure the organization's success. They are not only responsible for evaluating and improving the organization's internal controls, processes, and procedures, but they also have to adapt to changes within the organization and deal with resistance from management. In this chapter, we will discuss some insights and strategies for dealing with management resistance, managing workload and deadlines, and adapting to organizational changes.

Dealing with Management Resistance

As a CIA, you may encounter resistance from management when performing your audits. This can be due to various reasons such as fear of being exposed, lack of understanding about the role of internal audit, or disagreements about the findings of the audit. It requires a delicate approach to manage this resistance and ensure a productive audit. One way to deal with management resistance is to establish a good working relationship with them. This includes communication and transparency in the audit process. It is crucial to involve management in the audit planning and keep them informed about the audit progress. By involving them, they are more likely to understand the purpose and importance of your work.

Another strategy is to emphasize the benefits of internal audit to management. This includes identifying areas for improvement, reducing risks, and promoting transparency and accountability within the organization. By highlighting these benefits, management may be more open to working with internal audit and addressing any resistance.

Managing Workload and Deadlines

Internal auditors often face heavy workloads and tight deadlines. They are constantly under pressure to complete their audits while ensuring accuracy and quality. To effectively manage workload and deadlines, it is essential to prioritize tasks and set realistic timelines. One way to prioritize tasks is to use the risk-based approach in internal auditing. This means focusing on areas with high risks instead of performing audits on all areas. This approach not only helps in managing the workload but also provides valuable insights for the organization to mitigate risks.

It is also crucial to communicate effectively with the audit team and stakeholders to set realistic deadlines. This includes discussing timelines and potential challenges that may arise during the audit process. It is better to have a longer and achievable deadline than setting an unrealistic one and rushing through the audit, compromising its quality.

Adapting to Organizational Changes

Organizations are constantly evolving, and internal auditors need to be able to adapt to these changes. This may include changes in the organization's structure, processes, or policies. It requires a flexible and forward-thinking approach from CIAs to effectively adapt to these changes. One way to adapt is to continuously update your knowledge and skills. This includes staying updated with the latest internal audit practices, changes in regulations, and emerging technologies. Constant learning and development allow CIA to be prepared for any changes within the organization.

Communication is also key in adapting to organizational changes. It is important to stay in touch with different departments and stakeholders to understand their roles, processes, and concerns. This allows CIAs to have a holistic view of the organization and adapt their audit approach accordingly.

In conclusion, as a CIA, you may face challenges and changes in your role, but it is essential to embrace these challenges and utilize them to improve the organization's internal controls and processes. By establishing a good relationship with management, effectively managing workload and deadlines, and adapting to organizational changes, CIAs can contribute to the organization's success and ensure a productive audit. Continuous learning and development, effective communication, and a flexible approach are key in dealing with these challenges and changes in

internal audit.

Chapter 20: Audit Risk Management

Audit risk is an inherent part of the internal auditing process, as it involves identifying potential risks and evaluating their potential impact on an organization. As a certified internal auditor (CIA), it is crucial to understand the various types of audit risk and how to effectively manage and mitigate them. In this chapter, we will delve into the concept of audit risk management and explore different ways to assess and manage audit risk.

Types of Audit Risk

Audit risk can be categorized into three major types: inherent, control, and detection risk. Each of these risks represents a potential failure to achieve the objectives of an audit. Inherent risk refers to the susceptibility of an organization to material misstatements, whether due to error or fraud. This risk is influenced by factors such as the complexity of the business, the nature of transactions, and the competence of management.

Control risk, on the other hand, is the risk that the internal controls in place are inadequate to prevent or detect material misstatements. This type of risk is dependent on the effectiveness of an organization's internal control structure and can be influenced by factors such as management's integrity and the competence of internal control personnel. Detection risk is the risk that an auditor fails to detect a material misstatement in the financial statements. This type of risk can occur due to factors such as inadequate audit procedures, sampling error, or the failure to properly interpret audit evidence.

Understanding the different types of audit risk is crucial for a CIA in order to effectively plan and execute an audit, as each type of risk requires a different approach in the audit process.

Assessing and Managing Audit Risk

Assessing and managing audit risk is a continuous process that should be integrated into every stage of the audit. As a CIA, it is imperative to have a comprehensive understanding of the organization's internal controls, processes, and risk management strategies in order to effectively assess and manage audit risk. The first step in assessing audit risk is to identify potential risks by conducting a thorough risk assessment. This includes understanding the organization's business objectives, mapping out key processes and transactions, and identifying areas that are most susceptible to material misstatements. A risk assessment matrix can be used to prioritize and rank risks based on their likelihood and impact.

Once risks have been identified, the next step is to plan the audit accordingly. This includes developing an audit strategy and determining the level of assurance required for each area based on the assessed risks. It is important to note that the level of assurance required may vary for different types of audit risk.

To effectively manage audit risk, an auditor must have a deep understanding of the organization's internal control structure and assess its effectiveness. A thorough evaluation of internal controls can help identify potential weaknesses and areas for improvement, which can then be addressed to reduce the overall audit risk.

Audit Risk Model

The audit risk model is a tool used by auditors to guide the audit process and determine the appropriate level of assurance required for different types of audit risk. The model is based on the formula: $AR = IR \times CR \times DR$, where AR is audit risk, IR is inherent risk, CR is control risk, and DR is detection risk. By understanding and considering the different components of the audit risk model, a CIA can effectively plan and execute an audit that provides the desired level of assurance while minimizing the overall audit risk.

Some key factors that can affect each component of the audit risk model include the organization's size and complexity, the industry it operates in, and the reliability of the financial information being audited. By fully considering these factors, a CIA can ensure that the audit is tailored to the specific risks and needs of the organization.

In conclusion, audit risk is an integral part of the internal audit process and it is essential for a CIA to possess a strong understanding of the various types of audit risk and how to effectively assess and manage them. By conducting a thorough risk assessment, planning the audit accordingly, and utilizing the audit risk model, a CIA can provide valuable insights and assurance to an

organization's stakeholders.

Chapter 21: Understanding International Auditing Standards

Understanding the Basics of International Auditing Standards

When it comes to conducting global audits, one must have a good understanding of international auditing standards. These standards are a set of guidelines and principles that govern the practice of auditing around the world. They ensure consistency and quality in the audit process and help auditors maintain objectivity and integrity in their work. The standards are developed and maintained by various organizations such as the International Auditing and Assurance Standards Board (IAASB) and the International Federation of Accountants (IFAC).

Cultural Differences in Audit Practices

One of the biggest challenges in conducting global audits is dealing with cultural differences. Every country and region has its own unique culture, customs, and practices. These can greatly influence the way audits are conducted. For example, in some cultures, direct communication and confrontation are seen as offensive, while in others, it is seen as a sign of respect. This can have a significant impact on how auditors gather information and communicate findings.

Cultural differences can also affect the understanding and application of auditing standards. For instance, in some cultures, there is a strong emphasis on hierarchy and authority, which can lead to auditors being more deferential and less assertive in their interactions with management. In contrast, in other cultures, there may be a more egalitarian approach, where auditors are expected to be more direct and challenging in their communication.

Conducting Global Audits

When conducting global audits, it is important for auditors to be aware of and sensitive to cultural differences. This begins with understanding the cultural context of the country or region they are working in. This includes being familiar with the local language, customs, and business practices. It also involves being aware of any political or social factors that may impact the audit process. Additionally, auditors must tailor their approach to fit the cultural context. This means adapting their communication style, questioning techniques, and even their audit procedures to fit the cultural norms of the country. For example, in some cultures, written documentation is given more weight, while in others, verbal agreements hold more importance. Auditors must be able to adjust their methods to accommodate these variations.

Another aspect of conducting global audits is being mindful of potential language barriers. This is especially important when working with translators or interpreters. Miscommunication can easily occur if the translator is not familiar with the technical terms used in auditing. Auditors must ensure that they communicate clearly and effectively to avoid misunderstandings.

Finally, it is crucial for auditors to maintain objectivity and professionalism in the face of cultural differences. This means not letting personal biases or cultural stereotypes influence the audit process or conclusions. Auditors must strive to uphold ethical principles and maintain their independence, regardless of cultural pressures.

In conclusion, understanding international auditing standards and being aware of cultural differences is essential for conducting global audits. With the increasing globalization of businesses, auditors must be prepared to work in diverse cultural environments and be able to adapt their practices accordingly.

Chapter 22: External Auditors and Internal Auditors

External and internal auditors play crucial roles in ensuring the accuracy and integrity of a company's financial reporting and overall operations. While they both have similar aims, there are distinct differences between the two types of auditors. In this chapter, we will explore these differences and how collaboration between external and internal auditors can be beneficial for organizations.

Differences Between External and Internal Auditors

External auditors are typically independent professionals hired by a company to review their financial statements, internal controls, and other financial reporting processes. They are often certified public accountants (CPAs) and are responsible for ensuring that a company's financial statements are accurate and in compliance with accounting standards and regulations. On the other hand, internal auditors are employees of the organization and are responsible for evaluating the effectiveness of internal controls and processes, identifying potential risks, and providing recommendations for improvement. One of the main differences between external and internal auditors lies in their objectives. External auditors focus on providing assurance to shareholders and other external stakeholders by giving an independent opinion on the accuracy of a company's financial statements. On the other hand, internal auditors have a broader focus and provide assurance to management and the board of directors on the overall internal control environment and risk management practices of the organization.

Another significant difference is the scope of their work. External auditors are usually hired to perform annual audits of the company's financial statements, while internal auditors have a broader scope and can conduct audits on various aspects of the organization's operations, including financial, operational, and compliance areas. Additionally, external auditors are required to strictly adhere to auditing standards and regulations, while internal auditors have more flexibility in their approach and can tailor their audit procedures based on the organization's specific needs.

Collaboration between External and Internal Audit

While external and internal auditors have different roles and responsibilities, collaboration between the two can be highly beneficial for organizations. External auditors can gain valuable insights from internal auditors' work, which can help them better understand the organization's business processes and risks. On the other hand, internal auditors can benefit from external auditors' knowledge and experience in applying auditing standards and regulations. Collaboration between external and internal audit can also result in cost savings for organizations. By working together, they can avoid duplication of efforts and streamline audit procedures, leading to more efficient and effective audits. Furthermore, external auditors can rely on the work performed by internal auditors and reduce their testing procedures, which can save time and costs for organizations.

One area where collaboration between external and internal auditors is essential is in the evaluation of internal controls. External auditors are required to assess the design and effectiveness of internal controls, while internal auditors are responsible for ongoing monitoring and testing of controls. By sharing their findings and working together, both auditors can get a more comprehensive view of the organization's internal control environment, leading to more accurate and reliable assessments. Moreover, collaboration between external and internal auditors can result in a more robust risk management process. Internal auditors, who regularly assess risks across various areas of the organization, can provide valuable insights to external auditors in identifying potential areas of concern. This collaboration can ensure that all significant risks are adequately addressed, and the organization has a robust risk management framework in place.

In conclusion, while external and internal auditors have distinct roles and responsibilities, their collaboration can result in numerous benefits for organizations. Through effective and efficient collaboration, both auditors can gain a better understanding of the organization's operations and risks, leading to more reliable and accurate audit findings. By working together, these auditors can contribute to the overall effectiveness and efficiency of the organization's internal control and risk management processes.

Chapter 23: Compliance and Internal Audit: Navigating the Complex Landscape

As internal auditors, our primary responsibility is to ensure that our organizations are in compliance with all relevant laws, regulations, and internal policies. This is no easy task, as the compliance landscape is constantly evolving and becoming increasingly complex. In this chapter, we will explore the importance of compliance, the process of compliance risk assessment, and the methods for evaluating and reporting on compliance.

Importance of Compliance

Compliance is crucial for any organization, regardless of its size or industry. Not only does it ensure that the company is operating ethically and within the boundaries of the law, but it also helps to build a reputation of trust and integrity with stakeholders. In today's globalized business world, where companies operate in multiple jurisdictions with different regulations, compliance has become even more critical. In addition to maintaining a positive image, compliance also protects the organization from potential legal and financial risks. Failure to comply with regulations can result in penalties, fines, and even criminal charges, which can have severe consequences for the company's financial stability and reputation.

As internal auditors, it is our responsibility to assist management in identifying and assessing potential compliance risks and proposing effective controls to mitigate them. By doing so, we help the organization stay on the right side of the law and avoid costly consequences.

Compliance Risk Assessment

One of the first steps in achieving compliance is conducting a thorough risk assessment. This involves identifying all relevant laws, regulations, and internal policies that the organization must comply with. It also involves understanding the potential risks associated with non-compliance and assessing the likelihood and impact of these risks. To conduct a comprehensive compliance risk assessment, internal auditors must have a deep understanding of the organization's operations, systems, and processes. This includes identifying any potential gaps in compliance due to inadequate policies or processes.

It is also essential to involve key stakeholders, such as legal, risk management, and compliance personnel, in the risk assessment process. This will ensure that all relevant perspectives are considered and that the organization has a more holistic view of its compliance risks.

Evaluating and Reporting on Compliance

Once the compliance risk assessment is complete, internal auditors must evaluate the effectiveness of the organization's compliance controls. This involves testing the controls and identifying any weaknesses or deficiencies that may exist. The results of these tests should be reported to management, along with recommendations for improvement. When reporting on compliance, it is crucial to use a risk-based approach. This means focusing on the most significant risks and ensuring that the organization's controls adequately address them. It is also important to provide clear and concise recommendations that management can understand and implement effectively.

In addition to evaluating and reporting on compliance internally, auditors may also be asked to provide assurance to external stakeholders, such as regulators or investors. In such cases, it is essential to maintain independence and objectivity and provide reliable and accurate information.

In Conclusion

Compliance is an ever-evolving and complex landscape that requires continuous attention and monitoring. As internal auditors, it is our duty to help organizations navigate this landscape and ensure their operations are in line with relevant laws, regulations, and internal policies. By conducting comprehensive risk assessments, evaluating and reporting on compliance, and providing effective recommendations, we play a crucial role in helping organizations maintain their integrity and avoid legal and financial risks.

Chapter 24: Fraud Risk Management

Characteristics of Fraud Risk

Fraud is a pervasive issue in today's corporate world, affecting businesses of all sizes and industries. It is a complex and constantly evolving problem that can have significant financial and reputational consequences. In order to effectively manage fraud risks, it is important to understand the characteristics of fraud and the ways in which it can manifest itself. Here are some key characteristics of fraud risk to keep in mind: - Fraud is intentional and deceptive. This may seem obvious, but it is important to recognize that fraud is not a mistake or an unintentional error. It is an intentional act of deception carried out with the aim of obtaining personal gain.

- Fraud can take many forms. While most people associate fraud with financial theft, it can also include acts such as corrupt practices, bribery, and misuse of assets or resources. It is important for businesses to be aware of the various forms that fraud can take and to implement measures to prevent and detect them.

- Fraud can be committed by anyone. Often, people assume that fraud is only carried out by external parties or lower level employees. However, fraud can be committed by anyone within an organization, including senior management. This is why it is crucial to have strong internal controls and oversight in place.

- Fraud can occur at any time. Fraud can be committed at any stage in an organization's operations, from the initial planning to the execution and cover-up. It is important to have measures in place to prevent and detect fraud at each stage.

Assessing Fraud Risk

In order to effectively manage fraud risks, it is necessary to first assess and understand the specific risks that are present in an organization. This can be done through a thorough fraud risk assessment, which involves identifying potential areas of vulnerability and evaluating the likelihood and impact of potential fraud scenarios. Here are some key steps to consider when conducting a fraud risk assessment: - Identify key fraud risks. The first step in assessing fraud risk is to identify the areas of the organization that are most susceptible to fraud. This may include processes such as procurement, cash handling, and financial reporting, as well as high-risk departments or functions.

- Assess the likelihood of fraud. Once key fraud risks have been identified, the next step is to evaluate the likelihood of these risks materializing. This can be done by considering the controls that are currently in place and their effectiveness in preventing and detecting fraud.

- Evaluate the impact of potential fraud. In addition to assessing the likelihood of fraud, it is important to consider the potential impact on the organization if fraud does occur. This can include financial losses, damage to reputation, and legal consequences.

- Consider external factors. When assessing fraud risk, it is important to also consider external factors such as the overall regulatory and economic environment, as well as any specific risks associated with the industry or region in which the organization operates.

Implementing Fraud Prevention and Detection Measures

Once fraud risks have been identified and assessed, the next step is to implement measures to prevent and detect fraud. Here are some key considerations when developing fraud prevention and detection strategies: - Establish a code of ethics and conduct. A clear and comprehensive code of ethics and conduct can help set the tone for the organization and promote a culture of honesty and integrity. It should outline expected behaviors and consequences for non-compliance.

- Develop and implement internal controls. Internal controls are policies and procedures designed to protect assets, ensure accurate financial reporting, and prevent and detect fraud. These controls should be tailored to the specific risks identified in the fraud risk assessment.

- Conduct background checks. Before hiring new employees, it is important to conduct thorough background checks, especially for positions that involve handling sensitive information or assets. This can help identify any red flags or past incidents of fraud.

- Encourage reporting of suspicious activity. Employees should be encouraged to report any suspicious or unethical behavior, with clear avenues for reporting and protection for whistleblowers. This can help the organization detect fraud at an early stage.

- Utilize data analytics and technology. Data analytics tools can help identify patterns and anomalies in data that may indicate fraudulent activity. Technology can also be used to automate and enhance internal controls, reducing the potential for human error or manipulation.

- Conduct regular fraud risk assessments. Fraud risk is not a one-time consideration. It is important to conduct regular reviews and assessments to ensure that risks are continually identified, evaluated, and managed.

In conclusion, effective fraud risk management requires an understanding of fraud characteristics, thorough risk assessment, and the implementation of appropriate prevention and detection measures. By taking a proactive and comprehensive approach to fraud risk, organizations can protect themselves from financial losses, reputational damage, and legal consequences.

Chapter 25: Internal Audit and IT Governance

In today's digital world, the role of internal audit in IT governance is increasingly important. With the rise of technology, organizations must have effective IT governance frameworks in place to ensure the proper management and use of their information systems. As internal auditors, it is crucial to understand the role and impact of IT governance on an organization's overall performance. This chapter will delve into the relationship between internal audit and IT governance, including how to evaluate IT governance frameworks and best practices for effective IT governance.

Role of Internal Audit in IT Governance

As the guardians of an organization's operations, internal auditors play a critical role in ensuring the effectiveness of IT governance. They act as an independent third-party, providing an unbiased assessment of the organization's IT governance practices. Internal auditors work closely with IT governance professionals to identify potential risks and gaps in the governance framework. They also provide recommendations for improvements and help management in implementing necessary changes.

One of the primary responsibilities of internal audit in IT governance is to assess the design and implementation of controls within IT systems. This involves reviewing the policies, processes, and procedures related to IT governance and identifying any weaknesses that may exist. By conducting thorough audits, internal auditors can help mitigate risks and protect the organization's IT assets.

Evaluating IT Governance Frameworks

IT governance frameworks are essential tools for managing and directing an organization's IT activities. They provide a structured approach to aligning IT strategy with business objectives, managing risk, and maintaining compliance. As internal auditors, it is essential to understand the various IT governance frameworks and how they impact an organization. One of the most well-known and widely used IT governance frameworks is COBIT (Control Objectives for Information and Related Technology). COBIT provides a comprehensive framework for managing and governing IT systems, covering areas such as strategy, risk management, and performance measurement. As internal auditors, it is essential to familiarize ourselves with COBIT and assess its effectiveness in the organization we are auditing.

Another popular IT governance framework is ITIL (Information Technology Infrastructure Library), which focuses on service management and delivery. ITIL provides a set of best practices for IT service delivery, including processes for incident management, problem management, and service level management. Internal auditors can evaluate the implementation of ITIL in an organization and identify any areas for improvement.

IT Governance Best Practices

In addition to utilizing established frameworks, there are also several key best practices for effective IT governance. Firstly, it is crucial to have clear and defined roles and responsibilities for IT governance. Without proper alignment and understanding of roles and responsibilities, there can be confusion and gaps in decision-making. Internal auditors can review the organization's governance structure and ensure that roles and responsibilities are clearly defined and allocated.

Secondly, communication and collaboration are essential for effective IT governance. This includes communication between IT and business departments and between different levels of management. Internal auditors can assess the communication channels within the organization and identify any areas for improvement. Furthermore, regular monitoring and reporting are crucial for maintaining effective IT governance. Internal auditors can review the organization's monitoring and reporting processes to ensure that they are providing accurate and timely information to support decision-making. It is also essential to have a continuous improvement mindset when it comes to IT governance. Internal auditors can help identify areas for improvement and provide recommendations for changes to enhance the effectiveness of the governance framework.

Lastly, it is crucial to consider the ever-changing technology landscape and adapt IT governance practices accordingly. With new risks and opportunities emerging constantly, internal auditors must stay abreast of technological advancements and their impact on the organization's IT governance.

In conclusion, the relationship between internal audit and IT governance is a crucial one. As organizations continue to rely on technology for their operations, it is essential to have robust and effective IT governance practices in place. Internal auditors are well-positioned to play a significant role in evaluating and enhancing IT governance, thereby contributing to the overall success and performance of the organization. By understanding the role of internal audit in IT governance, evaluating IT governance frameworks, and promoting IT governance best practices, we can ensure that our organizations are well-equipped for the ever-changing digital landscape.

Chapter 26: The Power of Data Analytics in Internal Audit

In today's fast-paced business world, data is king. Every company and organization relies on data to make informed decisions and drive growth. This same concept applies to internal audit, where the use of data analytics has become increasingly important in enhancing the effectiveness and efficiency of audit processes.

Benefits of Data Analytics in Internal Audit

The benefits of incorporating data analytics in internal audit practices are numerous and far-reaching. By leveraging data and technology, auditors can gain valuable insights and identify potential risks and weaknesses in a company's operations. This allows for a more proactive and thorough approach to audits, providing stakeholders with a better understanding of the organization's performance and mitigating potential risks. But beyond just identifying risks, data analytics in internal audit can also improve the overall efficiency of the audit process. By automating tasks such as data collection and analysis, auditors can save time and resources, allowing them to focus on more critical areas of the audit. This can also lead to a more streamlined and standardized approach to auditing, eliminating human bias and increasing accuracy. The use of data analytics in internal audit can also provide a competitive advantage for the organization by revealing insights and trends that may have otherwise gone undetected. This can lead to innovative solutions and strategies that drive business growth and success.

Implementing Data Analytics in Audit Processes

Incorporating data analytics into internal audit processes may seem like a daunting task, but with careful planning and implementation, it can be a seamless and beneficial addition. The key to success lies in understanding the organization's data and having a solid strategy in place. The first step is to identify the data sources that will be used in the audit. This can include financial data, operational data, and other key performance indicators. It is essential to work closely with the organization's IT department to ensure access to data and to establish protocols for data security and privacy. Next, auditors must determine the appropriate data analytics tools and techniques to be used. These can range from basic spreadsheet software to more advanced data visualization and predictive analytics tools. It is crucial to choose tools that are user-friendly and align with the organization's needs and capabilities.

Once the tools are in place, it is essential to train auditors on how to effectively use them and integrate them into the audit process. This may require additional training or hiring external experts to assist in the implementation and execution of data analytics techniques.

Finally, it is crucial to continuously assess and improve the organization's data analytics capabilities. This can involve refining processes, investing in new technologies, and staying up-to-date with emerging trends in data analytics.

Data Analytics Tools and Techniques

There are numerous data analytics tools and techniques that can be used in internal audit, and the key is to find the right combination that fits the organization's needs. Some of the most commonly used tools and techniques include: - Data mining: This involves sifting through large amounts of data to identify patterns, trends, and anomalies that may be indicative of potential risks.

- Statistical analysis: Statistical methods such as regression analysis and correlation can help identify relationships between variables and provide insights into the organization's performance.

- Data visualization: Data visualization tools, such as dashboards and charts, can help auditors present data in a more meaningful and understandable way.

- Text analytics: With the growing amount of unstructured data, such as emails and social media posts, text analytics tools can help auditors identify key themes and sentiment analysis.

- Predictive analytics: By using historical data and algorithms, predictive analytics can help identify potential risks and future trends.

In conclusion, the use of data analytics in internal audit plays a crucial role in today's constantly evolving business environment. It provides auditors with the ability to gain valuable insights, enhance efficiency and effectiveness, and stay ahead of potential risks. By understanding the benefits, implementing the right tools and techniques, and continuously improving, organizations can harness the power of data to drive success and growth.

Chapter 27: Understanding Continuous Auditing and Monitoring

What is Continuous Auditing and Monitoring?

Continuous auditing and monitoring (CAM) refers to the use of technology and data analytics to continuously and automatically assess an organization's financial and operational performance. It goes beyond traditional internal audit methods, which are usually performed at specific intervals, to provide ongoing and real-time insights into an organization's internal controls, processes, and risks. CAM allows organizations to stay ahead of potential issues and identify areas for improvement, resulting in a more efficient and effective audit process.

The Evolution of Continuous Auditing and Monitoring

Continuous auditing and monitoring is not a new concept. It has been around for over three decades, starting in the 1980s when technology was first used to automate audit activities. Over the years, advancements in technology and the availability of vast amounts of data have further improved the capabilities and adoption of continuous auditing and monitoring.

Initially, CAM was mostly used in large organizations with complex systems and processes. As technology became more accessible and affordable, it has been increasingly adopted by smaller organizations as well. Today, CAM is considered a best practice in internal audit and is recommended by professional organizations such as the Institute of Internal Auditors (IIA).

Implementing Continuous Auditing and Monitoring Programs

The implementation of a continuous auditing and monitoring program requires careful planning and consideration of various factors. Some of the key steps involved in implementing CAM include:

- Assessing the organization's current internal audit processes and identifying areas that can benefit from continuous auditing and monitoring.
- Understanding the organization's data sources and availability of data for CAM activities.
- Identifying and evaluating suitable technology and data analytics tools that can support CAM activities.
- Developing a CAM framework that outlines the scope, objectives, and processes involved in the program.
- Training internal auditors and other relevant stakeholders on the use of technology and

data analytics in CAM.
- Establishing protocols for data collection, storage, and security to ensure the reliability and integrity of CAM activities.
- Conducting regular assessments and updates to ensure the effectiveness and efficiency of the CAM program.

Benefits of Continuous Auditing and Monitoring

The adoption of continuous auditing and monitoring programs brings numerous benefits to organizations, including: CAM provides real-time insights into an organization's internal controls, processes, and risks, allowing for prompt identification and mitigation of potential issues.

Real-time insights:Improved efficiency and effectiveness:
By automating audit processes and utilizing data analytics, CAM allows for a more efficient and effective audit process, reducing the time and resources needed for traditional audits.

Increased coverage:
With CAM, auditors can cover a larger amount of data and transactions, providing a more comprehensive understanding of an organization's operations.

Better risk management:
Continuous monitoring of data and processes enables organizations to identify and address potential risks in a timely manner, reducing the likelihood of fraud and errors.

Enhanced compliance:
CAM can assist organizations in maintaining compliance with regulatory requirements and internal policies by identifying and addressing potential issues quickly.

Challenges of Continuous Auditing and Monitoring

Despite the numerous benefits, there are some challenges associated with the adoption of continuous auditing and monitoring programs, including: Organizations that lack the necessary technology infrastructure and resources may struggle to implement CAM effectively.

Technology limitations:Data quality and accessibility:
The success of CAM relies heavily on the availability and quality of an organization's data. If data is not readily accessible or of poor quality, it can affect the reliability and effectiveness of CAM activities.

Costs:
Implementing a continuous auditing and monitoring program can involve significant upfront costs, including investments in technology and training.

Resistance to change:
Introducing CAM requires a cultural shift within an organization, and some employees may be resistant to the idea of relying on technology and data analytics for auditing processes.

Continuous auditing and monitoring is a rapidly developing field that offers many benefits to organizations, including real-time insights, improved efficiency and effectiveness, and better risk management. However, its successful implementation requires careful planning, consideration of challenges, and a willingness to embrace technological advancements in internal auditing. Companies that embrace CAM can improve their overall performance and mitigate potential risks, making it a valuable tool for any organization's internal audit practices.

Chapter 28: Auditing in Crisis and Emergency Situations

Auditing during a Crisis

Auditing is an essential process for organizations to ensure proper checks and balances are in place and goals are met. However, when a crisis or emergency situation arises, the auditing process can become more challenging. Whether it's a natural disaster, a cyberattack, or a financial crisis, organizations must be prepared to handle the situation while still maintaining efficiency and compliance.

During a crisis, auditors must adapt quickly to the changing environment and prioritize their tasks accordingly. This may mean shifting their focus from routine audits to critical areas that are affected by the crisis. They must also be able to work effectively with other departments, such as risk management and crisis management, to gather necessary information and assess the impact on the organization.

Emergency Preparedness

One of the most critical aspects of auditing during a crisis is the organization's emergency preparedness. A well-prepared organization will have developed a crisis management plan that outlines the steps to be taken in various emergency scenarios. Auditors must ensure that these plans are not only in place but also regularly reviewed and updated.

Along with the crisis management plan, a critical component of emergency preparedness is assessing risk and implementing risk mitigation strategies. Auditors must review the organization's risk management procedures and determine if they are effective in preparing for potential crises. In addition, they should also assess the financial impact of a crisis on the organization and whether proper financial controls are in place to mitigate these risks.

Assessing the Effectiveness of Crisis Management Plans

During a crisis, it's crucial for organizations to have a well-developed and regularly practiced crisis management plan. However, simply having a plan in place does not guarantee its effectiveness. Auditors must thoroughly assess the crisis management plan to determine if it is comprehensive, up-to-date, and tailored to the organization's specific needs. They must also evaluate whether the crisis management plan is communicated effectively to all stakeholders, as well as the level of awareness and understanding among employees. This includes testing the plan through simulations and drills to identify any weaknesses and make necessary improvements.

Moreover, auditors should review the organization's response to previous crisis situations and identify areas for improvement. This could include examining the effectiveness of communication channels, decision-making processes, and resource allocation.

Unforeseen Challenges in Auditing during a Crisis

While organizations may have a well-developed crisis management plan in place, there may still be unforeseen challenges during a crisis that can impact the auditing process. These could include a shortage of resources, changes in laws or regulations, or disruptions in the organization's operations.

Auditors must be agile and adaptive in dealing with these challenges and adjust their strategies accordingly. They should also keep stakeholders informed of any changes or difficulties that may arise during the auditing process.

Utilizing Technology in Auditing during a Crisis

Technology plays a vital role in auditing, and this is especially true during a crisis. With the advancement of data analytics and artificial intelligence, auditors can now gather and analyze vast amounts of data quickly. This can be especially beneficial during a crisis when time is of the essence.

Also, with the rise of remote work, technology allows auditors to conduct audits and communicate with stakeholders without being physically present. This can be incredibly useful during a crisis situation when travel may not be feasible.

Collaboration with Other Departments

During a crisis, it is essential for all departments to work together to coordinate efforts and mitigate risks. Auditors must play a crucial role in this collaboration, working closely with departments such as risk management, crisis management, and IT to gather necessary information and provide insights on the effectiveness of crisis management strategies.

By collaborating with other departments, auditors can gain a deeper understanding of the organization's overall preparedness and response to the crisis. They can also identify any potential gaps or areas for improvement in the crisis management plan.

The Role of Auditors in Building Resilience

Crisis situations are inevitable, and how well an organization can weather these storms depends on its resilience. As such, it is essential for auditors to play a role in building resilience within the organization. This includes regularly reviewing and testing crisis management plans, providing insights for improvements, and emphasizing the importance of risk management in preparing for potential crises.

Moreover, auditors should also evaluate the organization's response to a crisis and identify areas for improvement. This can include lessons learned from the crisis that can be incorporated into future crisis management plans.

Conclusion

Auditing during a crisis or emergency situation is crucial for organizations to assess their preparedness and response to potential risks. Auditors must be adaptable, collaborative, and utilize technology to effectively navigate the auditing process during a crisis. By working closely with other departments and prioritizing emergency preparedness, auditors can help build resilience within the organization and ensure it is better equipped to handle future crises.

Chapter 29: The Future of Internal Audit

With the rapid changes in technology, globalization, and business practices, the role of internal audit is constantly evolving. As organizations strive to remain competitive and adapt to ever-changing market conditions, internal audit is becoming an essential function in ensuring the effectiveness of risk management, control, and governance processes.

Benefits and Risks of Outsourcing Internal Audit

Outsourcing internal audit functions has become a popular solution for organizations looking to enhance their internal audit capabilities. By outsourcing, organizations can access specialized expertise, increase efficiency, and reduce costs. However, as with any business decision, there are also risks that must be carefully considered. One of the most significant benefits of outsourcing internal audit is the access to specialized expertise. External audit firms often have a deep pool of experienced professionals with specialized skills and knowledge. This can be particularly valuable for small to medium-sized organizations that may not have the resources to hire and retain such talent in-house.

Outsourcing also allows organizations to focus on their core competencies while leaving the internal audit function to experts. This can lead to increased efficiency and cost savings, as the organization does not have to invest in building and maintaining an internal audit team. However, outsourcing does come with its own set of risks. The most significant risk is the potential loss of control and objectivity. When outsourcing internal audit, organizations must ensure that the external auditors remain independent and objective in their assessments. It is essential to establish clear expectations and maintain open communication to mitigate this risk.

Another potential risk is the risk of leakage of confidential information. Organizations must carefully select a reputable and trustworthy external auditor to ensure the protection of sensitive information.

Best Practices for External/Internal Audit Relationship

For a successful outsourcing arrangement, strong collaboration and partnership between the external and internal auditors are essential. Here are some best practices to foster a positive working relationship:

1. Establish Clear Objectives and Expectations

It is crucial to have a clear understanding of the scope and objectives of the external audit engagement. Both parties must agree on the expectations and deliverables to avoid misunderstandings and conflicts down the line.

2. Establish and Maintain Open Communication

Effective communication is key to a successful collaborative relationship between external and internal auditors. Regular communication and timely reporting of audit findings and recommendations can help ensure that corrective action is taken promptly.

3. Coordinate Audit Plans

To avoid duplication of efforts and confusion, both internal and external auditors should collaborate in developing audit plans. This will also help ensure that all key areas are covered and no significant risks are overlooked.

4. Respect Roles and Boundaries

It is essential for both internal and external auditors to understand their respective roles and boundaries. External auditors should respect the internal audit function and not try to replace it. On the other hand, internal auditors should not see external auditors as a threat but rather as a valuable resource.

Maintaining Objectivity in Outsourcing Arrangements

Maintaining objectivity is critical to the integrity and effectiveness of the internal audit function. When outsourcing, organizations must take steps to ensure the independence and objectivity of external auditors.

Here are some best practices to maintain objectivity in outsourcing arrangements:

1. Avoid conflicts of interest

Organizations must carefully select an external auditor that does not have any conflicts of interest that could compromise their objectivity. This includes ensuring that the external auditor is not providing other services to the organization that could create a conflict of interest.

2. Implement Quality Assurance Procedures

Quality assurance procedures, such as independent reviews and monitoring, can help ensure that external auditors maintain objectivity and adhere to professional standards.

3. Clearly Define Reporting Lines

To avoid any influence or pressure from management, external auditors should have a direct reporting line to the Audit Committee or the Board of Directors.

4. Conduct Regular Assessments

Organizations should conduct regular assessments of their outsourcing arrangements to identify any potential threats to objectivity and take corrective action promptly.

In Conclusion

Outsourcing internal audit functions can provide significant benefits to organizations, such as access to specialized expertise and increased efficiency. However, it is crucial to carefully consider the risks and take necessary measures to maintain objectivity and foster a strong working relationship between internal and external auditors. By following best practices and regularly reassessing outsourcing arrangements, organizations can ensure the continued effectiveness and relevance of their internal audit function in the future.

Chapter 30: Corporate Social Responsibility Audits

Corporate social responsibility (CSR) has become an increasingly important aspect of business operations in recent years. Companies are now expected to not only deliver profits, but also to act in a socially responsible manner towards their stakeholders, communities, and the environment. As a result, many companies have implemented CSR policies and practices to demonstrate their commitment to ethical and sustainable business practices.

However, ensuring that these policies and practices are actually being implemented and followed can be a challenging task. This is where the role of internal auditors comes in. As the guardians of good governance, internal auditors are well positioned to conduct CSR audits and provide assurance to stakeholders that the company's CSR efforts are aligned with its values and objectives. In this chapter, we will explore the scope of CSR audits, the evaluation of CSR policies and practices, and reporting on CSR activities.

Scope of Corporate Social Responsibility Audits

When talking about CSR audits, it is important to first define the scope of these audits. Generally, CSR audits cover a wide range of areas including human rights, labor practices, environmental sustainability, business ethics, and community involvement. Auditors need to have a thorough understanding of the company's CSR policies and practices in order to effectively assess their alignment with international standards and industry best practices. One key aspect of CSR audits is ensuring compliance with relevant laws and regulations. Businesses are subject to a variety of laws and regulations related to CSR, including those pertaining to human rights, labor rights, and environmental protection. As such, internal auditors need to have a deep understanding of these laws and regulations and how they may impact the business. This requires keeping up-to-date with any changes and developments in these areas.

Another important aspect of CSR audits is evaluating the effectiveness of the company's CSR program. This involves looking beyond policies and procedures and assessing their actual implementation and impact. Internal auditors may use various tools and techniques such as surveys, interviews, and site visits to gather this information.

Evaluating CSR Policies and Practices

In order to effectively evaluate CSR policies and practices, internal auditors need to have a thorough understanding of the company's culture and values. This includes understanding the company's approach to CSR and the level of support and commitment from top management. Auditors should also assess the level of integration of CSR in the company's operations and decision-making processes. Are CSR considerations being taken into account when developing new products or entering new markets? Are supplier relationships being monitored and managed in line with ethical standards? These are just some examples of questions that auditors may ask when evaluating the integration of CSR in the company's activities.

Furthermore, auditors should also evaluate the effectiveness of communication and reporting mechanisms for the company's CSR efforts. Are stakeholders receiving accurate and timely information about the company's CSR activities? Are there any gaps or discrepancies between what is reported and what is actually being done? These are important considerations in determining the overall effectiveness of the company's CSR program.

Reporting on CSR Activities

Reporting on CSR activities is a crucial aspect of CSR audits. It serves as a means of communicating the company's commitment to responsible and ethical business practices to its stakeholders. In fact, some companies have even started to publish standalone CSR reports to provide a comprehensive overview of their CSR efforts. One key aspect of reporting on CSR activities is transparency. Companies should be transparent about their policies, practices, and performance in the area of CSR. This includes both positive and negative information. Reporting on negative impact and incidents may not be easy, but it is a sign of a company's commitment to responsible and ethical business practices.

In addition, reporting on CSR also involves measuring and tracking performance against established goals and targets. This allows the company to demonstrate progress and improvements in its CSR efforts. It also helps to identify areas for improvement and set new targets for the future.

Internal auditors play a critical role in reviewing and providing assurance on the accuracy and reliability of CSR reporting. Their independent and objective assessment adds credibility to the company's CSR program and enhances stakeholders' trust in the company.

Conclusion

In today's socially conscious world, companies need to not only deliver profits, but also demonstrate their commitment to ethical and sustainable business practices. CSR audits play a crucial role in providing assurance to stakeholders that companies are acting in a socially responsible manner. Internal auditors have a unique position to provide independent and objective assessment of a company's CSR program, and thus, play a critical role in promoting responsible and ethical business practices.

Chapter 31: Sampling and Analytical Techniques in Internal Audit

As an internal auditor, you are responsible for evaluating and testing the organization's internal control procedures and processes. In order to do so, you must have a deep understanding of sampling and analytical techniques. These techniques enable you to gather and analyze data to identify patterns, trends, and anomalies that could indicate potential areas of risk or inefficiency.

Sampling Methods

Sampling refers to the process of selecting a subset of data from a larger population to represent the entire population. This can be a valuable tool for internal auditors when they are conducting testing and analysis. There are several sampling methods that can be used:

1. Random Sampling

Random sampling involves selecting a random sample from the population. This method ensures that each item in the population has an equal chance of being selected. It is useful when the population is large and uniform, and when there is no prior knowledge or bias in the selection process.

2. Stratified Sampling

In stratified sampling, the population is divided into subgroups or strata based on certain characteristics. A sample is then selected from each stratum in proportion to its representation in the population. This method is useful when the population is diverse and you want to ensure that each subgroup is represented in the sample.

3. Systematic Sampling

Systematic sampling involves selecting every "kth" item from the population according to a predefined pattern. For example, you could select every fifth item from a list of employees. This method is useful when you want to include a large number of items in the sample and when the population is organized in a particular order.

Analytical Procedures

Analytical procedures involve the analysis of data and information to identify potential risks and areas of concern. It is a powerful tool for internal auditors as it enables them to detect patterns and trends that could indicate potential fraud or inefficiency. Some common analytical procedures include:

1. Trend Analysis

Trend analysis involves comparing data from multiple periods to identify any significant changes or trends. This can be useful for identifying potential areas of risk or inefficiency over time.

2. Comparative Analysis

Comparative analysis involves comparing data from different departments, locations, or time periods to identify any significant differences or anomalies. This can be useful for identifying potential control weaknesses or inconsistencies within the organization.

3. Ratio Analysis

Ratio analysis involves calculating and comparing ratios from financial data to identify any discrepancies or areas of concern. This can be a powerful tool for detecting potential financial statement fraud.

Interviews and Questionnaires

Interviews and questionnaires are important tools that internal auditors can use to gather information from employees and management. These methods provide an opportunity for internal auditors to gain insight into the operations of the organization and to identify any potential issues or concerns. Some important considerations for conducting interviews and questionnaires include:

1. Objectivity

It is important for internal auditors to maintain objectivity when conducting interviews and creating questionnaires. This means asking unbiased and non-leading questions and avoiding any personal opinions or biases.

2. Confidentiality

Employees should feel comfortable providing honest and accurate information during interviews and questionnaires. It is the responsibility of the internal auditor to maintain confidentiality and ensure that the information gathered is used for audit purposes only.

3. Effectiveness

The quality of information gathered through interviews and questionnaires is dependent on the effectiveness of the process. This includes having well-designed and relevant questions, as well as efficient and organized data collection and analysis.

Observation Techniques

Observation involves watching and recording processes and procedures to gain an understanding of how they are carried out. This can be a valuable tool for internal auditors when conducting process and control evaluations. Some important considerations for observation techniques include:

1. Non-participant vs. Participant Observation

Non-participant observation involves observing processes and procedures without directly participating in them. This can provide an unbiased view of the processes. On the other hand, participant observation involves actively participating in the process being observed. This can provide a more detailed understanding of the process but can also impact objectivity.

2. Simulated vs. Actual Observation

Simulated observation involves creating a hypothetical scenario to observe how a process would be carried out in a specific situation. This can be useful for identifying potential areas of risk or inefficiency. Actual observation involves observing a process in real-time. This can provide a more accurate understanding of how the process is actually carried out.

3. Follow-up Interviews

After conducting observations, it can be useful to follow up with interviews to get a deeper understanding of the processes and procedures observed. This can provide valuable insights and enable auditors to identify potential areas for improvement.

Conclusion

Sampling and analytical techniques are crucial skills for any CIA. These tools and methods enable internal auditors to gather and analyze data efficiently and effectively, leading to valuable insights and the ability to detect potential risks and inefficiencies. By utilizing these techniques, internal auditors can effectively fulfill their role in evaluating and improving the organization's internal control processes and procedures.

Chapter 32: Audit Manual Creation and Maintenance

In the fast-paced world of internal auditing, having an effective and up-to-date audit manual is crucial. An audit manual serves as a guide, providing auditors with the necessary framework to conduct audits in a consistent and efficient manner. It establishes the standards and procedures for the internal audit function and ensures that the audit team is aligned with the goals and objectives of the organization. In this chapter, we will explore the components of an audit manual, how to keep it updated, and best practices for audit manual maintenance.

Components of an Audit Manual

An audit manual typically consists of a set of policies and procedures that govern the internal audit function. These components serve as the building blocks for a successful audit program. Let's take a closer look at each one.

1. Audit Policy

The audit policy outlines the purpose, authority, and responsibility of the internal audit function within the organization. It defines the scope of the internal audit function and the principles that govern its operation. The audit policy is typically approved by the board of directors or a designated audit committee and serves as the foundation for the audit manual.

2. Audit Procedures

Audit procedures provide detailed instructions on how to conduct specific audits. They are designed to ensure that all audits are performed consistently and in accordance with established standards. These procedures should cover all stages of the audit process, from planning and fieldwork to reporting and follow-up.

3. Risk Assessment Methodology

An effective audit manual should include a risk assessment methodology that outlines how the internal audit function identifies, assesses, and prioritizes risks. This methodology should be tailored to the organization's specific needs and take into consideration any regulatory requirements. A thorough risk assessment methodology is essential for identifying areas of high risk that will require more attention during the audit process.

4. Reporting Standards

Reporting standards define the format, content, and timeline for internal audit reports. These standards should be aligned with the organization's reporting requirements and provide a clear and concise overview of audit findings and recommendations.

5. Quality Assurance Procedures

A quality assurance process is essential for ensuring the effectiveness and quality of the internal audit function. This includes procedures for monitoring, evaluating, and improving the performance of the audit team. It also outlines the responsibilities of the quality assurance function within the internal audit department.

Updating the Audit Manual

An audit manual should be viewed as a living document that is constantly evolving to meet the changing needs of the organization. Regular updates are necessary to ensure that the audit manual remains relevant and effective. Here are some best practices for updating your audit manual:

1. Conduct Regular Reviews

It is essential to review the audit manual on a regular basis, at least once a year. This review should involve all key stakeholders, including the audit team, management, and the audit committee. Any changes or updates should be documented and communicated to relevant parties.

2. Keep Up to Date with Changes in Laws and Regulations

The internal audit function must stay informed about changes in laws and regulations that may impact the organization. This includes updating the audit manual to reflect any changes in regulatory requirements.

3. Incorporate Best Practices

Regularly reviewing and updating the audit manual also allows for the incorporation of best practices. This could include the latest auditing techniques, industry trends, and technologies.

4. Seek Feedback

Audit manual updates can benefit from feedback from auditees and other stakeholders. Soliciting their feedback can help identify any areas for improvement and ensure that the audit manual remains relevant and effective.

Best Practices for Audit Manual Maintenance

Maintaining an effective audit manual is just as important as creating one. Here are some best practices for ensuring your audit manual remains relevant and useful.

1. Provide Proper Training

Proper training is necessary for ensuring that the audit team understands and follows the procedures outlined in the audit manual. This includes not only initial training but also ongoing training as updates are made to the manual.

2. Keep Communication Channels Open

Effective communication is essential for maintaining an up-to-date audit manual. Having open communication channels between the audit team, management, and the audit committee can help identify any areas for improvement and facilitate smooth updates to the manual.

3. Implement a Feedback System

Implementing a feedback system can help identify any issues or challenges with the audit manual. This can include surveys or regular check-ins with audit team members to gather their insights and experiences.

4. Regularly Review and Test Audit Procedures

In addition to updating the audit manual itself, it is important to regularly review and test audit procedures to ensure they are effective and relevant. This could include conducting mock audits or incorporating peer reviews into the audit process.

Conclusion

An effective and up-to-date audit manual is crucial for the success of the internal audit function. It serves as a guide for auditors, providing them with the necessary framework to conduct audits in a consistent and efficient manner. By regularly reviewing and updating the audit manual and implementing best practices for maintenance, organizations can ensure that their audit program remains aligned with their goals and objectives.

Chapter 33: Planning, Organizing, and Managing Internal Audit Projects

Planning and Organizing Audit Projects

As a Certified Internal Auditor (CIA), one of your primary responsibilities is to plan and organize audit projects to ensure they are completed successfully and efficiently. This involves identifying the objectives and scope of the audit, assessing the risks involved, and creating a detailed plan of action. To effectively plan an audit project, it is essential to understand the business and its operations. This includes the identification and evaluation of key processes and controls, as well as understanding the organization's governance structure and risk management processes.

Once the objectives and scope of the audit have been established, the next step is to determine the appropriate audit methodology to be used. This could include a risk-based approach, compliance-based approach, or a combination of both. It is important to select the most suitable methodology for each specific project to ensure the audit is carried out effectively. In addition to planning and organization, it is crucial to assess the resources and budget needed for the audit project. This includes considering the skills and expertise required, as well as the time and cost involved. Adequate allocation of resources and budget is essential to ensure the project runs smoothly and achieves its objectives.

Managing Resources and Budget

Effective management of resources and budget is crucial for the success of any audit project. As a CIA, you must ensure that resources are allocated appropriately, and the budget is managed efficiently to ensure the project is completed within the designated time and cost constraints. Managing resources involves identifying the team members' roles and responsibilities and ensuring they have the necessary skills and knowledge to carry out their tasks effectively. It is also essential to establish clear communication channels and mechanisms to keep the team aligned and working towards the project's objectives.

In terms of budget management, it is crucial to maintain accurate records of expenses and review them regularly to identify potential cost-saving opportunities. This could include using technology to streamline processes or renegotiating contracts with suppliers. Effective budget management not only ensures the project stays within budget but also reflects positively on the internal audit department's overall performance.

Effective Communication with Stakeholders

One of the critical elements of internal audit project management is effective communication with stakeholders. This includes both internal stakeholders, such as senior management and the audit team, as well as external stakeholders, such as regulators, shareholders, and other relevant parties. Communication with stakeholders should start at the beginning of the project and continue throughout its duration. It is essential to establish and maintain regular communication channels and provide timely updates on the project's progress, any significant findings, and potential areas of concern. It is also vital to tailor communication to suit different stakeholder groups. For example, senior management may require a high-level overview, while the audit team may need more detailed and technical information. Tailoring communication ensures that each stakeholder receives the information most relevant to them, thus increasing their engagement and buy-in to the project's objectives.

Uncommon and Insightful Concepts in Project Management

In addition to the above key elements of project management, there are a few uncommon and insightful concepts that CIAs should keep in mind when planning and organizing an internal audit project. One such concept is the use of benchmarking. Benchmarking involves comparing your audit project's performance and processes with other similar projects to identify potential areas for improvement. Benchmarking can help CIAs identify best practices and adopt them in their project management approach, leading to more effective and efficient audits. Another concept is the consideration of cultural and social factors. As businesses become more globalized, internal audit projects may involve working with teams and stakeholders from diverse backgrounds. Understanding and respecting cultural and social differences can improve communication and collaboration, ultimately leading to a more successful audit project.

Finally, CIAs should also be mindful of utilizing technology in project management. There are many tools and software available that can help streamline project planning, resource management, and communication with stakeholders. Embracing technology can improve the efficiency and effectiveness of internal audit projects and free up time for CIAs to focus on more critical tasks.

In Conclusion

Effective internal audit project management requires careful planning, organization, and management of resources, budget, and communication with stakeholders. As a CIA, it is essential to understand and apply these concepts to ensure that audit projects are completed successfully and contribute to the overall success of the organization. By utilizing uncommon and insightful concepts, CIAs can elevate their project management skills and deliver even more valuable and impactful audits.

Chapter 34: Ensuring Excellence: Quality Assurance in Internal Audit

In any organization, maintaining high-quality standards is crucial for sustainable success. This is especially true in the field of internal audit, where the credibility and reliability of the audit function depends on the quality of the audits conducted. Quality assurance ensures that internal audit practices are consistently meeting the required standards and delivering value to the organization. In this chapter, we will explore the importance of quality assurance in internal audit, commonly used Quality Assurance Frameworks, and the process of conducting internal quality assessments.

Importance of Quality Assurance

The primary purpose of quality assurance in internal audit is to uphold the integrity, accuracy, and effectiveness of the audit function. A robust quality assurance framework ensures that the internal audit function is delivering quality and timely audits that address the organization's risks and meet stakeholder expectations. Quality assurance not only ensures the quality of the audits but also strengthens the overall internal audit process by identifying areas for improvement and promoting continuous learning and development. Moreover, quality assurance helps in building stakeholder confidence in the internal audit function. By conducting regular assessments and providing evidence of the quality of the audits, internal audit can demonstrate its value and enhance its credibility within the organization. This also creates a culture of accountability and commitment to quality within the internal audit team.

Quality Assurance Frameworks

There are various frameworks that organizations can adopt to implement a quality assurance program for their internal audit function. These frameworks provide a structured approach to assess the effectiveness and efficiency of the internal audit process. One such widely recognized framework is the International Standards for the Professional Practice of Internal Auditing (Standards) issued by The Institute of Internal Auditors (IIA). The IIA Standards consist of 10 core principles that establish the foundation for the internal audit process. They also include mandatory elements that define the essential elements of an effective internal audit function. Adhering to these standards helps in building a strong quality assurance program and ensures that internal audit practices align with international best practices.

Another popular framework is the Quality Assurance Improvement Program (QAIP) developed by the IIA. It is designed to help chief audit executives assess and improve their internal audit function's overall effectiveness and make recommendations for continuous improvement. The QAIP consists of three stages - self-assessment, independent external assessment, and a follow-up review to address any findings and recommendations.

185

Conducting Internal Quality Assessments

Conducting internal quality assessments is an essential part of quality assurance for internal audit. It involves reviewing the internal audit function's activities and processes to ensure they adhere to relevant standards, procedures, and best practices. Internal quality assessments can be conducted either by an internal quality assessment team or by independent consultants. The self-assessment process includes reviews of the internal audit activity's relevance, effectiveness, efficiency, and compliance with professional standards and protocols. It also involves evaluating the internal audit team's skills, capabilities, and competencies required to meet the organization's objectives. Additionally, self-assessments also help identify any gaps or areas for improvement and develop a plan to address them.

External assessments are conducted by independent consultants and are a critical component of quality assurance. They provide an objective evaluation of the internal audit function's effectiveness and adherence to standards and best practices. External assessments provide a more comprehensive and impartial view of the internal audit function that can help identify areas for improvement and validate the organization's internal audit processes.

In Conclusion

Quality assurance is a crucial aspect of maintaining the integrity, credibility, and effectiveness of the internal audit function. It provides assurance to stakeholders that the internal audit process is consistently meeting the required standards and delivering value to the organization. By adopting a quality assurance framework and conducting regular internal quality assessments, internal audit can continuously improve its processes and contribute to the organization's success with confidence and reliability.

Chapter 35: Realizing the Full Potential of Internal Audit through Measuring Outcomes and Evaluating Performance

Internal audit plays a crucial role in organizations by providing independent assurance and advisory services that help improve the effectiveness and efficiency of operations, enhance reliability of financial reporting, and ensure compliance with laws and regulations. However, it is not enough for internal audit to simply conduct audits and report their findings. In order to truly excel in their function, internal audit needs to continually evaluate its own performance and measure the outcomes of its efforts. In this chapter, we will explore the importance of measuring internal audit outcomes and evaluating performance, and how to use these tools to find opportunities for improvement within the internal audit function.

Measuring Internal Audit Outcomes

In today's dynamic business environment, it is essential for internal audit to stay relevant and add value to the organization. This can only be achieved if internal audit is able to demonstrate its impact and effectiveness. This is where measuring outcomes becomes crucial. Measuring outcomes not only helps internal audit assess its performance, but also provides valuable insights on the organization's risks, control environment, and overall performance. It allows internal audit to identify areas for improvement and better align its efforts with the organization's strategic objectives. One way to measure internal audit outcomes is by tracking key performance indicators (KPIs). These are metrics that are used to measure specific aspects of internal audit's performance, such as the number and types of audits conducted, number of recommendations made, stakeholder satisfaction, and timeliness of audit reports. By regularly tracking and analyzing these KPIs, internal audit can identify patterns and trends that can help pinpoint areas for improvement.

Another useful tool for measuring internal audit outcomes is a maturity model. This is a framework that helps assess the maturity and effectiveness of internal audit practices and processes. By evaluating internal audit against a maturity model, organizations can identify gaps in their current practices and develop a roadmap for improvement. A maturity model can also help internal audit benchmark against other organizations and stay current with best practices.

Evaluating the Performance of Internal Audit

Measuring internal audit outcomes is just one piece of the puzzle. In order to truly improve, internal audit must also conduct a thorough evaluation of its performance. This involves looking at its processes, methodologies, and resources to determine if they are aligned with the organization's goals and objectives. An effective evaluation should also consider factors such as stakeholder feedback, audit quality, and staff capabilities. One way to evaluate internal audit performance is through a self-assessment. This involves internal audit conducting an objective evaluation of its own practices and processes. By involving all members of the internal audit team in this self-assessment, a more comprehensive and accurate picture can be obtained. This self-evaluation can then be compared to external standards and best practices to identify areas for improvement.

Utilizing external assessments can also be beneficial in evaluating internal audit's performance. These can be conducted through peer reviews, external quality assessments, or external quality assurance reviews. These assessments provide an objective view of internal audit's practices and processes and can uncover blind spots that may not have been identified through a self-assessment.

Finding Opportunities for Improvement

Measuring outcomes and evaluating performance not only helps internal audit assess its own effectiveness, but it also provides valuable insights and opportunities for improvement. By regularly tracking KPIs and conducting evaluations, internal audit can identify areas for improvement and make necessary adjustments to its processes and practices. This not only helps internal audit stay relevant and add value to the organization, but also positions it as a strategic partner in achieving the organization's goals. Continuous improvement is at the core of high-performing organizations. By regularly measuring outcomes and evaluating performance, internal audit can adapt and evolve to meet the changing needs of the organization. It is important for internal audit to foster a culture of learning and improvement, where feedback and constructive criticism are welcomed and utilized to drive positive change.

In addition to measuring outcomes and evaluating performance, internal audit can also look for improvement opportunities through stakeholder feedback and conducting root cause analysis on audit findings. Engaging with stakeholders and understanding their needs and expectations can help internal audit tailor their approach and delivery, leading to improved satisfaction and performance. Conducting root cause analysis on audit findings not only helps internal audit identify the underlying issues, but also allows for proactive and preventive actions to be taken in the future.

In conclusion, measuring internal audit outcomes and evaluating performance are essential for the internal audit function to reach its full potential and effectively support the organization. By regularly evaluating its own performance and seeking out improvement opportunities, internal audit can continually enhance its effectiveness and value to the organization. Let us embrace a culture of continuous improvement and chart the course towards excellence in internal audit.

Chapter 36: Collaboration and Partnership with Other Departments

Internal audit is not a standalone function within an organization. It relies heavily on collaboration and partnership with other departments to effectively carry out its duties and responsibilities. In this chapter, we will explore how working with finance, compliance, and legal departments can impact audit effectiveness. We will also delve into effective communication and coordination strategies that can enhance collaboration between internal audit and other departments.

Working with Finance, Compliance, and Legal Departments

One of the key roles of internal audit is to provide assurance on the financial statements and processes of an organization. This makes finance department a crucial partner for internal audit. By working closely with the finance team, auditors can gain a deeper understanding of the financial processes and identify potential risks. Moreover, finance department can also provide relevant data and analysis to help auditors in their risk assessment and planning. By involving finance department in the audit process, internal audit can also gather insights from their perspective and gain a more comprehensive view of the organization's financial health.

Compliance and legal departments also play a vital role in internal audit. Compliance teams ensure that the organization is adhering to laws, regulations, and internal policies. By including them in the audit process, internal auditors can ensure that their findings and recommendations align with compliance requirements.

In addition, legal teams can provide valuable insights on legal implications of audit findings and help internal audit in evaluating the effectiveness of controls and mitigating risks. Collaborating with compliance and legal departments can also help internal audit in identifying potential compliance issues and minimizing legal risks.

Impact of Collaboration on Audit Effectiveness

One of the key benefits of collaboration between internal audit and other departments is its impact on audit effectiveness. When working together, departments can share knowledge and expertise, leading to more comprehensive and effective audits. This collaboration can also enhance the value of the audit process and build credibility for internal audit within the organization.

Moreover, involving other departments in the audit can help in gaining their buy-in and support for audit recommendations. By collaborating with finance, compliance, and legal departments, internal audit can also gain a better understanding of the organization's risk appetite and culture, allowing them to tailor their audit approach accordingly.

Effective Communication and Coordination Strategies

Collaboration is not possible without effective communication and coordination strategies. Internal audit should establish clear channels of communication with other departments to share information and updates on the audit process. Regular meetings and status updates can help in aligning efforts and addressing any potential roadblocks. Coordination among departments is also crucial to ensure that the audit process is carried out smoothly. By coordinating audit timelines and schedules with other departments, internal audit can avoid any conflicts and complete the audit efficiently.

In addition, communication with other departments should continue even after the audit is completed. This allows for a better understanding of the implementation of audit recommendations and helps in evaluating their effectiveness.

Collaboration - The Key to Success

In conclusion, collaboration and partnership with other departments is a crucial aspect of internal audit. By working closely with finance, compliance, and legal departments, internal audit can enhance its effectiveness and bring more value to the organization. Effective communication and coordination strategies are essential for successful collaboration, which can ultimately lead to a stronger and more efficient internal audit function within the organization.

Chapter 37: Internal Audit in Nonprofit Organizations

Nonprofit organizations play a vital role in society, serving various needs and causes that benefit the greater public. As such, they are subject to unique considerations when it comes to internal audit practices. In this chapter, we will explore the specific challenges and opportunities that arise when conducting internal audits in nonprofit organizations.

The Importance of Nonprofit Governance

Governance is the system by which organizations are directed, controlled, and held accountable. Nonprofit governance is particularly crucial as it ensures that the organization fulfills its mission and provides meaningful impact to its beneficiaries. It also ensures that the organization is run ethically and transparently.

When conducting internal audits in nonprofit organizations, the auditor must have a thorough understanding of the organization's governance structure, policies, and practices. This includes understanding the role of the board of directors, executive leadership, and other stakeholders in decision-making processes. It is also essential to assess the effectiveness and independence of the board in overseeing the organization's operations, finances, and compliance.

Unique Considerations for Auditing Nonprofits

Nonprofit organizations are subject to different laws, regulations, and reporting requirements than for-profit organizations. This requires internal auditors to have a specialized knowledge of the unique challenges and risks faced by nonprofits. Some of these considerations include: - Funding Sources: Nonprofit organizations rely heavily on donations, grants, and other forms of funding to support their operations. Therefore, it is essential to understand the organization's funding sources and any associated restrictions or compliance requirements.

- Restricted Funds: Nonprofits often receive donations that are designated for specific programs or projects. These funds are subject to restrictions and must be used for their intended purpose. Internal auditors must evaluate the organization's processes for tracking and reporting on restricted funds to ensure they are used appropriately.

- Tax-exempt Status: Many nonprofit organizations are exempt from paying taxes. This status comes with specific regulations that must be adhered to, such as limitations on lobbying and political activities. Internal auditors must understand these regulations and assess the organization's compliance.

- Public Trust: Nonprofit organizations rely heavily on the trust of the public and their donors. Any fraud, mismanagement, or ethical lapses can severely damage the organization's reputation and ability to continue its operations. Therefore, internal auditors must pay special attention to areas that could erode public trust, such as conflicts of interest, related party transactions, and proper use of funds.

Compliance and Internal Controls

Compliance is a critical aspect of nonprofit organizations, as they have a responsibility to ensure that funds and resources are used appropriately to fulfill their mission. Internal auditors must assess the organization's compliance with laws, regulations, and internal policies and procedures.

Internal controls are the measures put in place to ensure that an organization's operations are effective, efficient, and in compliance with laws and regulations. In nonprofit organizations, internal controls must also consider the unique risks of dealing with donors, volunteers, and vulnerable beneficiaries. Internal auditors must evaluate the adequacy and effectiveness of internal controls, particularly in areas of risk such as cash handling, fundraising, and program implementation.

Striving for Excellence in Nonprofit Internal Audit

While internal auditing in nonprofit organizations presents its challenges, it also provides an opportunity to make a meaningful impact. Here are some tips to ensure your nonprofit internal audit practices are effective and in line with best practices: - Stay Educated: Nonprofit organizations are subject to an ever-changing regulatory environment. Therefore, it is essential to stay updated on any changes that may impact the organization and its operations. Joining professional organizations and attending conferences and training sessions can help you stay informed.

- Foster a Collaborative Environment: Nonprofit organizations typically have limited resources and rely heavily on volunteers and community support. Internal auditors must work closely with different departments and stakeholders to understand their challenges and risks fully. This will enable them to provide valuable insights and recommendations that align with the organization's mission and goals.

- Embrace Technology: Nonprofits are increasingly turning to technology to streamline their operations and improve transparency and accountability. Internal auditors must have a good understanding of the organization's technology landscape and assess the adequacy and effectiveness of controls in place to protect sensitive data.

- Focus on Results: Nonprofit organizations are mission-driven, and their success is measured by the impact they make. When conducting internal audits, focus on assessing the effectiveness in achieving the organization's goals rather than just checking compliance boxes.

Conclusion

Internal auditing in nonprofit organizations presents unique challenges that require specialized knowledge and skills. It also provides an opportunity to contribute to the betterment of society by ensuring that nonprofits are fulfilling their missions in an ethical, transparent, and accountable manner. By understanding the importance of governance, compliance, and internal controls in nonprofit organizations, internal auditors can provide meaningful insights and recommendations that help these organizations achieve their goals and make a positive impact on the world.

Chapter 38: Enterprise Risk Management: Collaboration and Partnership with Internal Audit

Understanding Enterprise Risk Management When discussing enterprise risk management (ERM), it is important to first understand what it is and how it differs from traditional risk management. ERM is a holistic approach to identifying, assessing, and managing risks across an entire organization, rather than focusing on individual departments or functions. It takes into consideration both internal and external risks, and emphasizes the integration of risk management throughout the organization's operations.

ERM is not meant to replace traditional risk management practices, but rather to enhance them. By taking a broader view of risks and their potential impact, ERM enables organizations to better prioritize and allocate resources to mitigate those risks. It also encourages collaboration and communication among different departments and functions, leading to a more comprehensive and effective risk management approach.

Identifying and Prioritizing Risks

In order to effectively manage risks, it is crucial to first identify and prioritize them. This is where internal auditors play a significant role in the ERM process. Being familiar with the organization's operations and processes, internal auditors are in a unique position to identify potential risks and their impact.

By conducting risk assessments and gathering input from various departments, internal auditors can help identify risks that may have been overlooked by individual departments. They can also provide valuable insights on the likelihood and potential impact of these risks. This information is crucial for the organization's risk management team to develop strategies and allocate resources appropriately.

Collaborating with ERM Teams

Effective collaboration between internal auditors and the organization's ERM team is essential for a successful ERM program. Internal auditors can provide valuable support to ERM teams by leveraging their knowledge of the organization's operations and processes. They can also assist in developing risk management plans and monitoring the effectiveness of those plans.

Furthermore, collaboration between internal audit and ERM teams allows for the integration of risk management into the organization's governance and decision-making processes. By working together, these teams can ensure that risks are considered in all aspects of the organization's strategic planning and decision-making.

One of the key benefits of collaboration between internal auditors and ERM teams is the efficiency and effectiveness it brings to the risk management process. By leveraging each team's expertise and knowledge, time and resources can be optimized, leading to a more streamlined and robust ERM program.

In addition, it is important for internal auditors and ERM teams to maintain open and transparent communication. This allows for the continuous sharing of information and updates on risk management activities, leading to a more proactive approach in identifying and mitigating risks.

Conclusion

In today's constantly evolving business landscape, organizations face a diverse range of risks that could potentially impact their operations and objectives. ERM offers a holistic approach to managing these risks, and internal auditors play a critical role in this process. By collaborating and partnering with ERM teams, internal auditors can contribute their unique expertise and knowledge to identify, assess, and manage risks throughout the organization. This not only strengthens the organization's risk mitigation strategies, but also enables a more efficient and effective risk management process. By incorporating ERM practices into their work, internal auditors can make a significant contribution to the overall success and sustainability of the organization.

Chapter 39: International Internal Audit Practices

Internal audit has become an essential function in organizations around the world, regardless of their size, industry, or location. With businesses expanding their operations globally, internal audit has also evolved to take on an international reach. This chapter explores the differences and challenges of international internal audit practices, and how auditors can navigate cultural, legal, and environmental differences to ensure compliance with international regulations and standards.

Differences Between Domestic and International Auditing

While the fundamentals of internal audit remain the same, there are significant differences when it comes to conducting audits internationally. Domestic audits are typically carried out within one country, with a focus on national laws and regulations. However, international audits require a broader scope, encompassing multiple countries, currencies, and regulations. One key difference between domestic and international audits is the complexity of the business environment. As organizations expand globally, they enter into new markets with diverse cultures, legal systems, and business practices. This creates a more complex and challenging audit environment, as auditors must navigate unfamiliar territory and adapt to different protocols.

Another significant difference is the influence of international bodies and regulations. While domestic audits primarily adhere to national laws and regulations, international audits also adhere to guidelines set by international organizations such as the International Auditing and Assurance Standards Board (IAASB) and the International Organization for Standardization (ISO).

Understanding Cultural, Legal, and Environmental Differences

Internal auditors must have a deep understanding of cultural, legal, and environmental differences when conducting international audits. This understanding is crucial to effectively evaluate risks and controls in different regions and ensure compliance with international standards. Cultural differences can significantly impact the audit process, as culture dictates how business is conducted, communication style, and relationships between management and employees. It is essential for auditors to be aware of these cultural nuances and adapt their approach accordingly to build trust and rapport.

Legal differences also pose a challenge for international audits. Each country has its unique legal system, and auditors must have a solid understanding of these laws to identify any non-compliance issues. It is also crucial for auditors to stay updated with any changes in laws and regulations in the countries they operate in, to ensure compliance during audits.

Environmental differences also play a significant role in international audits. For example, a company operating in a developing country may face different environmental laws and regulations compared to a developed country. These regulations may also vary within different regions of the same country. Auditors must have sound knowledge of these laws and regulations to identify risks and recommend appropriate solutions.

Adapting to International Regulations and Standards

Adhering to international regulations and standards can be challenging for internal auditors, especially if they are not familiar with them. International organizations such as the IAASB and ISO have set global standards and guidelines for internal auditing to promote consistency and best practices across different countries. To ensure compliance with these standards, it is essential for auditors to stay updated with any changes or updates in regulations and standards. This would require ongoing training and development to keep up with the evolving global landscape.

Auditors must also adapt their audit approach to suit the requirements of international standards. This may involve using different sampling techniques, evaluating the effectiveness of internal controls, and reporting standards. It is crucial for auditors to communicate clearly and effectively with stakeholders to ensure a thorough understanding and alignment with international regulations and standards.

Another aspect to consider is the use of technology in international audits. With the digital transformation of businesses, auditors must embrace technology to streamline processes and improve efficiency. This may include the use of data analytics to identify risks and opportunities or implementing continuous auditing and monitoring to uphold compliance with international standards.

In Conclusion

Conducting international audits requires a unique set of skills and a deep understanding of cultural, legal, and environmental differences. Auditors must be open-minded, adaptable, and stay updated with international regulations and standards to ensure compliance and provide valuable insights to stakeholders. With the continuous expansion of businesses globally, the role of international internal audit will only continue to evolve and play a vital role in maintaining effective internal controls and mitigating risks.

Practice Exam Questions

Book 1

Practice Questions Set 1

1) What is the primary purpose of internal auditing?
A) To identify areas for cost-cutting within the organization
B) To detect fraudulent activities
C) To provide assurance that the organization's goals and objectives are being met
D) To perform external financial audits

2) Which of the following is NOT a key milestone in the development of internal auditing?
A) Creation of The Institute of Internal Auditors
B) Publication of the International Professional Practices Framework
C) Introduction of the CPA certification
D) Sarbanes-Oxley Act of 2002

3) Which of the following frameworks is often used by internal auditors to assess an organization's control environment?
A) COSO
B) GAAP
C) IFRS
D) COBIT

4) Which of the following skills is NOT essential for an internal auditor?
A) Communication
B) Analytical skills
C) Technical expertise in a specific area
D) Emotional intelligence

5) What is the first step in the risk assessment process?
A) Identifying risks
B) Analyzing risks
C) Evaluating risks
D) Reporting

6) Which of the following is NOT a type of risk?
A) Operational risks
B) Compliance risks
C) Environmental risks
D) Strategic risks

7) Which of the following is NOT a component of internal control?
A) Information and communication
B) Risk assessment
C) Asset management
D) Monitoring

8) What is the main purpose of a compliance audit?
A) To identify areas for cost-cutting within the organization
B) To detect fraudulent activities
C) To ensure adherence to laws and regulations
D) To review the organization's financial statements

9) What qualifies an individual to take the CIA exam?
A) A bachelor's degree in accounting or a related field
B) Five years of experience in internal auditing or a related field
C) Proficiency in a foreign language
D) A high school diploma

10) What does the CIA exam consist of?
A) Multiple choice questions only
B) Essays only
C) A combination of multiple choice and essay questions
D) Only oral questioning by a panel of examiners

11) What is the primary responsibility of internal auditors?
A) To prepare financial statements
B) To conduct external audits
C) To provide independent assurance on an organization's operations
D) To make management decisions on behalf of the organization

12) What is the purpose of the International Professional Practices Framework?
A) To establish international accounting standards for all audits
B) To provide guidelines for the internal audit profession
C) To ensure compliance with local regulations in different countries
D) To set the standards for ethical conduct in the business world

13) How has technology impacted the field of internal auditing?
A) It has reduced the need for internal audits
B) It has made internal audits more expensive
C) It has made internal audits more efficient and effective
D) It has decreased the level of risk assessment needed for internal audits

14) What is the main goal of risk assessment in internal auditing?
A) To identify all risks within an organization
B) To eliminate all risks within an organization
C) To prioritize risks based on their potential impact
D) To transfer all risks to a third party

15) What type of risk is associated with the potential for financial loss?
A) Operational risk
B) Compliance risk
C) Reputational risk
D) Strategic risk

16) Which of the following is NOT a component of internal control as defined by COSO?
A) Monitoring
B) Risk assessment
C) Fraud prevention
D) Control environment

17) What is the role of internal auditors in corporate governance?
A) To make managerial decisions for the organization

B) To report to external stakeholders on the organization's performance

C) To ensure compliance with laws and regulations

D) To provide independent assurance on the organization's operations

18) How can internal auditors best build rapport with auditees?

A) By using formal language

B) By being overly critical

C) By being approachable and building trust

D) By never revealing their findings

19) What is a common and accepted approach to audit planning?

A) Setting objectives and then determining the business's goals

B) Starting with identifying risks and then evaluating them

C) Determining the objectives and then identifying the risks

D) Setting the tone and then establishing objectives

20) Which of the following is NOT an auditing technique used by internal auditors?

A) Data analysis

B) Surveying external stakeholders

C) Sampling

D) Document review

21) Which of the following is NOT a key area of focus for an operational audit?

A) Internal controls

B) Financial statements

C) Cost cutting

D) Business processes

22) Who is responsible for identifying and reporting on financial risks within an organization?

A) External auditors

B) Management

C) Internal auditors

D) Stakeholders

23) What is an effective way to mitigate risks within an organization?

A) Avoiding all risks

B) Transferring risks to a third party

C) Evaluating risks on a case-by-case basis

D) Embracing all risks

24) In which of the following situations would a compliance audit be most helpful?

A) When assessing the effectiveness of internal controls

B) When evaluating the accuracy of financial statements

C) When determining the level of operational risk

D) When checking for adherence to laws and regulations

25) What is the main focus of a financial audit?

A) Ensuring compliance with laws and regulations

B) Identifying areas for cost reduction

C) Providing assurance on the accuracy of financial statements

D) Evaluating the effectiveness of internal controls

26) What sets the CIA certification apart from other certification programs?

A) Its focus on operational risk

B) Its international recognition

C) Its requirement of a foreign language proficiency

D) Its emphasis on financial auditing

27) Which of the following is NOT a component of the International Professional Practices Framework?
A) Code of Ethics
B) Standards for the Professional Practice of Internal Auditing
C) Control-based approaches for compliance audits
D) Practice advisories

28) What impact does a strong control environment have on an organization?
A) It reduces the need for internal audits
B) It increases the risk of fraud
C) It improves the organization's overall performance
D) It eliminates all risk

29) In an operational audit, what is the main focus of data analysis?
A) To identify potential fraud
B) To evaluate the accuracy of financial statements
C) To assess the effectiveness of internal controls
D) To determine areas for cost reduction

30) What does the risk assessment process include?
A) Identifying risks only
B) Analyzing risks only
C) Evaluating risks only
D) All of the above

31) What is a key responsibility of internal auditors in corporate governance?
A) To make management decisions for the organization
B) To report on the organization's financial performance
C) To ensure compliance with laws and regulations
D) To evaluate the performance of external auditors

32) What is the main role of internal auditors in risk management?
A) To eliminate all risks within an organization
B) To prioritize risks and recommend mitigation strategies
C) To transfer all risks to a third party
D) To ignore any risks that are identified

33) What is an effective way for internal auditors to communicate their findings to stakeholders?
A) By using technical jargon
B) By presenting data and analysis in an easy-to-understand format
C) By keeping all findings confidential
D) By delegating the responsibility to someone else

Practice Questions Set 2

1. What is the purpose of internal auditing?

2. What is the difference between internal auditing and external auditing?

3. Internal auditors must have knowledge of which areas of an organization?

4. What are the three overarching principles of the International Standards for the Professional Practice of Internal Auditing (Standards)?

5. What is the difference between a financial audit and an operational audit?

6. What is the role of the audit committee?

7. What is the importance of independence for internal auditors?

8. What is a control self-assessment?

9. What is the purpose of a risk assessment?

10. What is the difference between inherent risk and residual risk?

11. What is the purpose of testing in internal auditing?

12. What is the importance of communicating audit findings to management and stakeholders?

13. What is the role of technology in internal auditing?

14. What is the purpose of a fraud detection technique?

15. What are the ethical standards for auditors?

16. What is the purpose of an audit report?

17. How can auditors track management's response to audit findings?

18. What is the role of the audit committee in overseeing auditors?

19. What is the integrated approach to risk management?

20. What are the components of an audit report?

21. What is the purpose of evaluating business processes in auditing?

22. How does internal auditing add value to an organization?

23. What is the importance of adaptability and inclusivity in the digital age of auditing?

24. What is the purpose of performance-based auditing?

25. What are the challenges and considerations of international internal auditing?

26. What is the difference between an internal auditor and a compliance officer?

27. What is the purpose of a self-assessment in internal auditing?

28. What are the primary responsibilities of internal auditors?

29. What is the difference between an internal auditor and a fraud examiner?

30. What is the purpose of conducting a follow-up audit?

31. What is the importance of professionalism in internal auditing?

32. What is the difference between a control and a risk?

33. What is the role of an internal auditor in evaluating business operations?

34. What is the purpose of governance in an organization?

35. What is the goal of an internal audit function?

36. What is the difference between assurance and consulting services provided by internal auditors?

37. What is the difference between a financial statement audit and a performance audit?

38. What is the purpose of an audit scope and objectives?

39. How do internal auditors add value to an organization?

40. What is the key component of effective communication for internal auditors?

41. What is the role of the internal audit function in enterprise risk management?

42. What is the difference between a financial audit and an internal controls audit?

43. What is the importance of objectivity for internal auditors?

44. What is the purpose of a risk assessment matrix?

45. How can internal auditors build strong relationships with stakeholders?

46. What is the role of the audit committee in enhancing the effectiveness of the internal audit function?

47. What is the purpose of a mid-year risk assessment?

48. What are the objectives of a code of ethics for internal auditors?

49. How can internal auditors help an organization achieve its objectives?

50. What is the purpose of risk management in an organization?

Practice Questions Set 3

1. What is the primary role of internal auditing for an organization?

2. What is the purpose of an internal audit charter?

3. What is the difference between an assurance engagement and a consulting engagement?

4. In the context of internal auditing, what is risk?

5. What are the three lines of defense in an organization's risk management structure?

6. What is the purpose of a risk assessment within the internal audit process?

7. What is the difference between a financial statement audit and an internal audit?

8. What is the purpose of a control self-assessment?

9. What are the elements of the internal control system?

10. What is the difference between a preventive control and a detective control?

11. What is the purpose of a fraud risk assessment?

12. What is the difference between fraud and misconduct?

13. When should internal audit activities be disclosed to the audit committee?

14. What is the primary purpose of an audit report?

15. What is the purpose of a root cause analysis?

16. What is the best way to manage potential conflicts of interest within the internal audit function?

17. What are the different levels of assurance that can be provided by an internal auditor?

18. What is an engagement letter and why is it important?

19. What are the components of the internal audit process?

20. What is the purpose of an internal audit work program?

21. What is the purpose of a quality assurance and improvement program for the internal audit function?

22. What are the roles and responsibilities of internal audit staff?

23. What are the common challenges that internal audit teams face?

24. How can internal audit teams ensure efficiency and effectiveness in their work?

25. In a virtual world, what are the main challenges for conducting audits remotely?

26. What is the importance of providing adequate training and development opportunities for internal auditors?

27. How is audit quality evaluated?

28. What are some governmental and regulatory requirements that may impact the internal audit function?

29. What is the role of internal auditors in corporate social responsibility (CSR) auditing?

30. What is the purpose of auditing environmental, social, and governance (ESG) criteria?

31. What are the key considerations when managing audit findings and recommendations?

32. What is a root cause analysis and how is it used in the internal audit process?

33. What is the role of technology in the evolution of internal auditing?

34. How can internal auditors track and monitor the implementation of audit recommendations?

35. What is the future of internal auditing?

36. What is the role of management in an organization's risk management structure?

37. What are the primary responsibilities of the risk and compliance functions?

38. What is the purpose of a risk assessment?

39. What is the relationship between an organization's objectives and its risks?

40. What is the difference between a preventive control and a detective control?

41. What is the purpose of a control environment?

42. How does information and communication contribute to an effective internal control system?

43. What is the purpose of monitoring in the internal control system?

44. What is the primary role of internal auditors in fraud risk management?

45. What is the difference between fraud and misconduct?

46. When should an internal auditor disclose potential conflicts of interest?

47. What is the difference between reasonable assurance and limited assurance?

48. What is the purpose of an engagement letter in the internal audit process?

49. What are the key components of the internal audit process?

50. Why is it important for internal auditors to maintain independence and objectivity in their work?

Practice Questions Set 4

1. What is the primary responsibility of an internal auditor?
a) Detect fraud
b) Provide financial advice to the organization
c) Maintain financial records
d) Provide assurance on the effectiveness of risk management, control, and governance processes

2. In which of the following situations is independence NOT required for an internal auditor?
a) When conducting an operational audit
b) When performing a consulting engagement
c) When reviewing financial statements for accuracy
d) When reviewing personnel files for compliance issues

3. Which of the following is NOT a component of the internal audit activity's governance structure?
a) Ethics and integrity
b) Independence and objectivity
c) Operations management
d) Quality assurance and improvement program

4. Which of the following is the most important skill for an auditor to possess?
a) Technical accounting knowledge
b) Analytical and critical thinking skills
c) Communication and interpersonal skills
d) Understanding of laws and regulations

5. Which of the following is the primary reason for conducting an internal audit?
a) To recommend changes to organizational structure
b) To identify areas of potential fraud
c) To improve the efficiency and effectiveness of operations
d) To review the accuracy of financial statements

6. Which of the following is NOT a responsibility of the internal audit function?
a) Developing organizational policies and procedures
b) Evaluating and monitoring risks
c) Reviewing the effectiveness of controls
d) Providing recommendations for improvement

7. Which of the following is a characteristic of effective internal audit reports?
a) Brief and concise
b) Highly technical and detailed
c) Only include positive findings
d) Written in the first person

8. Which of the following is NOT a risk management activity that internal auditors can assist with?
a) Identifying risks
b) Mitigating risks
c) Transferring risks
d) Determining the acceptability of risks

9. Which of the following is NOT a key responsibility of an internal auditor during an organizational change or restructuring?
a) Implementing changes to processes
b) Reviewing and assessing the effectiveness of the change
c) Identifying potential risks associated with the change
d) Communicating the change to stakeholders

10. Which of the following is NOT a component of a company's organizational structure?
a) Control environment
b) Risk appetite
c) Human resources
d) Policies and procedures

11. In order to maintain objectivity, an internal auditor should:
a) Perform consulting engagements for the same department they audit
b) Engage in social activities with management
c) Be involved in the day-to-day operations of the organization
d) Not have any financial interest in the organization

12. Which of the following is NOT a characteristic of a well-functioning internal audit activity?
a) The audit team has regular meetings with senior management
b) The audit team only reports to the audit committee
c) The audit team has access to all areas of the organization
d) The audit team has a high level of independence and objectivity

13. Which of the following is NOT a component of the International Standards for the Professional Practice of Internal Auditing (Standards)?
a) Performance standards
b) Attribute standards
c) Reporting standards
d) Quality assurance and improvement program (QAIP)

14. Which of the following is NOT a characteristic of quality assurance and improvement programs (QAIPs)?
a) They are aligned with the internal audit activity's objectives
b) They focus on improving the organization's operations
c) They include regular evaluation and improvement of the audit activity
d) They are established by external stakeholders

15. Which of the following is NOT a component of an organization's control environment?
a) Integrity and ethical values
b) Communication and information
c) Risk management
d) Human resources policies and procedures

16. The primary purpose of understanding an organization's objectives and strategies is to:
a) Develop an annual audit plan
b) Report on the effectiveness of risk management processes
c) Identify potential risks and controls
d) Gain an understanding of the organization's operations

17. Which of the following is NOT a tool or technique used by internal auditors during an audit engagement?
a) Observation
b) Benchmarking
c) Questionnaires
d) Performing accounting tasks

18. Which of the following is NOT a key element of effective communication skills for an internal auditor?
a) Active listening
b) Using technical jargon
c) Verbal and written communication
d) Nonverbal communication

19. Which of the following documents outlines the scope and objective of an audit engagement?
a) Audit program
b) Audit plan
c) Audit report
d) Engagement letter

20. Which of the following is NOT a common financial statement audit procedure?
a) Reviewing internal controls
b) Analyzing financial ratios
c) Confirming account balances with third parties
d) Performing inventory counts

21. When should internal auditors communicate with external auditors during an audit engagement?
a) Before the internal audit engagement begins
b) After the internal audit engagement is completed
c) Only if a significant issue is identified during the internal audit engagement
d) Throughout the entire internal audit engagement process

22. Which of the following is NOT a common responsibility of internal auditors during a performance audit?
a) Assessing compliance with laws and regulations
b) Evaluating the effectiveness of controls
c) Reviewing financial statements for accuracy
d) Identifying areas for organizational improvement

23. Which of the following statéments is TRUE regarding the use of data analytics in internal auditing?
a) Data analytics can only be used in financial statement audits
b) Data analytics is only used for fraud detection and prevention
c) Internal auditors do not need to have any technical skills to use data analytics
d) Data analytics can help identify patterns and trends within large sets of data

24. In order to assess the quality and effectiveness of an organization's control system, internal auditors should:
a) Observe control activities in action
b) Review management reports
c) Consult with external stakeholders
d) Use statistical sampling methods

25. Which of the following is a key responsibility of internal auditors during a consulting engagement?
a) Communicating findings to the audit committee
b) Reviewing the effectiveness of controls
c) Providing assurance on the accuracy of financial statements
d) Offering recommendations for improving operations

26. Which of the following activities is NOT a part of the internal audit engagement planning process?
a) Defining the scope and objectives of the audit
b) Developing the audit program
c) Performing fieldwork
d) Obtaining an understanding of the organization's operations

27. Which of the following best describes the purpose of management's response to internal audit findings?
a) To address and correct the identified issues

b) To deny the findings and prevent further audits
c) To shift responsibility to external stakeholders
d) To dismiss the internal audit report entirely

28. Which of the following statements is TRUE regarding the external assessment of the internal audit activity?
a) The external assessment must be conducted by an external auditor.
b) The external assessment is only required every five years.
c) The external assessment is not necessary if the internal audit activity has a QAIP.
d) The external assessment must meet all standards for external quality assessments.

29. Which of the following is NOT a key characteristic of a strong fraud risk management program?
a) Effective communication with stakeholders
b) Regular assessments of the organization's fraud risks
c) A punitive approach to handling fraud incidents
d) Ongoing monitoring and assessment of internal controls

30. In order to effectively manage conflicts of interest, an internal auditor should:
a) Disclose their personal financial interests to management
b) Limit interactions with stakeholders
c) Avoid any conflicts of interest entirely
d) Report any potential conflicts of interest to senior management

31. In order to maintain objectivity, internal auditors should:
a) Avoid any involvement in risk management activities
b) Only provide consulting services, not assurance services
c) Conduct all engagements independently, without any assistance
d) Maintain a balanced perspective and exercise professional skepticism

Book 2 - Internal Audit Practices

Practice Questions Set 1

1. What is the primary purpose of internal audit?
A. Detecting fraud
B. Ensuring compliance
C. Improving control processes
D. Providing financial advice

2. When was the internal audit function established?
A. 1950s
B. 1960s
C. 1970s
D. 1980s

3. What is the role of a CIA?
A. Ensuring the integrity of financial statements
B. Conducting risk assessments
C. Evaluating control processes
D. All of the above

4. Which of the following is not one of the principles of internal control?
A. Control environment
B. Risk assessment
C. Communication
D. Compensation

5. What is the first step in assessing and enhancing internal control?
A. Conduct a risk assessment
B. Evaluate existing control activities
C. Implement additional control measures
D. Communicate changes to stakeholders

6. Which of the following is not a red flag of fraud?
A. Excessive spending
B. Personal financial difficulties
C. Lack of segregation of duties
D. Transparency in financial reporting

7. What is the main purpose of an internal audit plan?
A. Identify risk areas
B. Develop audit procedures
C. Communicate changes to stakeholders
D. All of the above

8. What is the purpose of gathering evidence in an internal audit?
A. To identify potential fraud

B. To make recommendations for improvement
C. To assess the effectiveness of control processes
D. All of the above

9. What is the most common sampling technique used in internal auditing?
A. Judgmental sampling
B. Random sampling
C. Systematic sampling
D. Stratified sampling

10. What is the purpose of IT auditing?
A. Identify financial risks
B. Ensure data integrity
C. Evaluate employee performance
D. Increase company revenue

11. What is the most effective technique for assessing the effectiveness of IT controls?
A. Network and system scanning
B. Data analytics
C. Vulnerability assessments
D. Continuous monitoring

12. Why is effective report writing important for internal auditors?
A. To communicate findings to management
B. To meet regulatory requirements
C. To make recommendations for improvement
D. All of the above

13. Which of the following is not a responsibility of the internal audit function in corporate governance?
A. Ensuring compliance with laws and regulations
B. Evaluating the effectiveness of risk management processes
C. Detecting and reporting fraud
D. Making financial decisions for management

14. What is the purpose of the International Standards for the Professional Practice of Internal Auditing?
A. Provide guidance for conducting IT audits
B. Ensure ethical behavior in internal auditing
C. Establish best practices for risk management
D. All of the above

15. What is the primary focus of a quality assurance and improvement program for internal auditors?
A. Evaluating individual performance
B. Identifying areas for improvement
C. Ensuring compliance with laws and regulations
D. Enhancing control processes

16. What type of skills are essential for a CIA to possess?
A. Technical skills
B. Communication skills
C. Analytical skills
D. All of the above

17. Which of the following is not considered a soft skill for a CIA?
A. Leadership
B. Communication
C. Accounting

D. Time management

18. How can diversity and inclusivity be incorporated into the CIA program?
A. By hiring a diverse workforce
B. By including diversity in risk assessments
C. By providing diversity training
D. All of the above

19. What is the role of an IT auditor in risk management?
A. Identifying potential risks
B. Developing control measures
C. Evaluating the effectiveness of control processes
D. All of the above

20. Which of the following is not considered a best practice for conducting an IT audit?
A. Data analytics
B. Network and system scanning
C. Manual data entry
D. Vulnerability assessments

21. Who is responsible for overseeing the internal audit function?
A. External auditors
B. Company management
C. Regulatory agencies
D. Shareholders

22. What is the primary goal of internal control?
A. Detect and prevent fraud
B. Ensure compliance with laws and regulations
C. Improve efficiency and effectiveness of operations
D. All of the above

23. Which of the following is not a component of the control environment?
A. Risk assessment
B. Integrity and ethical values
C. Competence and accountability
D. Monitoring activities

24. What is the purpose of a risk assessment?
A. Identify potential risks
B. Develop control measures
C. Prioritize audit areas
D. All of the above

25. What is the primary responsibility of a CIA?
A. Prepare financial statements
B. Conduct risk assessments
C. Implement control processes
D. Give financial advice

26. Which of the following is not considered a control activity?
A. Human resources policies
B. Physical access controls
C. Risk assessment procedures
D. Personnel training programs

27. What is the purpose of monitoring activities?
A. Detect and prevent fraud
B. Evaluate the effectiveness of control processes
C. Identify potential risks
D. All of the above

28. What is the first step in the risk assessment process?
A. Identify potential risks
B. Develop control measures
C. Prioritize risks
D. Communicate with stakeholders

29. Which of the following is not an effective control implementation strategy?
A. Start with the highest risk areas
B. Involve key stakeholders
C. Utilize technology
D. Ignore recommendations from auditors

30. What is the primary role of internal auditors in fraud detection and prevention?
A. Conducting investigations
B. Identifying red flags of fraud
C. Developing control measures
D. Reviewing financial statements

31. What is the primary goal of IT auditing?
A. Identify and mitigate IT risks
B. Detect and prevent fraud
C. Ensure compliance with laws and regulations
D. Increase company revenue

32. What is the purpose of a code of ethics for internal auditors?
A. Ensure compliance with laws and regulations
B. Establish ethical standards for the profession
C. Provide guidance for conducting IT audits
D. Increase company profits

33. Which of the following is not considered a best practice for conducting an IT audit?
A. Network and system scanning
B. Data analytics
C. Continuous monitoring
D. Manual data entry

34. What is the primary purpose of an internal audit report?
A. Identify potential risks
B. Communicate findings and recommendations to management
C. Ensure compliance with laws and regulations
D. All of the above

35. Why is continuous monitoring of IT controls important?
A. To identify potential risks
B. To ensure the effectiveness of controls
C. To increase company profits
D. All of the above

36. How can technology be utilized in the internal audit process?
A. Sampling techniques

B. Data analytics
C. Gathering evidence
D. All of the above

37. Which of the following is not a key responsibility of the internal audit function in corporate governance?
A. Identifying potential risks
B. Evaluating the effectiveness of risk management processes
C. Making financial decisions for management
D. Reporting to the audit committee

38. What is the purpose of a quality assurance and improvement program for internal auditors?
A. Ensure compliance with laws and regulations
B. Evaluate the performance of individual auditors
C. Identify areas for improvement
D. All of the above

39. How can a CIA contribute to diversity and inclusivity in the workplace?
A. By hiring a diverse workforce
B. By including diversity in risk assessments
C. By providing diversity training
D. All of the above

40. What is the primary focus of an IT auditor in risk management?
A. Identifying potential risks
B. Evaluating the effectiveness of control processes
C. Developing control measures
D. All of the above

Practice Questions Set 2

1. What is the primary responsibility of internal auditing?
A. Monitor employee performance
B. Assess financial reporting accuracy
C. Improve organizational operations
D. Ensure regulatory compliance

2. Which of the following is not one of the three primary categories of internal auditing?
A. Operational auditing
B. Financial auditing
C. Compliance auditing
D. Risk management auditing

3. Which of the following is not a typical role of an internal auditor?
A. Setting goals and objectives for the organization
B. Evaluating the effectiveness of internal controls
C. Identifying potential areas of risk
D. Providing recommendations for improvements

4. One of the primary focuses of internal auditing is to provide assurance to stakeholders. What does this mean?
A. Ensuring that the organization is fulfilling its mission
B. Protecting the company's assets
C. Enforcing internal policies and procedures
D. Implementing changes to improve efficiency

5. What is the difference between assurance and consulting within the context of internal auditing?
A. Consulting provides recommendations while assurance confirms accuracy.
B. Consulting provides recommendations while assurance monitors compliance.
C. Consulting improves operations while assurance ensures financial reporting accuracy.
D. Consulting improves risk management while assurance ensures regulatory compliance.

6. Which of the following is an example of operational effectiveness?
A. Ensuring regulatory compliance
B. Evaluating financial statements
C. Identifying areas of risk
D. Improving processes and procedures

7. How does internal auditing add value to the organization?
A. By identifying areas of risk
B. By providing assurance to stakeholders
C. By improving operational effectiveness
D. By enforcing company policies and procedures

8. How can independence and objectivity be maintained within an internal audit department?
A. Employing third-party auditors
B. Rotating assignments within the department
C. Reporting directly to upper management
D. All of the above

9. Which of the following is a primary purpose of an internal audit charter?
A. To define the scope and objectives of the internal audit function
B. To review financial statements for accuracy
C. To enforce internal policies and procedures
D. To protect the organization's assets

10. What is one way an organization can demonstrate its commitment to internal auditing?
A. By providing a larger budget for the internal audit department
B. By implementing recommendations made by the internal auditors
C. By hiring more internal auditors
D. By creating a separate division for internal auditing

11. What is the purpose of the International Standards for the Professional Practice of Internal Auditing?
A. To provide guidance for conducting internal audits
B. To outline the responsibilities of internal auditors
C. To set ethical standards for internal auditors
D. All of the above

12. What is the difference between a risk and a control?
A. Risks are potential threats while controls are actions to minimize those threats.
B. Risks are potential opportunities while controls are actions to maximize those opportunities.
C. Risks are potential issues while controls are actions to resolve those issues.
D. Risks are potential benefits while controls are actions to maximize those benefits.

13. Why is it important for an internal auditor to maintain independence from the activities they are auditing?
A. To ensure their objectivity
B. To avoid any conflicts of interest
C. To report accurate findings
D. All of the above

14. What is the purpose of conducting an internal audit risk assessment?
A. To identify potential areas of risk within the organization
B. To determine the cost of implementing internal controls
C. To evaluate the effectiveness of current internal controls
D. All of the above

15. Which of the following is not one of the six main categories of internal control activities?
A. Monitoring activities
B. Control environment
C. Risk assessment
D. Financial management

16. What is the role of an internal auditor in regards to fraud?
A. To prevent and detect fraudulent activities
B. To conduct financial investigations
C. To recommend changes to internal controls to prevent fraud
D. All of the above

17. How can an internal auditor ensure the accuracy of financial information?
A. Conducting tests of detail to verify accuracy
B. Comparing financial data to industry standards
C. Interviewing employees responsible for preparing the financial statements
D. All of the above

18. Which of the following is not a typical objective of an operational audit?
A. Assessing the efficiency of operations

B. Identifying potential areas of fraud
C. Evaluating internal controls
D. Identifying areas for cost savings

19. How can an internal auditor help improve an organization's risk management processes?
A. By conducting risk assessments
B. By identifying areas of risk during audits
C. By recommending changes to internal controls
D. All of the above

20. What is the purpose of conducting a compliance audit?
A. To evaluate the effectiveness of internal controls
B. To assess the accuracy of financial statements
C. To ensure compliance with laws and regulations
D. To identify potential areas of fraud

21. What is the primary responsibility of an internal audit manager?
A. Conducting audits and preparing reports
B. Hiring and training internal auditors
C. Setting goals and objectives for the internal audit department
D. Reporting audit findings to upper management

22. Who should the internal audit department report to within the organization?
A. The board of directors
B. The CEO
C. The CFO
D. All of the above

23. What is one advantage of outsourcing internal auditing?
A. It can provide more objective and independent results
B. It can reduce the cost of internal auditing
C. It can create better relationships with employees
D. It can streamline the reporting process

24. How can technology enhance the internal audit process?
A. By automating certain audit procedures
B. By improving the accuracy and speed of data analysis
C. By providing real-time access to financial information
D. All of the above

25. How often should an internal audit charter be reviewed and approved by the governing body?
A. Annually
B. Every three years
C. Every five years
D. Only when significant changes occur

26. What is the purpose of having a quality assurance and improvement program for internal audit?
A. To ensure that the internal audit activity is consistently meeting standards
B. To identify areas for improvement within the internal audit department
C. To provide evidence of the internal audit department's effectiveness
D. All of the above

27. Why is it important for internal auditors to have good communication skills?
A. To effectively report findings to management
B. To build relationships with employees
C. To communicate audit results to stakeholders

D. All of the above

28. What is the future outlook for the internal audit profession?
A. Significant growth opportunities
B. Fewer job opportunities
C. No significant changes anticipated
D. Increased focus on technology and data analysis

29. What is the primary purpose of an audit plan?
A. To determine the scope of the audit
B. To outline the steps of the audit process
C. To assign tasks and responsibilities to auditors
D. All of the above

30. Which of the following is not one of the main steps in conducting an audit engagement?
A. Planning
B. Conducting the audit activities
C. Reporting the results
D. Auditing the audit process

31. What is the minimum amount of time an internal audit report should cover?
A. One month
B. One quarter
C. One fiscal year
D. One calendar year

32. Which of the following is not an example of an internal control activity?
A. Segregation of duties
B. Independent verification
C. Hiring competent employees
D. Documenting policies and procedures

33. How can an internal auditor assess the effectiveness of internal controls?
A. By conducting tests of detail
B. By reviewing employee performance evaluations
C. By interviewing employees responsible for internal controls
D. All of the above

Practice Questions Set 3

1. In the CIA exam, external auditors are responsible for conducting audits for:

2. Which of the following is a characteristic of a successful internal audit team?

3. True or False: Effective risk assessment requires understanding the organization's objectives and key processes.

4. The primary objective of internal audit is to:

5. Which of the following is not a component of the internal audit profession's definition of internal auditing?
a) Providing assurance on the organization's financial statements.
b) Bringing a systematic, disciplined approach to evaluate and improve the effectiveness of governance, risk management, and control processes.
c) Enhancing external audit performance.
d) Helping organizations accomplish their objectives.

6. True or False: The scope of an internal audit may be limited by management's acceptance of certain risks.

7. The primary responsibility of internal auditors is to:

8. Which of the following is a key duty of an internal auditor?
a) Issuing management reports.
b) Ensuring compliance with laws and regulations.
c) Authorizing payments.
d) Developing policies and procedures.

9. True or False: Internal auditors have the authority to implement recommendations made in their audit reports.

10. An external auditor is responsible for:

11. Refer to the table below to answer the question.

Account Type	Value
Cash	$50,000
Accounts Receivable	$25,000
Inventory	$75,000

What is the total value of assets?

12. True or False: A culture of integrity and ethical behavior is not important for an organization's success.

13. Which of the following is an example of an internal control activity related to cash receipts?
a) Reviewing contracts for accurate pricing.
b) Monitoring changes in market trends.
c) Verifying receipt of goods from a supplier.
d) Reconciling bank statements.

14. True or False: Management is not responsible for establishing and maintaining an effective system of internal controls.

15. The probability that internal controls will not prevent or detect a material misstatement is known as:

16. True or False: The purpose of a control self-assessment is to uncover potential control weaknesses.

17. Which of the following is not a primary objective of the COSO Internal Control Framework?
a) Reliable financial and non-financial reporting.
b) Compliance with laws and regulations.
c) Development of organization culture.
d) Effectiveness and efficiency of operations.

18. In the COSO ERM Framework, which component addresses the organization's attitude toward risk?

19. True or False: Internal auditors should always remain completely independent from the organization they are auditing.

20. When conducting an internal audit, internal auditors should remain objective and unbiased. What is another term that refers to this principle?

21. True or False: Using technology can decrease the efficiency of an internal audit.

22. How often should an organization perform a risk assessment?

23. True or False: Management's procedures for risk management cannot be evaluated by internal audit.

24. Which type of audit focuses on evaluating the efficiency, effectiveness, and economy of using resources?

25. True or False: All audits are focused on finding and reporting errors and mistakes.

26. What type of audit is focused on evaluating controls and risk management processes?

27. True or False: A crucial aspect of a successful audit is establishing relevant audit criteria.

28. Which of the following is a key factor to consider when determining the frequency of audit procedures?
a) The size of the organization.
b) Management's risk assessment processes.
c) The number of employees.
d) The organization's industry.

29. True or False: Interviews and questionnaires are useful tools in sampling and analytical techniques for internal audits.

30. When conducting an internal audit, the auditor should always:

31. True or False: The scope of an internal audit is determined by the audit charter.

32. An organization has implemented enhanced internal controls to mitigate its risks. The next step for the

organization is to:

33. True or False: The external auditor is responsible for designing and implementing the internal control system.

34. Which of the following is not a key requirement for internal audit to fulfill its role of evaluating and improving the effectiveness of risk management, control, and governance processes?
a) Recognize that business functions are responsible for managing risks.
b) Design a program to provide reasonable assurance that objectives will be met.
c) Understand relevant laws and regulations.
d) Conduct an annual assessment of the control system.

35. Due professional care, independence, and confidentiality are all principles of:

36. True or False: The internal audit profession's Code of Ethics does not include principles of integrity.

37. Independence means that internal auditors are not influenced by:

38. True or False: Internal auditors should not collaborate with external auditors.

39. Which of the following is not a cultural difference that can impact audit practices?
a) Language barriers.
b) Time zones.
c) Customs and traditions.
d) Political climate.

40. True or False: Global audits require cultural sensitivity and local knowledge.

41. When external and internal auditors collaborate on an audit, the internal auditors should:
a) Increase their sample sizes to ensure accuracy.
b) Take over all tasks related to internal control testing.
c) Ensure that the external auditors conduct all of the audit work.
d) Coordinate audit plans and maintain open communication.

42. True or False: Conducting global audits can decrease the efficiency of the internal audit department.

43. What is a key component of effective compliance risk assessment?

44. True or False: Evaluating and reporting on compliance is not within the scope of internal audit.

45. Fraud risk management involves:

46. True or False: Fraud risk management only involves evaluating financial fraud risks.

47. To effectively evaluate IT governance frameworks, internal auditors should:

48. True or False: Data analytics can decrease the efficiency of an internal audit.

49. The primary benefit of continuous auditing and monitoring is:

50. True or False: During a crisis, auditors should focus on conducting audits as usual to maintain consistency.

Practice Questions Set 4

1. What is the primary responsibility of internal auditors?
A. Evaluating financial statements
B. Ensuring compliance with laws and regulations
C. Providing assurance on the organization's risk management processes
D. Preparing tax returns

2. Which of the following is NOT a primary function of internal audit?
A. Operational audits
B. Financial audits
C. Human resources audits
D. Compliance audits

3. Which of the following is NOT a characteristic of effective internal auditing?
A. Ethical behavior
B. Independence
C. External focus
D. Objectivity

4. What is the main purpose of internal control?
A. To ensure all employees are following policies and procedures
B. To prevent fraud and misuse of company assets
C. To monitor and improve company performance
D. To monitor employee productivity

5. Ineffective internal control can result in:
A. Improved efficiency and effectiveness
B. Increased risk of financial and reputational loss
C. Greater accuracy in financial reporting
D. Lower employee morale

6. Which of the following is NOT a component of the COSO Internal Control Framework?
A. Control environment
B. Risk assessment
C. Compliance
D. Information and communication

7. Which of the following is not a risk assessment technique used by auditors?
A. Process mapping
B. Observation
C. Interviews
D. Data analytics

8. The audit risk model considers:
A. Inherent risk, control risk, and detection risk
B. Financial risk and operational risk
C. Fraud risk and compliance risk
D. Business risk and enterprise risk

9. Which of the following is NOT a type of testing used by auditors?
A. Interviewing
B. Observing
C. Inspecting
D. Sampling

10. Which of the following is NOT a type of audit opinion?
A. Unqualified opinion
B. Qualified opinion
C. Management's assertion
D. Adverse opinion

11. What is the purpose of an internal audit engagement charter?
A. To outline the objectives of the audit
B. To assign tasks to audit team members
C. To provide evidence of the audit's findings
D. To outline the qualifications of the audit team

12. Which of the following is NOT a type of fraud?
A. Theft
B. Embezzlement
C. Management override
D. Error

13. According to the IIA Standards, auditors should maintain their independence and objectivity by:
A. Accepting gifts and entertainment from clients
B. Reporting directly to the CEO
C. Being assigned to audit the same area year after year
D. Reporting any potential conflicts of interest

14. Which of the following is NOT one of the four key elements of fraud?
A. Opportunity
B. Rationalization
C. Trust
D. Pressure

15. Proper segregation of duties means that:
A. One employee can handle all aspects of a transaction
B. Two employees are required to handle all aspects of a transaction
C. Responsibilities are divided among multiple employees
D. Employees are responsible for both recording and authorizing transactions

16. In COSO's Enterprise Risk Management Framework, which category identifies an organization's current and potential risks?
A. Event identification
B. Risk appetite
C. Objectives
D. Information and communication

17. The Committee of Sponsoring Organizations (COSO) was formed to:
A. Develop a comprehensive framework for internal controls
B. Assist organizations in implementing the Sarbanes-Oxley Act
C. Regulate the internal audit profession
D. Develop audit procedures for financial statement audits

18. Which of the following is NOT a type of data input control?

A. Autorun programs
B. Validity check
C. User identification and authorization
D. System logs

19. A process map shows:
A. The flow of data through a system
B. The number of transactions in a period
C. The location of important documents
D. The structure of the organization

20. The key advantage of using computer-assisted audit techniques (CAATs) is:
A. Greater reliability of results
B. Faster completion of audits
C. Lower cost of testing
D. Reduced potential for auditor bias

21. Management override of internal controls means:
A. Management's authorization of fraudulent activities
B. The implementation of internal controls by management
C. Management's involvement in the audit process
D. The bypassing or ignoring of internal controls by management

22. According to the IIA Standards, what is the primary responsibility of internal audit regarding its consulting services?
A. Ensuring compliance with laws and regulations
B. Objectivity and independence
C. Providing assurance on the organization's risk management processes
D. Communicating the results of consulting engagements with management

23. The most effective method for detecting fraud is through:
A. Management review
B. Continuous monitoring
C. Employee training
D. Internal audits

24. In an internal audit, risk assessment activities should:
A. Be performed annually
B. Only focus on financial risks
C. Consider both internal and external risks
D. Be performed only at the beginning of the audit

25. Which of the following is NOT a type of control environment?
A. Risk management processes
B. Tone at the top
C. Management's philosophy and operating style
D. Human resources policies and practices

26. The purpose of internal audit's continuous monitoring activities is to:
A. Ensure that processes are functioning as intended
B. Identify weaknesses in internal controls
C. Detect errors or fraud
D. Prepare for external audits

27. When conducting a financial statement audit, the primary objective of internal audit is to:
A. Detect fraud and errors in the financial statements

B. Ensure that all financial transactions are recorded accurately

C. Prepare the financial statements

D. Provide assurance on the accuracy and completeness of the financial statements

28. A well-designed internal audit report should include:

A. Audit team member names and qualifications

B. Recommendations for improving internal controls

C. Statements from management justifying any audit findings

D. Examples of fraudulent activities observed during the audit

29. Which of the following is NOT a characteristic of a strong risk management culture?

A. Strong internal controls

B. Encouraging risk-taking behaviors

C. Open communication

D. Good governance practices

30. In a risk assessment, likelihood refers to:

A. The severity of potential risks

B. The probability that a risk will occur

C. The frequency of risk events

D. The impact of potential risks

31. Which of the following is NOT a component of the fraud triangle?

A. Pressure

B. Rationalization

C. Segregation of duties

D. Opportunity

32. Which of the following is NOT a type of internal audit assurance engagement?

A. Financial audit

B. Compliance audit

C. Consulting engagement

D. Operational audit

33. A risk appetite statement outlines:

A. The risks the organization is willing to take

B. The risks the organization must avoid

C. The organization's goals and objectives

D. The organization's internal controls

34. The purpose of continuous auditing is to:

A. Reduce audit costs

B. Provide real-time monitoring and feedback

C. Increase the frequency of audits

D. Identify potential control deficiencies

35. In the COSO Enterprise Risk Management Framework, which of the following is NOT one of the eight components of internal control?

A. Control environment

B. Risk assessment

C. Compliance

D. Information and communication

36. Which of the following is NOT a benefit of performing internal audits?

A. Improved operational efficiency

B. Reduced risk of fraud

C. Compliance with external regulations
D. Enhanced employee morale

37. The primary role of the audit committee is to:
A. Prepare the company's financial statements
B. Monitor management's implementation of internal controls
C. Conduct internal audits
D. Report to stakeholders on the results of the audit

Practice Exam Questions w/ Answers

Book 1

Practice Questions Set 1

1) What is the primary purpose of internal auditing?
A) To identify areas for cost-cutting within the organization
B) To detect fraudulent activities
C) To provide assurance that the organization's goals and objectives are being met
D) To perform external financial audits

Answer: C) To provide assurance that the organization's goals and objectives are being met

2) Which of the following is NOT a key milestone in the development of internal auditing?
A) Creation of The Institute of Internal Auditors
B) Publication of the International Professional Practices Framework
C) Introduction of the CPA certification
D) Sarbanes-Oxley Act of 2002

Answer: C) Introduction of the CPA certification

3) Which of the following frameworks is often used by internal auditors to assess an organization's control environment?
A) COSO
B) GAAP
C) IFRS
D) COBIT

Answer: A) COSO

4) Which of the following skills is NOT essential for an internal auditor?
A) Communication
B) Analytical skills
C) Technical expertise in a specific area
D) Emotional intelligence

Answer: C) Technical expertise in a specific area

5) What is the first step in the risk assessment process?
A) Identifying risks
B) Analyzing risks
C) Evaluating risks
D) Reporting

Answer: A) Identifying risks

6) Which of the following is NOT a type of risk?
A) Operational risks
B) Compliance risks
C) Environmental risks
D) Strategic risks

Answer: C) Environmental risks

7) Which of the following is NOT a component of internal control?
A) Information and communication
B) Risk assessment
C) Asset management
D) Monitoring

Answer: C) Asset management

8) What is the main purpose of a compliance audit?
A) To identify areas for cost-cutting within the organization
B) To detect fraudulent activities
C) To ensure adherence to laws and regulations
D) To review the organization's financial statements

Answer: C) To ensure adherence to laws and regulations

9) What qualifies an individual to take the CIA exam?
A) A bachelor's degree in accounting or a related field
B) Five years of experience in internal auditing or a related field
C) Proficiency in a foreign language
D) A high school diploma

Answer: B) Five years of experience in internal auditing or a related field

10) What does the CIA exam consist of?
A) Multiple choice questions only
B) Essays only
C) A combination of multiple choice and essay questions
D) Only oral questioning by a panel of examiners

Answer: C) A combination of multiple choice and essay questions

11) What is the primary responsibility of internal auditors?
A) To prepare financial statements
B) To conduct external audits
C) To provide independent assurance on an organization's operations
D) To make management decisions on behalf of the organization

Answer: C) To provide independent assurance on an organization's operations

12) What is the purpose of the International Professional Practices Framework?
A) To establish international accounting standards for all audits
B) To provide guidelines for the internal audit profession
C) To ensure compliance with local regulations in different countries
D) To set the standards for ethical conduct in the business world

Answer: B) To provide guidelines for the internal audit profession

13) How has technology impacted the field of internal auditing?
A) It has reduced the need for internal audits
B) It has made internal audits more expensive
C) It has made internal audits more efficient and effective
D) It has decreased the level of risk assessment needed for internal audits

Answer: C) It has made internal audits more efficient and effective

14) What is the main goal of risk assessment in internal auditing?
A) To identify all risks within an organization
B) To eliminate all risks within an organization
C) To prioritize risks based on their potential impact
D) To transfer all risks to a third party

Answer: C) To prioritize risks based on their potential impact

15) What type of risk is associated with the potential for financial loss?
A) Operational risk
B) Compliance risk
C) Reputational risk
D) Strategic risk

Answer: A) Operational risk

16) Which of the following is NOT a component of internal control as defined by COSO?
A) Monitoring
B) Risk assessment
C) Fraud prevention
D) Control environment

Answer: C) Fraud prevention

17) What is the role of internal auditors in corporate governance?
A) To make managerial decisions for the organization
B) To report to external stakeholders on the organization's performance
C) To ensure compliance with laws and regulations
D) To provide independent assurance on the organization's operations

Answer: D) To provide independent assurance on the organization's operations

18) How can internal auditors best build rapport with auditees?
A) By using formal language
B) By being overly critical
C) By being approachable and building trust
D) By never revealing their findings

Answer: C) By being approachable and building trust

19) What is a common and accepted approach to audit planning?
A) Setting objectives and then determining the business's goals
B) Starting with identifying risks and then evaluating them
C) Determining the objectives and then identifying the risks
D) Setting the tone and then establishing objectives

Answer: C) Determining the objectives and then identifying the risks

20) Which of the following is NOT an auditing technique used by internal auditors?
A) Data analysis
B) Surveying external stakeholders
C) Sampling
D) Document review

Answer: B) Surveying external stakeholders

21) Which of the following is NOT a key area of focus for an operational audit?
A) Internal controls
B) Financial statements
C) Cost cutting
D) Business processes

Answer: B) Financial statements

22) Who is responsible for identifying and reporting on financial risks within an organization?
A) External auditors
B) Management
C) Internal auditors
D) Stakeholders

Answer: C) Internal auditors

23) What is an effective way to mitigate risks within an organization?
A) Avoiding all risks
B) Transferring risks to a third party
C) Evaluating risks on a case-by-case basis
D) Embracing all risks

Answer: B) Transferring risks to a third party

24) In which of the following situations would a compliance audit be most helpful?

A) When assessing the effectiveness of internal controls
B) When evaluating the accuracy of financial statements
C) When determining the level of operational risk
D) When checking for adherence to laws and regulations

Answer: D) When checking for adherence to laws and regulations

25) What is the main focus of a financial audit?
A) Ensuring compliance with laws and regulations
B) Identifying areas for cost reduction
C) Providing assurance on the accuracy of financial statements
D) Evaluating the effectiveness of internal controls

Answer: C) Providing assurance on the accuracy of financial statements

26) What sets the CIA certification apart from other certification programs?
A) Its focus on operational risk
B) Its international recognition
C) Its requirement of a foreign language proficiency
D) Its emphasis on financial auditing

Answer: B) Its international recognition

27) Which of the following is NOT a component of the International Professional Practices Framework?
A) Code of Ethics
B) Standards for the Professional Practice of Internal Auditing
C) Control-based approaches for compliance audits
D) Practice advisories

Answer: C) Control-based approaches for compliance audits

28) What impact does a strong control environment have on an organization?
A) It reduces the need for internal audits
B) It increases the risk of fraud
C) It improves the organization's overall performance
D) It eliminates all risk

Answer: C) It improves the organization's overall performance

29) In an operational audit, what is the main focus of data analysis?
A) To identify potential fraud
B) To evaluate the accuracy of financial statements
C) To assess the effectiveness of internal controls
D) To determine areas for cost reduction

Answer: D) To determine areas for cost reduction

30) What does the risk assessment process include?
A) Identifying risks only
B) Analyzing risks only

C) Evaluating risks only
D) All of the above

Answer: D) All of the above

31) What is a key responsibility of internal auditors in corporate governance?
A) To make management decisions for the organization
B) To report on the organization's financial performance
C) To ensure compliance with laws and regulations
D) To evaluate the performance of external auditors

Answer: C) To ensure compliance with laws and regulations

32) What is the main role of internal auditors in risk management?
A) To eliminate all risks within an organization
B) To prioritize risks and recommend mitigation strategies
C) To transfer all risks to a third party
D) To ignore any risks that are identified

Answer: B) To prioritize risks and recommend mitigation strategies

33) What is an effective way for internal auditors to communicate their findings to stakeholders?
A) By using technical jargon
B) By presenting data and analysis in an easy-to-understand format
C) By keeping all findings confidential
D) By delegating the responsibility to someone else

Answer: B) By presenting data and analysis in an easy-to-understand format

Practice Questions Set 2

1. What is the purpose of internal auditing?

Answer: To provide independent and objective assurance and consulting services to add value and improve an organization's operations.

2. What is the difference between internal auditing and external auditing?

Answer: Internal auditing focuses on evaluating and improving internal controls, while external auditing focuses on verifying the accuracy of financial statements.

3. Internal auditors must have knowledge of which areas of an organization?

Answer: Finance, operations, and governance.

4. What are the three overarching principles of the International Standards for the Professional Practice of Internal Auditing (Standards)?

Answer: Purpose, authority, and responsibility.

5. What is the difference between a financial audit and an operational audit?

Answer: A financial audit focuses on the accuracy of financial statements, while an operational audit focuses on the efficiency and effectiveness of processes and procedures.

6. What is the role of the audit committee?

Answer: To oversee the internal audit function and ensure its independence and effectiveness.

7. What is the importance of independence for internal auditors?

Answer: Independence ensures objectivity and credibility in the audit process.

8. What is a control self-assessment?

Answer: A process in which members of an organization evaluate the effectiveness of controls in their own areas of responsibility.

9. What is the purpose of a risk assessment?

Answer: To identify and prioritize areas of risk within an organization.

10. What is the difference between inherent risk and residual risk?

Answer: Inherent risk is the risk associated with a process or activity without considering controls, while residual risk is the risk that remains after controls have been implemented.

11. What is the purpose of testing in internal auditing?

Answer: To gather evidence and evaluate the effectiveness of controls.

12. What is the importance of communicating audit findings to management and stakeholders?

Answer: To inform them of potential risks and issues and provide recommendations for improvement.

13. What is the role of technology in internal auditing?

Answer: It can be used for data analytics, automation, and IT auditing to enhance the efficiency and effectiveness of the audit process.

14. What is the purpose of a fraud detection technique?

Answer: To identify potential fraudulent activities within an organization.

15. What are the ethical standards for auditors?

Answer: Objectivity, integrity, confidentiality, and competency.

16. What is the purpose of an audit report?

Answer: To communicate the results of an audit to management and stakeholders.

17. How can auditors track management's response to audit findings?

Answer: Through discussions and follow-up audits.

18. What is the role of the audit committee in overseeing auditors?

Answer: To ensure the independence and effectiveness of the internal audit function.

19. What is the integrated approach to risk management?

Answer: Integrating risk management into all areas of an organization to ensure alignment with objectives.

20. What are the components of an audit report?

Answer: Audit scope and objectives, executive summary, findings and recommendations, and communication to management and stakeholders.

21. What is the purpose of evaluating business processes in auditing?

Answer: To determine their effectiveness and identify areas for improvement.

22. How does internal auditing add value to an organization?

Answer: By identifying and mitigating risks, enhancing internal controls, and improving processes and procedures.

23. What is the importance of adaptability and inclusivity in the digital age of auditing?

Answer: To stay current with technological advancements and cater to a diverse stakeholder audience.

24. What is the purpose of performance-based auditing?

Answer: To evaluate the effectiveness and efficiency of an organization's operations.

25. What are the challenges and considerations of international internal auditing?

Answer: Differing cultural, legal, and regulatory environments.

26. What is the difference between an internal auditor and a compliance officer?

Answer: An internal auditor evaluates organizational processes, while a compliance officer ensures adherence to laws and regulations.

27. What is the purpose of a self-assessment in internal auditing?

Answer: To evaluate the effectiveness of controls in a specific area of an organization.

28. What are the primary responsibilities of internal auditors?

Answer: Evaluating internal controls, assessing risks, and making recommendations for improvement.

29. What is the difference between an internal auditor and a fraud examiner?

Answer: An internal auditor evaluates controls, while a fraud examiner investigates potential fraudulent activities.

30. What is the purpose of conducting a follow-up audit?

Answer: To assess whether management has taken corrective actions in response to audit findings.

31. What is the importance of professionalism in internal auditing?

Answer: To maintain objectivity and credibility in the audit process.

32. What is the difference between a control and a risk?

Answer: A control is a method of preventing or detecting a risk, while a risk is a potential event that could have a negative impact on an organization.

33. What is the role of an internal auditor in evaluating business operations?

Answer: To assess the effectiveness and efficiency of processes to identify areas for improvement.

34. What is the purpose of governance in an organization?

Answer: To establish and maintain policies, processes, and structures for effective leadership and oversight.

35. What is the goal of an internal audit function?

Answer: To add value and improve an organization's operations through independent and objective evaluations.

36. What is the difference between assurance and consulting services provided by internal auditors?

Answer: Assurance services involve evaluating the adequacy and effectiveness of controls, while consulting services involve providing advice and recommendations for improvement.

37. What is the difference between a financial statement audit and a performance audit?

Answer: A financial statement audit focuses on the accuracy of financial information, while a performance audit evaluates the effectiveness and efficiency of processes.

38. What is the purpose of an audit scope and objectives?

Answer: To define the boundaries and goals of an audit.

39. How do internal auditors add value to an organization?

Answer: By identifying risks, enhancing controls, and improving operations.

40. What is the key component of effective communication for internal auditors?

Answer: Tailoring the message to the intended audience.

41. What is the role of the internal audit function in enterprise risk management?

Answer: To assess and prioritize risks and assist management in developing strategies to mitigate them.

42. What is the difference between a financial audit and an internal controls audit?

Answer: A financial audit focuses on the accuracy of financial statements, while an internal controls audit evaluates the effectiveness of controls.

43. What is the importance of objectivity for internal auditors?

Answer: To ensure unbiased evaluations and maintain credibility.

44. What is the purpose of a risk assessment matrix?

Answer: To prioritize risks based on their likelihood and potential impact on an organization.

45. How can internal auditors build strong relationships with stakeholders?

Answer: By open and effective communication and demonstrating the value of the internal audit function.

46. What is the role of the audit committee in enhancing the effectiveness of the internal audit function?

Answer: To provide oversight and ensure the independence and objectivity of internal auditors.

47. What is the purpose of a mid-year risk assessment?

Answer: To identify emerging risks and adjust audit plans accordingly.

48. What are the objectives of a code of ethics for internal auditors?

Answer: To promote objectivity, integrity, confidentiality, and competence.

49. How can internal auditors help an organization achieve its objectives?

Answer: By identifying and addressing risks and providing recommendations for improvement.

50. What is the purpose of risk management in an organization?

Answer: To identify, assess, and manage potential risks to the achievement of objectives.

Practice Questions Set 3

1. What is the primary role of internal auditing for an organization?

Answer: To provide independent and objective assurance and consulting services aimed at improving the organization's operations.

2. What is the purpose of an internal audit charter?

Answer: To formally define the mission, authority, and responsibilities of the internal audit function within an organization.

3. What is the difference between an assurance engagement and a consulting engagement?

Answer: An assurance engagement is focused on evaluating and providing assurance on the organization's activities, while a consulting engagement is focused on providing recommendations and advice for improvement.

4. In the context of internal auditing, what is risk?

Answer: Risk is the potential for an event or action to impact the achievement of an organization's objectives.

5. What are the three lines of defense in an organization's risk management structure?

Answer: Management, risk and compliance functions, and internal audit.

6. What is the purpose of a risk assessment within the internal audit process?

Answer: To identify and prioritize areas of risk within an organization to guide the internal audit plan and activities.

7. What is the difference between a financial statement audit and an internal audit?

Answer: A financial statement audit is conducted by external auditors and focuses on the financial statements and compliance with accounting standards, while an internal audit is conducted by employees of the organization and focuses on the effectiveness and efficiency of operations.

8. What is the purpose of a control self-assessment?

Answer: To engage management and other stakeholders in the evaluation and improvement of controls within their areas of responsibility.

9. What are the elements of the internal control system?

Answer: Control environment, risk assessment, control activities, information and communication, and monitoring.

10. What is the difference between a preventive control and a detective control?

Answer: A preventive control aims to prevent errors or fraud from occurring, while a detective control is designed to detect and correct errors or fraud that have occurred.

11. What is the purpose of a fraud risk assessment?

Answer: To identify potential areas of fraud within an organization and implement controls to prevent, detect, and respond to fraudulent activities.

12. What is the difference between fraud and misconduct?

Answer: Fraud involves intentional deception for personal gain, while misconduct refers to actions that violate an organization's code of conduct or ethical standards.

13. When should internal audit activities be disclosed to the audit committee?

Answer: As part of the annual internal audit plan and significant changes to the plan.

14. What is the primary purpose of an audit report?

Answer: To communicate the results of the audit to management, the audit committee, and other stakeholders.

15. What is the purpose of a root cause analysis?

Answer: To identify underlying factors that contribute to problems or issues within an organization.

16. What is the best way to manage potential conflicts of interest within the internal audit function?

Answer: By implementing a conflict of interest policy and procedures for identifying, disclosing, and mitigating conflicts.

17. What are the different levels of assurance that can be provided by an internal auditor?

Answer: Reasonable assurance and limited assurance.

18. What is an engagement letter and why is it important?

Answer: An engagement letter outlines the scope, objectives, and responsibilities of both the internal auditor and the auditee for a specific engagement. It is important for defining expectations and reducing misunderstandings.

19. What are the components of the internal audit process?

Answer: Planning, fieldwork, reporting, and follow-up.

20. What is the purpose of an internal audit work program?

Answer: To document the procedures and steps to be undertaken during the audit process.

21. What is the purpose of a quality assurance and improvement program for the internal audit function?

Answer: To monitor and assess the effectiveness and quality of the internal audit function, with the goal of continuous improvement.

22. What are the roles and responsibilities of internal audit staff?

Answer: Conducting audits, maintaining independence and objectivity, and providing recommendations for improvement.

23. What are the common challenges that internal audit teams face?

Answer: Limited resources, organizational resistance, and management expectations.

24. How can internal audit teams ensure efficiency and effectiveness in their work?

Answer: Through proper staffing, budgeting, and time management.

25. In a virtual world, what are the main challenges for conducting audits remotely?

Answer: Access to information, maintaining confidentiality, and ensuring data security.

26. What is the importance of providing adequate training and development opportunities for internal auditors?

Answer: To bridge skills gaps and ensure auditors have the necessary knowledge and competencies to perform their roles effectively.

27. How is audit quality evaluated?

Answer: Through the use of performance metrics and monitoring for improvement.

28. What are some governmental and regulatory requirements that may impact the internal audit function?

Answer: Compliance audits, the Sarbanes-Oxley Act, and other legislation and guidelines.

29. What is the role of internal auditors in corporate social responsibility (CSR) auditing?

Answer: To assess and report on an organization's CSR initiatives and compliance with related laws and regulations.

30. What is the purpose of auditing environmental, social, and governance (ESG) criteria?

Answer: To evaluate an organization's impact and performance in these areas and identify areas for improvement.

31. What are the key considerations when managing audit findings and recommendations?

Answer: Due diligence, managing vendor relationships, and implementing recommendations in a timely manner.

32. What is a root cause analysis and how is it used in the internal audit process?

Answer: A root cause analysis is a method for identifying the underlying factors that contribute to an issue or problem. It is used by internal auditors to address the root causes and prevent future occurrences.

33. What is the role of technology in the evolution of internal auditing?

Answer: Technology has enabled auditors to perform their work more efficiently and effectively, and has the potential to transform the audit function in the future.

34. How can internal auditors track and monitor the implementation of audit recommendations?

Answer: Through follow-up procedures and engaging management in the resolution of outstanding issues.

35. What is the future of internal auditing?

Answer: To continue evolving and adapting to the changing business landscape and utilize technology and data analytics to provide insights and value to organizations.

36. What is the role of management in an organization's risk management structure?

Answer: To establish a risk management framework, identify and assess risks, and implement controls to mitigate risks.

37. What are the primary responsibilities of the risk and compliance functions?

Answer: To provide oversight, guidance, and support for the organization's risk management and compliance activities.

38. What is the purpose of a risk assessment?

Answer: To identify potential risks and prioritize areas for further review and evaluation.

39. What is the relationship between an organization's objectives and its risks?

Answer: Risks can impact an organization's ability to achieve its objectives, therefore should be managed and monitored to ensure objectives are met.

40. What is the difference between a preventive control and a detective control?

Answer: A preventive control aims to prevent errors or fraud from occurring, while a detective control is designed to detect and correct errors or fraud that have occurred.

41. What is the purpose of a control environment?

Answer: To set the tone for the organization and establish the importance of internal control and ethical behavior.

42. How does information and communication contribute to an effective internal control system?

Answer: By ensuring relevant and reliable information is captured and communicated throughout the organization.

43. What is the purpose of monitoring in the internal control system?

Answer: To assess the effectiveness of controls and ensure they are functioning as intended.

44. What is the primary role of internal auditors in fraud risk management?

Answer: To identify potential areas of fraud and implement controls to prevent, detect, and respond to fraudulent activities.

45. What is the difference between fraud and misconduct?

Answer: Fraud involves intentional deception for personal gain, while misconduct refers to actions that violate an organization's code of conduct or ethical standards.

46. When should an internal auditor disclose potential conflicts of interest?

Answer: As soon as it is identified and before beginning an engagement.

47. What is the difference between reasonable assurance and limited assurance?

Answer: Reasonable assurance provides a higher level of confidence in the conclusions of the audit, while limited assurance provides limited confidence due to scope or other constraints.

48. What is the purpose of an engagement letter in the internal audit process?

Answer: To outline the scope, objectives, and responsibilities of both the internal auditor and the auditee for a specific engagement.

49. What are the key components of the internal audit process?

Answer: Planning, fieldwork, reporting, and follow-up.

50. Why is it important for internal auditors to maintain independence and objectivity in their work?

Answer: To ensure they are not influenced by personal biases or conflicts of interest and can provide unbiased and accurate assessments of the organization's activities.

Practice Questions Set 4

1. What is the primary responsibility of an internal auditor?
a) Detect fraud
b) Provide financial advice to the organization
c) Maintain financial records
d) Provide assurance on the effectiveness of risk management, control, and governance processes

Answer: d) Provide assurance on the effectiveness of risk management, control, and governance processes

2. In which of the following situations is independence NOT required for an internal auditor?
a) When conducting an operational audit
b) When performing a consulting engagement
c) When reviewing financial statements for accuracy
d) When reviewing personnel files for compliance issues

Answer: d) When reviewing personnel files for compliance issues

3. Which of the following is NOT a component of the internal audit activity's governance structure?
a) Ethics and integrity
b) Independence and objectivity
c) Operations management
d) Quality assurance and improvement program

Answer: c) Operations management

4. Which of the following is the most important skill for an auditor to possess?
a) Technical accounting knowledge
b) Analytical and critical thinking skills
c) Communication and interpersonal skills
d) Understanding of laws and regulations

Answer: b) Analytical and critical thinking skills

5. Which of the following is the primary reason for conducting an internal audit?
a) To recommend changes to organizational structure
b) To identify areas of potential fraud
c) To improve the efficiency and effectiveness of operations
d) To review the accuracy of financial statements

Answer: c) To improve the efficiency and effectiveness of operations

6. Which of the following is NOT a responsibility of the internal audit function?
a) Developing organizational policies and procedures
b) Evaluating and monitoring risks
c) Reviewing the effectiveness of controls

d) Providing recommendations for improvement

Answer: a) Developing organizational policies and procedures

7. Which of the following is a characteristic of effective internal audit reports?
a) Brief and concise
b) Highly technical and detailed
c) Only include positive findings
d) Written in the first person

Answer: a) Brief and concise

8. Which of the following is NOT a risk management activity that internal auditors can assist with?
a) Identifying risks
b) Mitigating risks
c) Transferring risks
d) Determining the acceptability of risks

Answer: c) Transferring risks

9. Which of the following is NOT a key responsibility of an internal auditor during an organizational change or restructuring?
a) Implementing changes to processes
b) Reviewing and assessing the effectiveness of the change
c) Identifying potential risks associated with the change
d) Communicating the change to stakeholders

Answer: a) Implementing changes to processes

10. Which of the following is NOT a component of a company's organizational structure?
a) Control environment
b) Risk appetite
c) Human resources
d) Policies and procedures

Answer: b) Risk appetite

11. In order to maintain objectivity, an internal auditor should:
a) Perform consulting engagements for the same department they audit
b) Engage in social activities with management
c) Be involved in the day-to-day operations of the organization
d) Not have any financial interest in the organization

Answer: d) Not have any financial interest in the organization

12. Which of the following is NOT a characteristic of a well-functioning internal audit activity?
a) The audit team has regular meetings with senior management
b) The audit team only reports to the audit committee
c) The audit team has access to all areas of the organization
d) The audit team has a high level of independence and objectivity

Answer: b) The audit team only reports to the audit committee

13. Which of the following is NOT a component of the International Standards for the Professional Practice of Internal Auditing (Standards)?
a) Performance standards
b) Attribute standards
c) Reporting standards
d) Quality assurance and improvement program (QAIP)

Answer: c) Reporting standards

14. Which of the following is NOT a characteristic of quality assurance and improvement programs (QAIPs)?
a) They are aligned with the internal audit activity's objectives
b) They focus on improving the organization's operations
c) They include regular evaluation and improvement of the audit activity
d) They are established by external stakeholders

Answer: d) They are established by external stakeholders

15. Which of the following is NOT a component of an organization's control environment?
a) Integrity and ethical values
b) Communication and information
c) Risk management
d) Human resources policies and procedures

Answer: c) Risk management

16. The primary purpose of understanding an organization's objectives and strategies is to:
a) Develop an annual audit plan
b) Report on the effectiveness of risk management processes
c) Identify potential risks and controls
d) Gain an understanding of the organization's operations

Answer: d) Gain an understanding of the organization's operations

17. Which of the following is NOT a tool or technique used by internal auditors during an audit engagement?
a) Observation
b) Benchmarking
c) Questionnaires
d) Performing accounting tasks

Answer: d) Performing accounting tasks

18. Which of the following is NOT a key element of effective communication skills for an internal auditor?
a) Active listening
b) Using technical jargon
c) Verbal and written communication
d) Nonverbal communication

Answer: b) Using technical jargon

19. Which of the following documents outlines the scope and objective of an audit engagement?
a) Audit program
b) Audit plan
c) Audit report
d) Engagement letter

Answer: d) Engagement letter

20. Which of the following is NOT a common financial statement audit procedure?
a) Reviewing internal controls
b) Analyzing financial ratios
c) Confirming account balances with third parties
d) Performing inventory counts

Answer: c) Confirming account balances with third parties

21. When should internal auditors communicate with external auditors during an audit engagement?
a) Before the internal audit engagement begins
b) After the internal audit engagement is completed
c) Only if a significant issue is identified during the internal audit engagement
d) Throughout the entire internal audit engagement process

Answer: d) Throughout the entire internal audit engagement process

22. Which of the following is NOT a common responsibility of internal auditors during a performance audit?
a) Assessing compliance with laws and regulations
b) Evaluating the effectiveness of controls
c) Reviewing financial statements for accuracy
d) Identifying areas for organizational improvement

Answer: c) Reviewing financial statements for accuracy

23. Which of the following statements is TRUE regarding the use of data analytics in internal auditing?
a) Data analytics can only be used in financial statement audits
b) Data analytics is only used for fraud detection and prevention
c) Internal auditors do not need to have any technical skills to use data analytics
d) Data analytics can help identify patterns and trends within large sets of data

Answer: d) Data analytics can help identify patterns and trends within large sets of data

24. In order to assess the quality and effectiveness of an organization's control system, internal auditors should:
a) Observe control activities in action
b) Review management reports
c) Consult with external stakeholders
d) Use statistical sampling methods

Answer: a) Observe control activities in action

25. Which of the following is a key responsibility of internal auditors during a consulting engagement?
a) Communicating findings to the audit committee
b) Reviewing the effectiveness of controls
c) Providing assurance on the accuracy of financial statements
d) Offering recommendations for improving operations

Answer: d) Offering recommendations for improving operations

26. Which of the following activities is NOT a part of the internal audit engagement planning process?
a) Defining the scope and objectives of the audit
b) Developing the audit program
c) Performing fieldwork
d) Obtaining an understanding of the organization's operations

Answer: c) Performing fieldwork

27. Which of the following best describes the purpose of management's response to internal audit findings?
a) To address and correct the identified issues
b) To deny the findings and prevent further audits
c) To shift responsibility to external stakeholders
d) To dismiss the internal audit report entirely

Answer: a) To address and correct the identified issues

28. Which of the following statements is TRUE regarding the external assessment of the internal audit activity?
a) The external assessment must be conducted by an external auditor.
b) The external assessment is only required every five years.
c) The external assessment is not necessary if the internal audit activity has a QAIP.
d) The external assessment must meet all standards for external quality assessments.

Answer: d) The external assessment must meet all standards for external quality assessments.

29. Which of the following is NOT a key characteristic of a strong fraud risk management program?
a) Effective communication with stakeholders
b) Regular assessments of the organization's fraud risks
c) A punitive approach to handling fraud incidents
d) Ongoing monitoring and assessment of internal controls

Answer: c) A punitive approach to handling fraud incidents

30. In order to effectively manage conflicts of interest, an internal auditor should:
a) Disclose their personal financial interests to management
b) Limit interactions with stakeholders
c) Avoid any conflicts of interest entirely
d) Report any potential conflicts of interest to senior management

Answer: d) Report any potential conflicts of interest to senior management

31. In order to maintain objectivity, internal auditors should:

a) Avoid any involvement in risk management activities
b) Only provide consulting services, not assurance services
c) Conduct all engagements independently, without any assistance
d) Maintain a balanced perspective and exercise professional skepticism

Answer: d) Maintain a balanced perspective and exercise professional skepticism

Book 2 - Internal Audit Practices

Practice Questions Set 1

1. What is the primary purpose of internal audit?
A. Detecting fraud
B. Ensuring compliance
C. Improving control processes
D. Providing financial advice

Answer: C. Improving control processes

2. When was the internal audit function established?
A. 1950s
B. 1960s
C. 1970s
D. 1980s

Answer: B. 1960s

3. What is the role of a CIA?
A. Ensuring the integrity of financial statements
B. Conducting risk assessments
C. Evaluating control processes
D. All of the above

Answer: D. All of the above

4. Which of the following is not one of the principles of internal control?
A. Control environment
B. Risk assessment
C. Communication
D. Compensation

Answer: D. Compensation

5. What is the first step in assessing and enhancing internal control?
A. Conduct a risk assessment
B. Evaluate existing control activities
C. Implement additional control measures
D. Communicate changes to stakeholders

Answer: A. Conduct a risk assessment

6. Which of the following is not a red flag of fraud?
A. Excessive spending
B. Personal financial difficulties
C. Lack of segregation of duties
D. Transparency in financial reporting

Answer: D. Transparency in financial reporting

7. What is the main purpose of an internal audit plan?
A. Identify risk areas
B. Develop audit procedures
C. Communicate changes to stakeholders
D. All of the above

Answer: D. All of the above

8. What is the purpose of gathering evidence in an internal audit?
A. To identify potential fraud
B. To make recommendations for improvement
C. To assess the effectiveness of control processes
D. All of the above

Answer: D. All of the above

9. What is the most common sampling technique used in internal auditing?
A. Judgmental sampling
B. Random sampling
C. Systematic sampling
D. Stratified sampling

Answer: B. Random sampling

10. What is the purpose of IT auditing?
A. Identify financial risks
B. Ensure data integrity
C. Evaluate employee performance
D. Increase company revenue

Answer: B. Ensure data integrity

11. What is the most effective technique for assessing the effectiveness of IT controls?
A. Network and system scanning
B. Data analytics
C. Vulnerability assessments
D. Continuous monitoring

Answer: D. Continuous monitoring

12. Why is effective report writing important for internal auditors?
A. To communicate findings to management
B. To meet regulatory requirements
C. To make recommendations for improvement
D. All of the above

Answer: D. All of the above

13. Which of the following is not a responsibility of the internal audit function in corporate governance?
A. Ensuring compliance with laws and regulations
B. Evaluating the effectiveness of risk management processes
C. Detecting and reporting fraud
D. Making financial decisions for management

Answer: D. Making financial decisions for management

14. What is the purpose of the International Standards for the Professional Practice of Internal Auditing?
A. Provide guidance for conducting IT audits
B. Ensure ethical behavior in internal auditing
C. Establish best practices for risk management
D. All of the above

Answer: B. Ensure ethical behavior in internal auditing

15. What is the primary focus of a quality assurance and improvement program for internal auditors?
A. Evaluating individual performance
B. Identifying areas for improvement
C. Ensuring compliance with laws and regulations
D. Enhancing control processes

Answer: B. Identifying areas for improvement

16. What type of skills are essential for a CIA to possess?
A. Technical skills
B. Communication skills
C. Analytical skills
D. All of the above

Answer: D. All of the above

17. Which of the following is not considered a soft skill for a CIA?
A. Leadership
B. Communication
C. Accounting
D. Time management

Answer: C. Accounting

18. How can diversity and inclusivity be incorporated into the CIA program?

A. By hiring a diverse workforce
B. By including diversity in risk assessments
C. By providing diversity training
D. All of the above

Answer: D. All of the above

19. What is the role of an IT auditor in risk management?
A. Identifying potential risks
B. Developing control measures
C. Evaluating the effectiveness of control processes
D. All of the above

Answer: D. All of the above

20. Which of the following is not considered a best practice for conducting an IT audit?
A. Data analytics
B. Network and system scanning
C. Manual data entry
D. Vulnerability assessments

Answer: C. Manual data entry

21. Who is responsible for overseeing the internal audit function?
A. External auditors
B. Company management
C. Regulatory agencies
D. Shareholders

Answer: B. Company management

22. What is the primary goal of internal control?
A. Detect and prevent fraud
B. Ensure compliance with laws and regulations
C. Improve efficiency and effectiveness of operations
D. All of the above

Answer: D. All of the above

23. Which of the following is not a component of the control environment?
A. Risk assessment
B. Integrity and ethical values
C. Competence and accountability
D. Monitoring activities

Answer: A. Risk assessment

24. What is the purpose of a risk assessment?
A. Identify potential risks
B. Develop control measures

C. Prioritize audit areas
D. All of the above

Answer: D. All of the above

25. What is the primary responsibility of a CIA?
A. Prepare financial statements
B. Conduct risk assessments
C. Implement control processes
D. Give financial advice

Answer: B. Conduct risk assessments

26. Which of the following is not considered a control activity?
A. Human resources policies
B. Physical access controls
C. Risk assessment procedures
D. Personnel training programs

Answer: C. Risk assessment procedures

27. What is the purpose of monitoring activities?
A. Detect and prevent fraud
B. Evaluate the effectiveness of control processes
C. Identify potential risks
D. All of the above

Answer: B. Evaluate the effectiveness of control processes

28. What is the first step in the risk assessment process?
A. Identify potential risks
B. Develop control measures
C. Prioritize risks
D. Communicate with stakeholders

Answer: A. Identify potential risks

29. Which of the following is not an effective control implementation strategy?
A. Start with the highest risk areas
B. Involve key stakeholders
C. Utilize technology
D. Ignore recommendations from auditors

Answer: D. Ignore recommendations from auditors

30. What is the primary role of internal auditors in fraud detection and prevention?
A. Conducting investigations
B. Identifying red flags of fraud
C. Developing control measures
D. Reviewing financial statements

Answer: B. identifying red flags of fraud

31. What is the primary goal of IT auditing?
A. Identify and mitigate IT risks
B. Detect and prevent fraud
C. Ensure compliance with laws and regulations
D. Increase company revenue

Answer: A. Identify and mitigate IT risks

32. What is the purpose of a code of ethics for internal auditors?
A. Ensure compliance with laws and regulations
B. Establish ethical standards for the profession
C. Provide guidance for conducting IT audits
D. Increase company profits

Answer: B. Establish ethical standards for the profession

33. Which of the following is not considered a best practice for conducting an IT audit?
A. Network and system scanning
B. Data analytics
C. Continuous monitoring
D. Manual data entry

Answer: D. Manual data entry

34. What is the primary purpose of an internal audit report?
A. Identify potential risks
B. Communicate findings and recommendations to management
C. Ensure compliance with laws and regulations
D. All of the above

Answer: B. Communicate findings and recommendations to management

35. Why is continuous monitoring of IT controls important?
A. To identify potential risks
B. To ensure the effectiveness of controls
C. To increase company profits
D. All of the above

Answer: B. To ensure the effectiveness of controls

36. How can technology be utilized in the internal audit process?
A. Sampling techniques
B. Data analytics
C. Gathering evidence
D. All of the above

Answer: D. All of the above

37. Which of the following is not a key responsibility of the internal audit function in corporate governance?
A. Identifying potential risks
B. Evaluating the effectiveness of risk management processes
C. Making financial decisions for management
D. Reporting to the audit committee

Answer: C. Making financial decisions for management

38. What is the purpose of a quality assurance and improvement program for internal auditors?
A. Ensure compliance with laws and regulations
B. Evaluate the performance of individual auditors
C. Identify areas for improvement
D. All of the above

Answer: C. Identify areas for improvement

39. How can a CIA contribute to diversity and inclusivity in the workplace?
A. By hiring a diverse workforce
B. By including diversity in risk assessments
C. By providing diversity training
D. All of the above

Answer: D. All of the above

40. What is the primary focus of an IT auditor in risk management?
A. Identifying potential risks
B. Evaluating the effectiveness of control processes
C. Developing control measures
D. All of the above

Answer: D. All of the above

Practice Questions Set 2

1. What is the primary responsibility of internal auditing?
A. Monitor employee performance
B. Assess financial reporting accuracy
C. Improve organizational operations
D. Ensure regulatory compliance

Answer: B. Assess financial reporting accuracy

2. Which of the following is not one of the three primary categories of internal auditing?
A. Operational auditing
B. Financial auditing
C. Compliance auditing
D. Risk management auditing

Answer: D. Risk management auditing

3. Which of the following is not a typical role of an internal auditor?
A. Setting goals and objectives for the organization
B. Evaluating the effectiveness of internal controls
C. Identifying potential areas of risk
D. Providing recommendations for improvements

Answer: A. Setting goals and objectives for the organization

4. One of the primary focuses of internal auditing is to provide assurance to stakeholders. What does this mean?
A. Ensuring that the organization is fulfilling its mission
B. Protecting the company's assets
C. Enforcing internal policies and procedures
D. Implementing changes to improve efficiency

Answer: A. Ensuring that the organization is fulfilling its mission

5. What is the difference between assurance and consulting within the context of internal auditing?
A. Consulting provides recommendations while assurance confirms accuracy.
B. Consulting provides recommendations while assurance monitors compliance.
C. Consulting improves operations while assurance ensures financial reporting accuracy.
D. Consulting improves risk management while assurance ensures regulatory compliance.

Answer: A. Consulting provides recommendations while assurance confirms accuracy.

6. Which of the following is an example of operational effectiveness?
A. Ensuring regulatory compliance
B. Evaluating financial statements

C. Identifying areas of risk

D. Improving processes and procedures

Answer: D. Improving processes and procedures

7. How does internal auditing add value to the organization?

A. By identifying areas of risk

B. By providing assurance to stakeholders

C. By improving operational effectiveness

D. By enforcing company policies and procedures

Answer: C. By improving operational effectiveness

8. How can independence and objectivity be maintained within an internal audit department?

A. Employing third-party auditors

B. Rotating assignments within the department

C. Reporting directly to upper management

D. All of the above

Answer: D. All of the above

9. Which of the following is a primary purpose of an internal audit charter?

A. To define the scope and objectives of the internal audit function

B. To review financial statements for accuracy

C. To enforce internal policies and procedures

D. To protect the organization's assets

Answer: A. To define the scope and objectives of the internal audit function

10. What is one way an organization can demonstrate its commitment to internal auditing?

A. By providing a larger budget for the internal audit department

B. By implementing recommendations made by the internal auditors

C. By hiring more internal auditors

D. By creating a separate division for internal auditing

Answer: B. By implementing recommendations made by the internal auditors

11. What is the purpose of the International Standards for the Professional Practice of Internal Auditing?

A. To provide guidance for conducting internal audits

B. To outline the responsibilities of internal auditors

C. To set ethical standards for internal auditors

D. All of the above

Answer: D. All of the above

12. What is the difference between a risk and a control?

A. Risks are potential threats while controls are actions to minimize those threats.

B. Risks are potential opportunities while controls are actions to maximize those opportunities.

C. Risks are potential issues while controls are actions to resolve those issues.

D. Risks are potential benefits while controls are actions to maximize those benefits.

Answer: A. Risks are potential threats while controls are actions to minimize those threats.

13. Why is it important for an internal auditor to maintain independence from the activities they are auditing?
A. To ensure their objectivity
B. To avoid any conflicts of interest
C. To report accurate findings
D. All of the above

Answer: D. All of the above

14. What is the purpose of conducting an internal audit risk assessment?
A. To identify potential areas of risk within the organization
B. To determine the cost of implementing internal controls
C. To evaluate the effectiveness of current internal controls
D. All of the above

Answer: A. To identify potential areas of risk within the organization

15. Which of the following is not one of the six main categories of internal control activities?
A. Monitoring activities
B. Control environment
C. Risk assessment
D. Financial management

Answer: D. Financial management

16. What is the role of an internal auditor in regards to fraud?
A. To prevent and detect fraudulent activities
B. To conduct financial investigations
C. To recommend changes to internal controls to prevent fraud
D. All of the above

Answer: D. All of the above

17. How can an internal auditor ensure the accuracy of financial information?
A. Conducting tests of detail to verify accuracy
B. Comparing financial data to industry standards
C. Interviewing employees responsible for preparing the financial statements
D. All of the above

Answer: D. All of the above

18. Which of the following is not a typical objective of an operational audit?
A. Assessing the efficiency of operations
B. Identifying potential areas of fraud
C. Evaluating internal controls
D. Identifying areas for cost savings

Answer: B. Identifying potential areas of fraud

19. How can an internal auditor help improve an organization's risk management processes?
A. By conducting risk assessments
B. By identifying areas of risk during audits
C. By recommending changes to internal controls
D. All of the above

Answer: D. All of the above

20. What is the purpose of conducting a compliance audit?
A. To evaluate the effectiveness of internal controls
B. To assess the accuracy of financial statements
C. To ensure compliance with laws and regulations
D. To identify potential areas of fraud

Answer: C. To ensure compliance with laws and regulations

21. What is the primary responsibility of an internal audit manager?
A. Conducting audits and preparing reports
B. Hiring and training internal auditors
C. Setting goals and objectives for the internal audit department
D. Reporting audit findings to upper management

Answer: C. Setting goals and objectives for the internal audit department

22. Who should the internal audit department report to within the organization?
A. The board of directors
B. The CEO
C. The CFO
D. All of the above

Answer: D. All of the above

23. What is one advantage of outsourcing internal auditing?
A. It can provide more objective and independent results
B. It can reduce the cost of internal auditing
C. It can create better relationships with employees
D. It can streamline the reporting process

Answer: B. It can reduce the cost of internal auditing

24. How can technology enhance the internal audit process?
A. By automating certain audit procedures
B. By improving the accuracy and speed of data analysis
C. By providing real-time access to financial information
D. All of the above

Answer: D. All of the above

25. How often should an internal audit charter be reviewed and approved by the governing body?
A. Annually
B. Every three years
C. Every five years
D. Only when significant changes occur

Answer: A. Annually

26. What is the purpose of having a quality assurance and improvement program for internal audit?
A. To ensure that the internal audit activity is consistently meeting standards
B. To identify areas for improvement within the internal audit department
C. To provide evidence of the internal audit department's effectiveness
D. All of the above

Answer: D. All of the above

27. Why is it important for internal auditors to have good communication skills?
A. To effectively report findings to management
B. To build relationships with employees
C. To communicate audit results to stakeholders
D. All of the above

Answer: D. All of the above

28. What is the future outlook for the internal audit profession?
A. Significant growth opportunities
B. Fewer job opportunities
C. No significant changes anticipated
D. Increased focus on technology and data analysis

Answer: D. Increased focus on technology and data analysis

29. What is the primary purpose of an audit plan?
A. To determine the scope of the audit
B. To outline the steps of the audit process
C. To assign tasks and responsibilities to auditors
D. All of the above

Answer: D. All of the above

30. Which of the following is not one of the main steps in conducting an audit engagement?
A. Planning
B. Conducting the audit activities
C. Reporting the results
D. Auditing the audit process

Answer: D. Auditing the audit process

31. What is the minimum amount of time an internal audit report should cover?
A. One month

B. One quarter
C. One fiscal year
D. One calendar year

Answer: C. One fiscal year

32. Which of the following is not an example of an internal control activity?
A. Segregation of duties
B. Independent verification
C. Hiring competent employees
D. Documenting policies and procedures

Answer: C. Hiring competent employees

33. How can an internal auditor assess the effectiveness of internal controls?
A. By conducting tests of detail
B. By reviewing employee performance evaluations
C. By interviewing employees responsible for internal controls
D. All of the above

Answer: D. All of the above

Practice Questions Set 3

1. In the CIA exam, external auditors are responsible for conducting audits for:

Answer: External entities outside of the organization.

2. Which of the following is a characteristic of a successful internal audit team?

Answer: Clear communication and collaboration between members.

3. True or False: Effective risk assessment requires understanding the organization's objectives and key processes.

Answer: True.

4. The primary objective of internal audit is to:

Answer: Evaluate and improve the effectiveness of risk management, control, and governance processes.

5. Which of the following is not a component of the internal audit profession's definition of internal auditing?
a) Providing assurance on the organization's financial statements.
b) Bringing a systematic, disciplined approach to evaluate and improve the effectiveness of governance, risk management, and control processes.
c) Enhancing external audit performance.
d) Helping organizations accomplish their objectives.

Answer: c) Enhancing external audit performance.

6. True or False: The scope of an internal audit may be limited by management's acceptance of certain risks.

Answer: True.

7. The primary responsibility of internal auditors is to:

Answer: Conduct audits and provide recommendations to management.

8. Which of the following is a key duty of an internal auditor?
a) Issuing management reports.
b) Ensuring compliance with laws and regulations.
c) Authorizing payments.
d) Developing policies and procedures.

Answer: b) Ensuring compliance with laws and regulations.

9. True or False: Internal auditors have the authority to implement recommendations made in their audit reports.

Answer: False.

10. An external auditor is responsible for:

Answer: Conducting audits on behalf of external entities, such as investors or regulatory bodies.

11. Refer to the table below to answer the question.

Account Type	Value
Cash	$50,000
Accounts Receivable	$25,000
Inventory	$75,000

What is the total value of assets?

Answer: $150,000.

12. True or False: A culture of integrity and ethical behavior is not important for an organization's success.

Answer: False.

13. Which of the following is an example of an internal control activity related to cash receipts?
a) Reviewing contracts for accurate pricing.
b) Monitoring changes in market trends.
c) Verifying receipt of goods from a supplier.
d) Reconciling bank statements.

Answer: d) Reconciling bank statements.

14. True or False: Management is not responsible for establishing and maintaining an effective system of internal controls.

Answer: False.

15. The probability that internal controls will not prevent or detect a material misstatement is known as:

Answer: Control risk.

16. True or False: The purpose of a control self-assessment is to uncover potential control weaknesses.

Answer: True.

17. Which of the following is not a primary objective of the COSO Internal Control Framework?
a) Reliable financial and non-financial reporting.
b) Compliance with laws and regulations.
c) Development of organization culture.
d) Effectiveness and efficiency of operations.

Answer: c) Development of organization culture.

18. In the COSO ERM Framework, which component addresses the organization's attitude toward risk?

Answer: Culture and risk appetite.

19. True or False: Internal auditors should always remain completely independent from the organization they are auditing.

Answer: False.

20. When conducting an internal audit, internal auditors should remain objective and unbiased. What is another term that refers to this principle?

Answer: Integrity.

21. True or False: Using technology can decrease the efficiency of an internal audit.

Answer: False.

22. How often should an organization perform a risk assessment?

Answer: At least annually.

23. True or False: Management's procedures for risk management cannot be evaluated by internal audit.

Answer: False.

24. Which type of audit focuses on evaluating the efficiency, effectiveness, and economy of using resources?

Answer: Performance audit.

25. True or False: All audits are focused on finding and reporting errors and mistakes.

Answer: False.

26. What type of audit is focused on evaluating controls and risk management processes?

Answer: Compliance audit.

27. True or False: A crucial aspect of a successful audit is establishing relevant audit criteria.

Answer: True.

28. Which of the following is a key factor to consider when determining the frequency of audit procedures?
a) The size of the organization.
b) Management's risk assessment processes.

c) The number of employees.
d) The organization's industry.

Answer: b) Management's risk assessment processes.

29. True or False: Interviews and questionnaires are useful tools in sampling and analytical techniques for internal audits.

Answer: True.

30. When conducting an internal audit, the auditor should always:

Answer: Remain objective and unbiased.

31. True or False: The scope of an internal audit is determined by the audit charter.

Answer: True.

32. An organization has implemented enhanced internal controls to mitigate its risks. The next step for the organization is to:

Answer: Monitor and test the effectiveness of the controls.

33. True or False: The external auditor is responsible for designing and implementing the internal control system.

Answer: False.

34. Which of the following is not a key requirement for internal audit to fulfill its role of evaluating and improving the effectiveness of risk management, control, and governance processes?
a) Recognize that business functions are responsible for managing risks.
b) Design a program to provide reasonable assurance that objectives will be met.
c) Understand relevant laws and regulations.
d) Conduct an annual assessment of the control system.

Answer: a) Recognize that business functions are responsible for managing risks.

35. Due professional care, independence, and confidentiality are all principles of:

Answer: The internal audit profession's Code of Ethics.

36. True or False: The internal audit profession's Code of Ethics does not include principles of integrity.

Answer: False.

37. Independence means that internal auditors are not influenced by:

Answer: Personal relationships.

38. True or False: Internal auditors should not collaborate with external auditors.

Answer: False.

39. Which of the following is not a cultural difference that can impact audit practices?
a) Language barriers.
b) Time zones.
c) Customs and traditions.
d) Political climate.

Answer: b) Time zones.

40. True or False: Global audits require cultural sensitivity and local knowledge.

Answer: True.

41. When external and internal auditors collaborate on an audit, the internal auditors should:
a) Increase their sample sizes to ensure accuracy.
b) Take over all tasks related to internal control testing.
c) Ensure that the external auditors conduct all of the audit work.
d) Coordinate audit plans and maintain open communication.

Answer: d) Coordinate audit plans and maintain open communication.

42. True or False: Conducting global audits can decrease the efficiency of the internal audit department.

Answer: False.

43. What is a key component of effective compliance risk assessment?

Answer: Understanding relevant laws and regulations.

44. True or False: Evaluating and reporting on compliance is not within the scope of internal audit.

Answer: False.

45. Fraud risk management involves:

Answer: Assessing and mitigating potential fraud risks.

46. True or False: Fraud risk management only involves evaluating financial fraud risks.

Answer: False.

47. To effectively evaluate IT governance frameworks, internal auditors should:

Answer: Understand the organization's IT infrastructure and strategies.

48. True or False: Data analytics can decrease the efficiency of an internal audit.

Answer: False.

49. The primary benefit of continuous auditing and monitoring is:

Answer: Timely identification of potential issues and risks.

50. True or False: During a crisis, auditors should focus on conducting audits as usual to maintain consistency.

Answer: False.

Practice Questions Set 4

1. What is the primary responsibility of internal auditors?
A. Evaluating financial statements
B. Ensuring compliance with laws and regulations
C. Providing assurance on the organization's risk management processes
D. Preparing tax returns

Answer: C. Providing assurance on the organization's risk management processes

2. Which of the following is NOT a primary function of internal audit?
A. Operational audits
B. Financial audits
C. Human resources audits
D. Compliance audits

Answer: C. Human resources audits

3. Which of the following is NOT a characteristic of effective internal auditing?
A. Ethical behavior
B. Independence
C. External focus
D. Objectivity

Answer: C. External focus

4. What is the main purpose of internal control?
A. To ensure all employees are following policies and procedures
B. To prevent fraud and misuse of company assets
C. To monitor and improve company performance
D. To monitor employee productivity

Answer: B. To prevent fraud and misuse of company assets

5. Ineffective internal control can result in:
A. Improved efficiency and effectiveness
B. Increased risk of financial and reputational loss
C. Greater accuracy in financial reporting
D. Lower employee morale

Answer: B. Increased risk of financial and reputational loss

6. Which of the following is NOT a component of the COSO Internal Control Framework?
A. Control environment
B. Risk assessment

C. Compliance

D. Information and communication

Answer: C. Compliance

7. Which of the following is not a risk assessment technique used by auditors?

A. Process mapping

B. Observation

C. Interviews

D. Data analytics

Answer: B. Observation

8. The audit risk model considers:

A. Inherent risk, control risk, and detection risk

B. Financial risk and operational risk

C. Fraud risk and compliance risk

D. Business risk and enterprise risk

Answer: A. Inherent risk, control risk, and detection risk

9. Which of the following is NOT a type of testing used by auditors?

A. Interviewing

B. Observing

C. Inspecting

D. Sampling

Answer: A. Interviewing

10. Which of the following is NOT a type of audit opinion?

A. Unqualified opinion

B. Qualified opinion

C. Management's assertion

D. Adverse opinion

Answer: C. Management's assertion

11. What is the purpose of an internal audit engagement charter?

A. To outline the objectives of the audit

B. To assign tasks to audit team members

C. To provide evidence of the audit's findings

D. To outline the qualifications of the audit team

Answer: A. To outline the objectives of the audit

12. Which of the following is NOT a type of fraud?

A. Theft

B. Embezzlement

C. Management override

D. Error

Answer: D. Error

13. According to the IIA Standards, auditors should maintain their independence and objectivity by:
A. Accepting gifts and entertainment from clients
B. Reporting directly to the CEO
C. Being assigned to audit the same area year after year
D. Reporting any potential conflicts of interest

Answer: D. Reporting any potential conflicts of interest

14. Which of the following is NOT one of the four key elements of fraud?
A. Opportunity
B. Rationalization
C. Trust
D. Pressure

Answer: C. Trust

15. Proper segregation of duties means that:
A. One employee can handle all aspects of a transaction
B. Two employees are required to handle all aspects of a transaction
C. Responsibilities are divided among multiple employees
D. Employees are responsible for both recording and authorizing transactions

Answer: C. Responsibilities are divided among multiple employees

16. In COSO's Enterprise Risk Management Framework, which category identifies an organization's current and potential risks?
A. Event identification
B. Risk appetite
C. Objectives
D. Information and communication

Answer: A. Event identification

17. The Committee of Sponsoring Organizations (COSO) was formed to:
A. Develop a comprehensive framework for internal controls
B. Assist organizations in implementing the Sarbanes-Oxley Act
C. Regulate the internal audit profession
D. Develop audit procedures for financial statement audits

Answer: A. Develop a comprehensive framework for internal controls

18. Which of the following is NOT a type of data input control?
A. Autorun programs
B. Validity check
C. User identification and authorization
D. System logs

Answer: D. System logs

19. A process map shows:
A. The flow of data through a system
B. The number of transactions in a period
C. The location of important documents
D. The structure of the organization

Answer: A. The flow of data through a system

20. The key advantage of using computer-assisted audit techniques (CAATs) is:
A. Greater reliability of results
B. Faster completion of audits
C. Lower cost of testing
D. Reduced potential for auditor bias

Answer: B. Faster completion of audits

21. Management override of internal controls means:
A. Management's authorization of fraudulent activities
B. The implementation of internal controls by management
C. Management's involvement in the audit process
D. The bypassing or ignoring of internal controls by management

Answer: D. The bypassing or ignoring of internal controls by management

22. According to the IIA Standards, what is the primary responsibility of internal audit regarding its consulting services?
A. Ensuring compliance with laws and regulations
B. Objectivity and independence
C. Providing assurance on the organization's risk management processes
D. Communicating the results of consulting engagements with management

Answer: B. Objectivity and independence

23. The most effective method for detecting fraud is through:
A. Management review
B. Continuous monitoring
C. Employee training
D. Internal audits

Answer: B. Continuous monitoring

24. In an internal audit, risk assessment activities should:
A. Be performed annually
B. Only focus on financial risks
C. Consider both internal and external risks
D. Be performed only at the beginning of the audit

Answer: C. Consider both internal and external risks

25. Which of the following is NOT a type of control environment?

A. Risk management processes

B. Tone at the top

C. Management's philosophy and operating style

D. Human resources policies and practices

Answer: A. Risk management processes

26. The purpose of internal audit's continuous monitoring activities is to:

A. Ensure that processes are functioning as intended

B. Identify weaknesses in internal controls

C. Detect errors or fraud

D. Prepare for external audits

Answer: A. Ensure that processes are functioning as intended

27. When conducting a financial statement audit, the primary objective of internal audit is to:

A. Detect fraud and errors in the financial statements

B. Ensure that all financial transactions are recorded accurately

C. Prepare the financial statements

D. Provide assurance on the accuracy and completeness of the financial statements

Answer: D. Provide assurance on the accuracy and completeness of the financial statements

28. A well-designed internal audit report should include:

A. Audit team member names and qualifications

B. Recommendations for improving internal controls

C. Statements from management justifying any audit findings

D. Examples of fraudulent activities observed during the audit

Answer: B. Recommendations for improving internal controls

29. Which of the following is NOT a characteristic of a strong risk management culture?

A. Strong internal controls

B. Encouraging risk-taking behaviors

C. Open communication

D. Good governance practices

Answer: B. Encouraging risk-taking behaviors

30. In a risk assessment, likelihood refers to:

A. The severity of potential risks

B. The probability that a risk will occur

C. The frequency of risk events

D. The impact of potential risks

Answer: B. The probability that a risk will occur

31. Which of the following is NOT a component of the fraud triangle?
A. Pressure
B. Rationalization
C. Segregation of duties
D. Opportunity

Answer: C. Segregation of duties

32. Which of the following is NOT a type of internal audit assurance engagement?
A. Financial audit
B. Compliance audit
C. Consulting engagement
D. Operational audit

Answer: C. Consulting engagement

33. A risk appetite statement outlines:
A. The risks the organization is willing to take
B. The risks the organization must avoid
C. The organization's goals and objectives
D. The organization's internal controls

Answer: A. The risks the organization is willing to take

34. The purpose of continuous auditing is to:
A. Reduce audit costs
B. Provide real-time monitoring and feedback
C. Increase the frequency of audits
D. Identify potential control deficiencies

Answer: B. Provide real-time monitoring and feedback

35. In the COSO Enterprise Risk Management Framework, which of the following is NOT one of the eight components of internal control?
A. Control environment
B. Risk assessment
C. Compliance
D. Information and communication

Answer: C. Compliance

36. Which of the following is NOT a benefit of performing internal audits?
A. Improved operational efficiency
B. Reduced risk of fraud
C. Compliance with external regulations
D. Enhanced employee morale

Answer: C. Compliance with external regulations

37. The primary role of the audit committee is to:

A. Prepare the company's financial statements
B. Monitor management's implementation of internal controls
C. Conduct internal audits
D. Report to stakeholders on the results of the audit

Answer: B. Monitor management's implementation of internal controls

Made in the USA
Columbia, SC
20 September 2024

42666908R00152